Contents

New Jersey Sta
Camping
Recreation G

Scott Zamek

STACKPOLE
BOOKS

0   11557 03473   8

In memory of Mack Ness,
New Jersey's original conservationist,
1909–2004

Copyright ©2008 by Stackpole Books

Published by
STACKPOLE BOOKS
5067 Ritter Road
Mechanicsburg, PA 17055
www.stackpolebooks.com

Printed in the United States of America

10 9 8 7 6 5 4 3 2 1

FIRST EDITION

Design by Beth Oberholtzer
Cover design by Wendy Reynolds

Cover: Sawmill Lake Campground at High Point State Park

Library of Congress Cataloging-in-Publication Data

Zamek, Scott.
    New Jersey state parks camping and recreation guide / Scott Zamek.
— 1st ed.
        p.   cm.
    Includes bibliographical references and index.
    ISBN-13: 978-0-8117-3473-8 (pbk.)
    ISBN-10: 0-8117-3473-0 (pbk.)
    1. Outdoor recreation—New Jersey—Guidebooks. 2. Parks—New Jersey—Guidebooks. 3. Forest reserves—New Jersey—Guidebooks. 4. Recreation areas—New Jersey—Guidebooks. 5. Camping—New Jersey—Guidebooks. 6. Hiking—New Jersey—Guidebooks. 7. Backpacking—New Jersey—Guidebooks. 8. New Jersey—Guidebooks. I. Title.
GV191.42.N5Z36   2008
917.4904′44—dc22

                                                              2007015292

Foreword

I always thought I knew a lot about New Jersey and I do. I now know a lot more having read *New Jersey State Parks Camping & Recreation Guide*. And the value in reading it is significant. It is easy to talk about what we have built in this state, but this book gives us a chance to appreciate what we have left alone and how precious that can be. You will be impressed with the historical background accompanying much of the discussion. The rich, unspoiled New Jersey is a treat for anyone to experience, and Scott Zamek knows it and delivers it beautifully. We have not only an informative book but an enduring tool ready to guide you through untold New Jersey treasures.

Brendan T. Byrne
Former Governor of New Jersey

Preface

The theme of this book began when I returned from an around-the-world mountain bike journey and found myself in New Jersey. After camping, hiking, and mountain biking in regions like the Himalaya Mountains, India's Kanha National Park, and China's remote Xinjiang Province, I longed for similar experiences in New Jersey. Many residents claimed such wilderness areas did not exist in the Garden State, but I began seeking them out when my spirit needed an infusion of peace and serenity. This book is the culmination of my fifteen-year search. It is a list of destinations that, in this ever-growing world of ours, will make travelers feel apart from mechanized society and close to the wild.

Throughout my search for open space, I not only found New Jersey's critics to be wrong, but also discovered many areas that reminded me of those remote corners of the earth I had visited. New Jersey is a state of unbounded salt marshes on the Atlantic Ocean, high ridgetops along the Kittatinny Mountains, and a vast southern pineland that is recognized by the United Nations as one of the rarest ecosystems on the planet. It is a state where a trip to Ken Lockwood Gorge can remind you of the Rocky Mountains, or a journey to the Cohansey River Watershed can bring to mind a remote island beach.

New Jersey is also a state of dense population and industry, to be sure, but this book is written for anyone tired of crowded summer beaches. It is for anyone wishing to explore New Jersey's little-known corners, quiet campgrounds, and mountain corridors—places where a cell phone may serve as an efficient paperweight, but nothing more.

The completion of a guidebook of this kind requires the collective knowledge of many people. This book would not have been possible without the help of the staff and superintendents of New Jersey's individual state parks, as well as the officials of the Division of Parks and

Forestry in Trenton. A long list of anglers, hikers, mountain bikers, and others selflessly shared their knowledge, and my special thanks go to Joseph Wise, a longtime camping companion, who has fished the waters of New Jersey for more than forty years.

I am especially indebted to Michelle De Paola, who read the entire manuscript and field-tested many of the driving tours and directions within this guidebook. Others who added their expertise include Nicholas Friend, who provided an endless list of mountain-biking destinations; Paul Mulvey, a longtime fly fisherman and friend; and Edward Dusko, who has been hiking New Jersey's trails for almost fifty years. I also owe a debt of gratitude to Judi and Charlie Brown, who were gracious enough to loan me their Virginia hideaway, where I finished this manuscript; Charles King, an extraordinary graphic designer; and my family and friends, who put up with, even understood, my disappearance during the writing process.

Finally, I owe an enduring debt of gratitude to the late Mack Ness, who taught anyone willing to listen about conservation and land management in New Jersey.

Introduction

New Jersey harbors 122 wildlife management areas, 42 state parks and forests, and 7 national reserves, yet most residents will go a lifetime without setting foot on the Appalachian Trail or standing atop a Kittatinny Mountain overlook. Part of this contradiction is born from a perception that remote and exotic places cannot exist in the most densely populated state in the country. Informed travelers have long held a different perception and will point to areas within the Garden State more reminiscent of the Colorado River than the Delaware. The southern pinelands alone represent the largest protected tract of land on the Eastern Seaboard between Boston and Richmond, an area known as the Pinelands National Reserve. Add to that another 330,000 acres of park and forest land, 310,000 acres protected as wildlife management areas, and the 70,000-acre Delaware Water Gap National Recreation Area shared by Pennsylvania.

In a small and populated state such as New Jersey, it is even more important to understand the areas where we can recharge ourselves and breathe a clean sigh. The following pages offer suggestions that will leave the crowds behind, a compilation of scenic vistas, remote waterfalls, and secluded mountain trails. Destinations include Atlantic Ocean islands accessible by car, panoramic vistas at the end of long and rugged hikes, and more than eighty wildlife areas, ranging from the sheer cliffs of Kittatinny Ridge to the 1.1 million acres constituting New Jersey's southern Pine Barrens.

This book is also written with the notion that once campers pitch a tent, they are ready to climb an isolated peak, paddle a quiet river, or mountain bike along the base of a nearby ravine. Camping is covered in detail, but so are activities such as fishing, boating, birding, butterfly-watching, and scuba diving. The following pages combine all of the information necessary for a journey to New Jersey's state parks and natural areas, including trail descriptions with maps, a summary of the best and most private campsites, and advice about every conceivable activity near public camping in the Garden State. You will also find accounts of historical sites, serene beaches, horseback-riding trails, and a variety of winter pursuits such as cross-country skiing, snowshoeing, ice fishing, and dogsledding. With so many wildlife areas and activities described in depth, you should be able to find ideas that will suit a holiday weekend, an entire day, or just a few hours on a summer afternoon.

How to Use This Book

The Wildlife Areas

In an attempt to make this guidebook as comprehensive as possible, I've included thirty-seven of New Jersey's forty-two state parks and forests within its pages, in addition to all seven national reserves in the state and more than forty wildlife management areas, protected watersheds, historical sites, and nature preserves. It is a broad account, but by no means complete, and understanding the rationale I used to include or omit certain parks may be helpful. The five state parks I've excluded lie in developed areas that do not fit the theme of a wilderness escape, such as Liberty State Park in Jersey City and Washington Rock State Park near Plainfield. Six state marinas, although managed by the Division of Parks and Forestry, are covered in the fishing sections only where they apply to certain fishing destinations. A number of New Jersey's wildlife management areas are missing as well, as most of them consist of undeveloped tracts of land with no marked trails. What the book does include is a collection of parks, forests, and preserves chosen for their beauty or excellent contribution to a certain activity. A complete list of locations is shown on the map of Wildlife Areas by Chapter.

Chapters and Camping Regions

The chapters in this guidebook represent the eighteen parks within New Jersey equipped with camping facilities. One of the most rewarding ways to explore an area is to break camp at one park, explore the surrounding area, and pitch camp at the next park to the north or south. For that reason, parks in this guidebook are listed from north to south rather than alphabetically. This is meant to aid travelers who wish to visit one park after another on the same journey.

Similarly, a section in each chapter on surrounding points of interest describes wildlife areas within a twenty-minute drive of a given campground. This section is organized with the closest destination to the campground presented first, and suggestions vary from one-hour distractions to full-day side trips. You should check through the entire section before heading out, as certain wildlife areas may cater to specific pursuits, such as horseback riding, whereas others are of more interest to birders or mountain bikers. I compiled the list with an eye toward variety, although no outstanding park or preserve was omitted in preference to balance.

If you systematically explore New Jersey's campgrounds in the manner suggested, from High Point State Park in the north to Belleplain State Forest in the south, you will notice three completely different camping environments as you travel. The three regions in this guidebook—north, central, and south—do not conform to any geological standard, but they differ in three different and distinct wilderness experiences within New Jersey. Northern hardwood forests and mountains produce a wilder atmosphere than the central, developed areas of our state. The southern pinelands and coastline provide yet a third experience, defined by flat terrain, isolated campgrounds, and the 1.1-million-acre Pinelands National Reserve. Refer to the introduction preceding each region for a summary of camping conditions in parks throughout the area.

Campsite Recommendations

Campsite recommendations give priority to privacy and wilderness appeal, taking into account factors such as scenery, distance from the road, proximity to neighboring sites, amount of trees and vegetation around the site, overall privacy, and the wilderness feel of the campsite. The system is not perfect and will please campers seeking privacy and seclusion more than those who require a restroom nearby. The campground maps included in each chapter show the location of restrooms and other amenities and will help anyone interested in a more developed campsite.

Fishing Ratings

The New Jersey Division of Fish and Wildlife uses a scale of 1 (excellent), 2 (good), 3 (fair), and 4 (poor) to rank the quality of fishing in New Jersey's waters. Lakes and rivers in this guidebook are ranked similarly, and anglers should keep the rankings in mind when reading the fishing sections. The use of the word "excellent" means that a particular water body ranks a 1 on a scale from 1 to 4, "good" ranks a 2 on a scale from 1 to 4, and so on. For the purposes of this guidebook, the word "abundant" also denotes a 2 on the same scale.

4

WILDLIFE AREAS BY CHAPTER

1. High Point State Park
- 1a. Wallkill River NWR
- 1b. Bashakill WMA
- 1c. Shawangunk Ridge Trail

2. Stokes State Forest
- 2a. Flatbrook-Roy WMA
- 2b. Buttermilk Falls

3. Worthington State Forest
- 3a. Watergate Recreation Site
- 3b. Millbrook Village
- 3c. Walpack WMA
- 3d. Walpack
- 3e. Dingmans Falls
- 3f. Pocono Environmental Center
- 3g. Toms Creek Picnic Area
- 3h. Bushkill Falls
- 3i. Smithfield Beach
- 3j. McDade Trail
- 3k. Hialeah Picnic Area
- 3l. Mount Minsi

4. Swartswood State Park
- 4a. Paulinskill River WMA
- 4b. Whittingham WMA

5. Jenny Jump State Forest
- 5a. Pequest WMA

6. Stephens/Allamuchy Mt. State Parks
- 6a. Hackettstown Resevoir
- 6b. Kittatinny Valley State Park
- 6c. Hopatcong State Park
- 6d. Hackettstown Fish Hatchery
- 6e. Rockport Pheasant Farm

7. Wawayanda State Park
- 7a. Abram S. Hewitt State Forest
- 7b. Long Pond Ironworks State Park
- 7c. Ringwood State Park
- 7d. Ramapo Mountain State Forest
- 7e. Norvin Green State Forest
- 7f. Farny State Park

8. Voorhees State Park
- 8a. Ken Lockwood Gorge WMA
- 8b. Hacklebarney State Park

9. Spruce Run Recreation Area
- 9a. Clinton WMA
- 9b. Union Furnace Nature Preserve

10. Round Valley Recreation Area
- 10a. Cushetunk Mt. Nature Preserve
- 10b. Capoolong Creek WMA
- 10c. Great Swamp NWR

11. Delaware and Raritan Canal State Park
- 11a. Washington Crossing State Park
- 11b. Main Canal Towpath

12. Cheesequake State Park
- 12a. Sandy Hook Gateway NRA

13. Allaire State Park
- 13a. Manasquan River WMA
- 13b. Manasquan Reservoir
- 13c. Monmouth Battlefield State Park

14. Brendan T. Byrne State Forest
- 14a. Greenwood and Pasadena WMA
- 14b. Double Trouble State Park
- 14c. Manchester and Whiting WMAs
- 14d. Colliers Mills WMA
- 14e. Barnegat Bay
- 14f. Island Beach State Park

15. Wharton State Forest
- 15a. Penn State Forest

16. Bass River State Forest
- 16a. Stafford Forge WMA
- 16b. Great Bay Boulevard WMA
- 16c. Edwin B. Forsythe NWR

17. Parvin State Park
- 17a. Union Lake WMA
- 17b. Cohansey River Watershed
- 17c. Fort Mott State Park
- 17d. Supawna Meadows NWR
- 17e. Finn's Point Lighthouse

18. Belleplain State Forest
- 18a. Tuckahoe WMA
- 18b. Corson's Inlet State Park
- 18c. Cape May Point State Park
- 18d. Horseshoe Crab Spawning Areas
- 18e. Cape May NWR

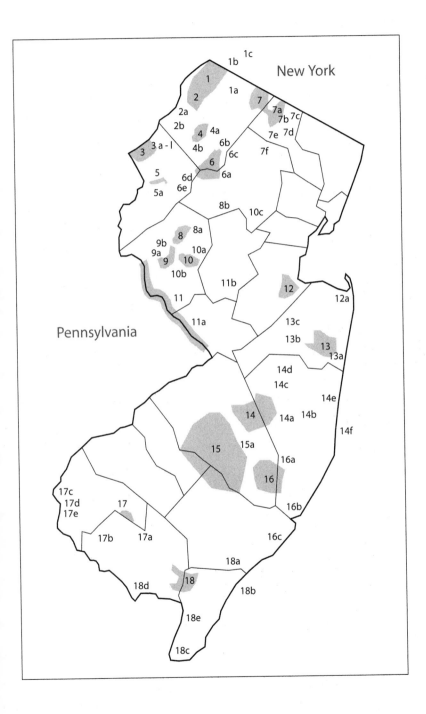

MAP AND TABLE LEGEND

Park road	Dirt road	Park trail	Interpark trail

25*	25	25	25	25
Recommended campsite	Lean-to	Shelter	Wooden platform	Yurt

Trail Tables

h Hiking

E Easy   b Snowmobiling   m Mountain biking

M Moderate   d Dogsledding   s Snowshoeing

D Difficult   e Horseback riding   X Cross-country skiing

Park Maps

- Appalachian Trail
- Appalachian Trail shelter
- Boat ramp
- Boat rentals
- Cabin
- Campground
- Canoe launch
- Fire tower
- Food concession
- Footbridge
- Historical site
- Natural area
- Observatory
- Overlook
- Parking
- Park office
- Picnic area
- Picnic shelter
- Playground
- Restrooms
- Restrooms with showers
- Swimming
- Trailer sanitary station
- Water

Maps and Directions

Although every effort has been made for accuracy, the fifty maps in this guidebook are meant as a general reference to be used in conjunction with local topographic maps. Given the large areas depicted in certain cases, it is sometimes not practical to include great detail or adhere to exact geography. This is especially true when a large area is represented on one small page, such as Wharton State Forest. Readers should always refer to the written directions or a local map. Where a smaller area is depicted, such as campgrounds, the maps adhere very closely to available information.

Specific directions are provided as often as possible, especially where a destination is difficult to find or roads are not marked or are too small to appear on standard maps. In certain instances, only a general location is given, and you must refer to a local map. This is often the case for New Jersey's many wildlife management areas, which may cover 30,000 acres with no central office or recreation area. The New Jersey Wild Places and Open Spaces Map shows the specific locations of all 122 of New Jersey's wildlife management areas. The map is available at many park offices and is recommended as an addendum to this guidebook.

These pages represent an accumulation of knowledge from many sources. I readily accept responsibility for any inaccuracies, but things do change over time. Please refer any errors to the publisher, and corrections will be researched for future editions. Enjoy the exploration!

The Northern Region: Sussex, Warren, Morris, Passaic, Bergen

Nothing is more inspiring to a wilderness camper, backpacker, or hiker than a land of high-altitude ridges and clear mountain streams. The hardwood forests along the Kittatinny Ridge in northern New Jersey simply produce a different experience than pinelands or coastline, an experience defined by sheer cliffs, sweeping vistas along the Appalachian Trail, and grand oak trees stretching to the horizon. This is bear country as well, and there's something about the need to take special care, the extra effort, that makes traveling through the northern parks a heartening endeavor. From remote trails surrounding Wawayanda Mountain to quiet fishing spots along the Delaware River, the following destinations will appeal to any wilderness seeker with the will to head north.

High Point State Park

1480 Route 23
Sussex, NJ 07461

Area. 15,827 acres.

Park office. Sussex County, 8 miles north of Sussex Borough on the west side of Route 23.

Highlights. High Point Monument, Dryden Kuser Natural Area, Appalachian Trail.

Activities. Camping, hiking, fishing, boating, picnicking, swimming, mountain biking, horseback riding, birding, hunting, ice fishing, cross-country skiing, snowshoeing, snowmobiling, dogsledding, ice skating.

Entrance fee. A fee is charged to enter the recreation area from Memorial Day weekend through Labor Day.

Park hours. Year-round, from dawn to dusk.

For additional information: (973) 875-4800

In 1909, environmentalist Anthony R. Kuser funded a 52,000-mile expedition across Asia to catalog pheasant species throughout the Orient, and in 1923, he donated 10,000 acres of his mountaintop estate to begin High Point State Park. Kuser then hired an architect to design the High Point Monument, which was completed in 1930 and marks the highest elevation in the state, at 1,803 feet. Sawmill Lake came into existence seven years later, when the Civilian Conservation Corps dammed the Flatbrook River to create the centerpiece of High Point's Family Campground, and the final blazes of the Appalachian Trail were laid soon after on the eastern edge of the park.

Kuser's Colonial-style mansion no longer stands on the highest bluff in New Jersey, but his legacy remains in a land that stretches from the New York border in the north to Stokes State Forest in the south. The Kittatinny Mountains line the east end of the park, looking down on three lakes, an Atlantic white cedar swamp, and 16,000 acres of mixed oak forest. Thirty miles of trails crisscross High Point, ranging in altitude from 900 to 1,800 feet and varying in difficulty from hikes along the ridge to quiet walks along a slow-moving stream. Campsites rest in a secluded setting surrounding the forested shores of Sawmill Lake, while most of the activity occurs 2 miles to the north at Lake Marcia, home to a modern recreation area, picnic tables, and a sandy beach.

Camping

High Point's one family campground, two group sites, and three cabins are located far from the recreation area. Tent sites surround Sawmill Lake about 2 miles south of the park office, and one group campground lies a mile to the west. The park's two family cabins look like grand hunting lodges on the shore of Steenykill Lake, and their wide porches will remind you of rocking chairs and lazy summer days. A third cabin sits by itself near the group campground and accommodates up to twenty-eight people. The basic amenities of a modern park are close at hand, but you will not find showers at either campground, nor will you find any sites that accommodate trailers. Both factors add to the quiet and solitude at High Point's picturesque campgrounds.

Family Campground

The Flatbrook River drains 20-acre Sawmill Lake, a clear mountain pool looking like a perfect oval at the bottom of a gently sloping basin. One road circles the campground about 30 feet above the lake, where you can look down and see the campsites ringing the shore. All of the campsites are well spaced, and many sit at the water's edge. Some rise above the road and look down on the scene. A thick cover of oak, maple, and hickory ring the campground, creating an unbroken chain of forest, ever rising, from the banks of Sawmill Lake to the Appalachian Trail.

Directions. Turn left out of the park office onto Route 23, drive .5 mile, and turn left on Sawmill Road. Proceed 1.9 miles to the campground on the left.

Sites and facilities. High Point's fifty tent sites are each equipped with fire rings and picnic tables. About twenty of the sites hold wooden platforms. Water and restrooms are evenly distributed throughout the campground, and you will find a boat ramp on the west end of Sawmill Lake. The restrooms do not contain showers, and none of the sites support trailers. The campground is open from April 1 through October 31.

Recommended sites. You could drop a fishing line into Sawmill Lake from sites 1 through 4, which touch the shore and offer enough space for privacy. Numbers 5 through 8 are almost as close to the water, and you will find a clear view and ample space between sites. Numbers 12

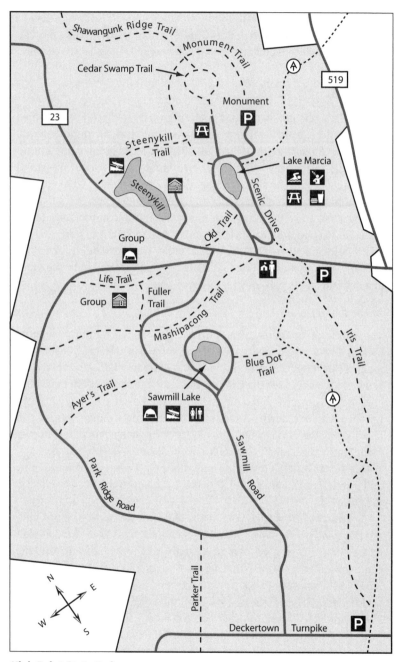

High Point State Park

through 14, although bunched together, are still worthy waterside sites. Number 27 lies on the shore and open to the road, and 23 and 24 offer privacy but do not lie directly on the lake. Many of the remaining sites border swampy sections of Sawmill Lake, but they still hold great views, including 15 through 20, 25, and 26. Take a look at the sites across the circular access road if you are searching for ultimate privacy, since several of them rest at the end of long paths leading into the woods, including 34 through 42, and 49. The terrain slopes toward Sawmill Lake, so consider a platform site if you prefer level ground.

Group Campground

High Point's two group campsites are isolated and private, situated more than a mile from the activity at Lake Marcia and 2 miles from Sawmill Lake. Both sites occupy a grass lawn backed by forest, but site A is slightly larger, with a capacity of thirty-five campers and an extra chemical toilet. Site B accommodates only twenty-five campers, but it benefits from more tree cover and lies farther from Route 23. Each site contains one fire pit, one grill, two picnic tables, and at least one chemical toilet. You will find water from ground pumps next to each site. Turn left out of the park office, drive .5 mile, and turn left on Sawmill Road. Proceed .1 mile and turn right on Park Ridge Road. Continue .2 mile to group campsite A or .3 mile to campsite B, both on the right side of the road. They are open from May 15 through October 15.

Cabins

High Point offers two family cabins on the east shore of Steenykill Lake and one group cabin on Park Ridge Road. The two family cabins look more like sprawling ranch houses, located at the end of a lonely access road about .7 mile north of the park office. A wraparound porch circles three-quarters of the cabin, and Steenykill Lake is within view. Each cabin contains three bedrooms, one furnished with a double-deck bunk and the others with twin beds. The living room contains a fireplace, table, and chairs. The kitchen is equipped with hot and cold running water, an electric stove, and refrigerator, and the bathroom holds a shower and modern toilet.

The group cabin is situated near the group campsites on Park Ridge Road. Two bedrooms each contain seven double-deck bunks, accommodating a total of 28 people. A kitchen and two bathrooms are identical to those in the family cabins. A wooden porch in the front faces a gravel parking area, and a grass lawn in the back is encircled by wood-

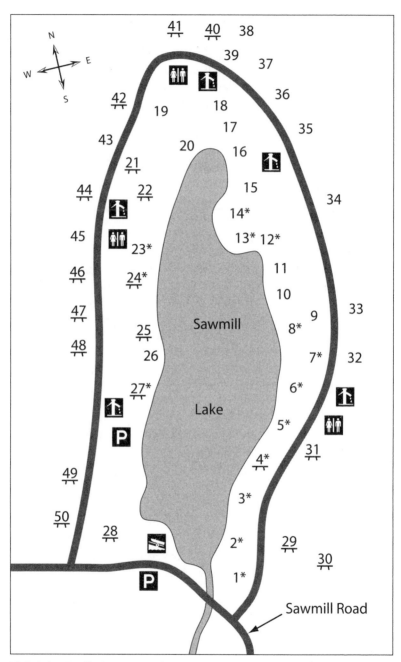

High Point Family Campground

land and holds a fire ring, grill, and two picnic tables. A woodburning stove heats the main room, which is furnished with wooden tables and benches. All three cabins, invariably booked solid a full twelve months in advance, are available from May 15 through October 15.

Trails

It is possible to hike more than 2,500 miles of continuous trails beginning at High Point State Park. About 9 miles of the Appalachian Trail cut through the park in the AT's 2,175-mile course from Mount Katahdin in Maine to Springer Mountain, Georgia. Another long-distance trail, the Shawangunk Ridge Trail, begins in High Point, extends 1.7 miles across the New York State border, and then continues another 33 miles to join the 300-mile Long Path trail in Wurtsboro Ridge State Forest. Eleven more marked trails weave through High Point, totaling more than 19 miles and varying in length from .4-mile mountain ascents ending atop the Kittatinny Ridge to 4.3-mile walks through cedar swamps, hardwood forest, and mountain valleys.

The difficult trails throughout High Point tend to be more scenic. The 3.7-mile Monument Trail, an undulating hike along the Kittatinny Ridge

Trail Mileage and Difficulty

TRAIL	MILES	DIFFICULTY	BLAZE	USES
Appalachian Trail	9.0	E–M	white	h
Ayer's Trail	0.9	E	black	b,d,e,h,m,s,x
Blue Dot Trail	0.4	D	blue	h
Cedar Swamp Trail	1.5	E	green	h
Fuller Trail	0.8	E	blue/red	b,d,e,h,m,s,x
Iris Trail	4.3	E	red	b,d,e,h,m,s,x
Life Trail	0.7	E	brown	b,d,e,h,m,s,x
Mashipacong Trail	2.8	E–M	yellow	b,d,e,h,m,s,x
Monument Trail	3.7	M–D	green/red	h,s,x
Old Trail	0.5	E	brown/yellow	e,h,m,x
Parker Trail	3.0	M	green	b,d,e,h,m,s,x
Shawangunk Ridge Trail	1.7	D	turquoise	h
Steenykill Trail	0.7	M	blue	e,h,m,x

through cedar swamp and pitch pine, produces vistas of the Shawangunk Mountains and Pocono Plateau. Blue Dot Trail is more like beginner's rock climbing, but it is a fast way to get to the Appalachian Trail from the campground and ends at an overlook of Sawmill Lake. Shawangunk Ridge Trail is almost as difficult, descending from over 1,500 feet to just under 1,000 feet as it crosses the border into New York State. One of High Point's longer trails, the 2.8-mile Mashipacong Trail, begins easily as it follows an old farm road leading through red maple and huckleberry, but the trail becomes a bit more difficult when it climbs a 300-foot ridge to the visitors center near Lake Marcia.

High Point offers a number of easier trails as well. Iris Trail gets you away from the recreation area and into the forest, stretching 4.3 miles past views of Lake Rutherford to the Appalachian Trail. Cedar Swamp Trail, perhaps the most rewarding nature walk in the park if you're looking for unique habitat, begins at the end of Scenic Drive north of Lake Marcia, then stretches 1.5 miles through an Atlantic white cedar swamp in the Dryden Kuser Natural Area. Another short walk, the .9-mile Ayer's Trail, leads past several stone foundations and the remnants of Ayer's Farm, a homestead tracing its origins almost to the Civil War. Parker Trail, although rated as moderate, extends 3 miles south into Stokes State Forest, where you encounter an entirely new set of twenty-five marked trails.

Activities

High Point's beauty radiates outward from three central lakes to the Big Flatbrook River and the Kittatinny Ridge. Thirty miles of trails crisscross the land, many of them open to various pursuits such as mountain biking, horseback riding, cross-country skiing, and dogsledding. Two boat ramps give access to Steenykill and Sawmill Lakes. The recreation area, complete with a beach, picnic tables, and hot showers, sits on the south shore of Lake Marcia in the shadow of the Kittatinny Mountains. The High Point Monument will always be the first stop for many visitors, but Dryden Kuser Natural Area caters to those interested in a quiet hike through Atlantic white cedar swamp and High Point's natural environment. This is one of the few parks that thrives during the colder months, when the High Point Cross Country Ski Center manufactures snow for 15 miles of groomed cross-country trails.

Scenic Drive

A picturesque route to the monument passes several isolated and solitary picnic tables as it heads toward Lake Marcia. Along this 1-mile drive, you will pass five small dirt parking areas, all giving access to the Appalachian Trail. A scenic overlook lies at .8 mile, where you will find an observation platform facing views of Wawayanda Mountain and the Wallkill River Valley to the east. Scenic Drive is the first right turn beyond the recreation area entrance booth. Drive 1 mile north along Scenic Drive; then turn right on Monument Drive to arrive at the monument.

High Point Monument

Composed of New Hampshire granite and local quartzite, the 220-foot High Point Monument was completed in 1930 to memorialize New Jersey's war veterans. The spire also stands as another legacy of Anthony R. Kuser, who hired an architect in 1927 to design the memorial. The monument reopened in 2005 after an eight-year, $75 million renovation, and visitors now line up on sunny days to climb the 292 steps to the top. The scene of the Shawangunk Mountains to the north, Pocono Plateau to the west, and Wallkill River Valley to the east makes the climb worthwhile. Two parking areas service the monument. Here you will find restrooms, a scenic overlook of Pochuck Mountain to the east, and access to the Monument Trail.

Dryden Kuser Natural Area

The 1.5-mile Cedar Swamp Trail takes you into the heart of Dryden Kuser Natural Area, where the highest-elevation Atlantic white cedar swamp in New Jersey lies at 1,500 feet above sea level. Black spruce, striped maple, and red oak represent just a few of the many species that inhabit a landscape ranging from marshland to ridgetop. A walk along the Cedar Swamp Trail puts you in the midst of an area that was carved out during the last ice age, and a habitat encompassing more than twenty-nine types of trees, 140 herbs, nineteen ferns, and fifty-six grasses, sedges, and rushes. Rhododendrons bloom in late June, dominating the scene at this 1,500-acre area on the northern border of High Point State Park. The access road leading to the Cedar Swamp Trail begins .1 mile west of Monument Drive.

Fishing and Boating

High Point's three lakes offer serene settings for anglers, and boats with electric motors are allowed on two of the lakes. A boat ramp lies on the west shore of 20-acre Sawmill Lake, where almost 1,500 trout are stocked every year. Largemouth bass and sunfish are abundant in the lake as well, and you will find a lesser population of catfish. At 30 acres,

Steenykill is the largest lake in High Point. A boat ramp sits on the north shore, and fishing is good for smallmouth bass, catfish, and sunfish, with a few largemouth bass and crappie in the mix. Boating is not allowed on 19-acre Lake Marcia, but fishing is permitted anywhere from the shore other than the beach area. You'll find an abundance of yellow perch, catfish, and sunfish, but only fair fishing for largemouth and smallmouth bass.

High Point is also the source of the Big Flatbrook River, which begins its journey toward the Delaware River at Sawmill Lake. Only a few feet wide at its source, the Flatbrook turns wilder farther south, and the upper reaches near High Point are stocked with nearly 2,000 trout each year. The lower section through Stokes State Forest draws more than 30,000 trout annually, and a 4-mile stretch of river below Route 206 is designated as a fly-fishing area. See the Stokes State Forest chapter for more information.

Picnicking

High Point offers five picnic areas within a mile of Lake Marcia. Tables line the main road near the recreation area, the cement sidewalk leading to the beach, and a hill overlooking the beach itself. Two additional picnic areas lie across the road from the beach in their own wooded groves. All of the sites provide grills, with drinking water, restrooms, and playgrounds nearby. The area on the hill near the beach holds a covered pavilion and can be reserved at least five days in advance by groups of up to seventy-five people. If you're looking to escape the crowds, a handful of solitary tables line Scenic Drive and the road leading to Dryden Kuser Natural Area. None of them provide grills, water, or restrooms, but they are unmatched for privacy. The tables along Scenic Drive each offer a small dirt parking space and access to the Appalachian Trail.

Swimming

The recreation area at Lake Marcia receives more visitors during the summer than any other area of the park. A strip of sand borders the south shore, where swimming is allowed from Memorial Day through Labor Day. The beach is backed by a grass lawn and a large parking area, and High Point Monument rises in the background beyond the north shore of Lake Marcia. A trailer serving as the food concession is open during the summer, offering hot dogs, pizza, hot pretzels, and soda. Restrooms, picnic tables, and a bathhouse with showers are nearby.

Mountain Biking

Most of the trails at High Point allow mountain bikes. The five exceptions are the Shawangunk Ridge, Monument, Cedar Swamp, Blue Dot, and Appalachian Trails. Many of the trails produce either short or rocky rides, but the beauty of the lakes and overlooks that are accessible to mountain bikers makes almost any ride worthwhile. Iris Trail, one of the longest in the park at 4.3 miles, encompasses a variety of terrain, including moderate ascents, a few stream crossings, and some rocky areas. Parker Trail is flat but still challenging, as it is pressed thin by brush and prone to flooding during wet weather.

Consider combining several of the shorter trails with paved forest roads to create a longer ride. Park Ridge Road travels along rolling hills and intersects a few side trails, including Mashipacong, Ayer's, Life, and Fuller. Sawmill Road produces a scenic tour along the Flatbrook River from Sawmill Lake to Deckertown Turnpike. You can turn right on Deckertown Turnpike to hit Parker Trail after about .4 mile (the trailhead is easy to miss). Turn right on Parker Trail to head back to Park Ridge Road, forming a loop. For a longer ride, turn left on Parker Trail to continue into Stokes State Forest and reach another set of twenty-five marked trails.

Horseback Riding

Horseback riding is permitted on the trails designated in the mountain-biking section. Iris Trail stretches through fairly easy terrain with a few gentle slopes, and you will find parking for horse trailers at the north end. See the trails table for mileage and difficulty.

Birding

High Point's varied habitat includes ridgetop forests, mountain lakes, cedar swamps, shallow rivers, and a microwave tower near the park office that attracts nesting northern ravens. Wind off the high ridges brings migrating hawks, and High Point operates a hawk watch from the nature center porch as well as from the base of High Point Monument. Dryden Kuser Natural Area is known for a variety of elusive birds, such as white-winged crossbills, barred owls, and northern waterthrushes. A number of warblers can also be found along the Cedar Swamp Trail, including blackburnian, golden-winged, Nashville, Canada, and yellow-rumped warblers. Drive along Park Ridge Road for occasional blue-headed vireos, alder flycatchers, and olive-sided flycatchers, along with more common residents such as hooded warblers, purple finches, and northern goshawks. During spring, look for a few species that have nested along Sawmill Road in the past, including brown creepers, golden-crowned kinglets, worm-eating warblers, cerulean warblers, black-billed cuckoos, and northern parulas.

Hunting

About 21 percent of the park, just over 3,200 acres, is open to the hunting of deer, small game, wild turkeys, and waterfowl. A little more than half of the park is designated as a special deer hunt area, requiring a separate permit and subject to a variety of regulations. The special deer hunt usually occurs around mid-November and attracts hunters to many of High Point's trails. The High Point State Park website posts specific times and annual regulation changes.

Winter Activities

Trails remain open to all sorts of activities during the winter. Some are even covered with artificial snow, and the High Point Cross Country Ski Center offers rentals, a fireplace, and hot meals. A basic rule governs trail use within High Point State Park during the winter. Trails and unplowed roads to the south of Route 23 are reserved for snowmobiling and dogsledding, and those to the north for cross-country skiing and snowshoeing.

Almost 10 miles of cross-country skiing trails north of Route 23 are groomed and covered by artificial snow. Five miles of groomed trails are open to snowshoeing, and 30 miles of unmarked trails are open to those who want to make their own way through High Point's 15,827 acres. Groomed ski routes include Steenykill Trail (rated as difficult), Scenic Drive (moderate to easy), and Cedar Swamp Trail (easy). Snowshoe routes include Monument Trail and the park access road on the west side of Lake Marcia. You will find parking at the recreation area; ski and snowshoe trails begin across the road.

The trails and roads south of Route 23 open to snowmobiling and dogsledding include Iris Trail, Fuller Trail, Ayer's Trail, Park Ridge Road, and Sawmill Road. Parker Trail is open as well, but only when snowfall exceeds 8 inches. You can also head into Stokes, where another 18.7 miles of trails and roads allow snowmobiles. The New Jersey Sled Dog Club schedules a race at High Point every year, but the race is sometimes canceled because of a lack of snow.

High Point Cross Country Ski Center functions much like a downhill ski resort, charging fees for trail passes by the day, half day, or season. The lodge offers hot food, a central fireplace, and sales and rental of ski and snowshoe equipment, ice skates, poles, boots, bindings, and clothing. You can even ice skate next to the lodge, given safe conditions on Lake Marcia, and ice fishing is allowed on all of High Point's lakes. The center schedules tours, lessons, and other events throughout the winter.

Flora and Fauna

Habitats within High Point State Park vary greatly. Much of the area is a reflection of the Kittatinny Ridge section of the Highlands, rarely falling below 1,000 feet. Other areas include Atlantic white cedar swamp, mountain lakes, high ridges, and at least four types of forest. The number of oaks alone found in the park—white, scarlet, chestnut, red, and black—exemplify High Point's diversity. Pitch pine, hawthorn, and sassafras inhabit the high-altitude ridgetops, and the edges of the streams and bogs support eastern hemlock, white pine, black spruce, and yellow, gray, and river birches. A few endangered plants have adapted to existence in high-altitude swamps, including the three-toothed cinquefoil, a very rare white rose distinguished by three jagged points on each leaf.

The varied forest supports a wide range of animals, from black bears found throughout the park to beavers that depend on mountain streams and lakes. More than 200 types of birds occur in the forest, including nesting species such as the barred owl and hermit thrush. Common animal life is similar to that of Stokes State Forest to the south, but High Point and the Kittatinny Ridge support a number of rare species as well. Bobcats, bald eagles, timber rattlesnakes, and long-tailed salamanders are just a few threatened and endangered animals that rely on High Point State Park and the New Jersey Highlands for food, shelter, and breeding sites in the northeastern United States.

Surrounding Points of Interest

Head north along the Shawangunk Ridge Trail and you will come to a number of beautiful nature preserves beyond the New York border. Bashakill Wildlife Management Area begins only 17 miles to the north, but the Shawangunk Ridge Trail continues through seven more state parks and preserves leading to the Catskill Mountains. Depending on how far you want to venture into New York, the area could easily keep a hiker busy for months. If you want to stay within New Jersey, Wallkill River National Wildlife Refuge lies 10 miles east of High Point and is one of only seven national wildlife areas in the state. High Point also sits on the northern border of the 70,000-acre Delaware Water Gap

National Recreation Area, which is covered in the Stokes State Forest and Worthington State Forest chapters.

Wallkill River National Wildlife Refuge

This 5,100-acre sanctuary lies about 10 miles east of High Point and extends from Route 23 to the New York border. The Wallkill River flows northward through the Great Valley, an area bounded by the Kittatinny Ridge to the west and New Jersey Highlands to the east. American sycamore, red maple, green ash, and marsh marigold line the riverbank, while higher elevations hold white oak, shagbark hickory, and flowering dogwood. Sweeping meadows fill with wildflowers during the spring and summer, attracting butterflies by the hundreds. More than 225 species of birds occur at the refuge as well, including rare visitors to New Jersey such as white-rumped sandpipers, Tennessee warblers, and rough-legged hawks.

The best way to explore the preserve is by canoe, and the river moves slowly, making for easy round-trip canoeing. The water level fluctuates seasonally and is usually highest during the spring and fall. Summer droughts may cause the river to be impassable. Two canoe access points in New Jersey are located where Routes 565 and 642 cross the Wallkill River, but the Route 565 access point does not offer parking. You will find another access point in New York, about .3 mile north of the New Jersey border, where Oil City Road crosses the river.

A number of trails weave through the wildlife area as well. The Dagmar Dale Nature Trail leaves from the refuge headquarters in the southern section of the park. The trail actually consists of two loops, the 1.7-mile North Loop (marked in blue) and the 1-mile South Loop (marked in yellow). The South Loop runs through alternating meadow and woodland, leading to a small cascade and a wooden bench about .2 mile from the office. The North Loop travels along the river's edge before climbing up to circle a vast meadow of wildflowers, an advisable destination for butterfly-watchers during midsummer. You will find a good view of the river valley at the beginning of the North Loop, about .2 mile east of the park office.

Two other trails stretch through the refuge, one near the park office and one on the New York border about 6.5 miles to the north. The 1.5-mile Wood Duck Nature Trail begins 1.4 miles south of the office, on the west side of Route 565, and runs wide and flat to the Wallkill River. The 2.5-mile Liberty Loop crosses the New York border on the northern end of the refuge, cutting through grassland to join a section of the Appalachian Trail. All of the trails allow hiking, cross-country skiing, and snowshoeing. Drive 9.6 miles south of the High Point office on Route 23 and turn left on Route 565 (Glenwood Road). Proceed 1.5 miles to the Wallkill River headquarters on the left.

Bashakill Wildlife Management Area, New York

This 3,000-acre wildlife management area not only represents the largest freshwater wetlands in southeastern New York, but also serves as a scenic route to Wurtsboro and the Shawangunk Ridge Trail farther north. A 10-mile rail trail follows the defunct Ontario and Western Railway line along the east bank of the Bashakill River, where a dozen parking areas, two boat ramps, and three canoe launch areas give access to the wetlands. Several of the parking areas offer sweeping vistas of Bashakill Wetlands backed by the 1,500-foot Mongaup Hills to the west and the Shawangunk Mountains to the north and east. Fishing is good for trout, largemouth bass, and pickerel. The parking areas are popular birding spots for rarities such as the Virginia rail, sora, and common moorhen.

Drive 4.7 miles north of the High Point office on Route 23 and turn left on Route 6 west, following the sign for Port Jervis. Proceed 1.4 miles and turn right on Route 209 north. Follow Route 209 for 11.2 miles and turn right on Otisville Road (Route 61). Beware: Otisville Road is difficult to see and not marked at the turn. Drive .4 mile and turn left on South Road. A dozen parking areas line South Road, but proceed 1.5 miles to one of the more scenic parking areas on the left. Continue another 1.7 miles north, turn left on Haven Road, and stop at the bridge for a canoe access point and a view of the Mongaup Hills. If you want to head farther north to the Shawangunk Ridge Trail, follow the directions below to the trailhead.

Shawangunk Ridge Trail, New York

The 36-mile Shawangunk Ridge Trail is a spectacular hike if you have the time, especially the 10 miles along the ridgetop north of Wurtsboro. The trail weaves along the white cliffs and waterfalls of the Shawangunk Mountains, with stunning views of the Catskills in the distance. Eight state parks and preserves line the 36-mile trail, many of them inaccessible to cars. From south to north, the trail crosses through the Neversink Preserve, Bashakill Wildlife Management Area, Wurtsboro Ridge State Forest, Roosa Gap State Forest, Shawangunk Ridge State Forest, Bear Hill Preserve, Sam's Point Preserve, and the trail's end at Minnewaska State Park Preserve.

You can begin the trail at High Point State Park, but the most scenic section requires a short drive. Follow the directions for Bashakill Wildlife

Management Area. From the corner of Haven Road and South Road, drive north on South Road for 3.5 miles to Sullivan Street in Wurtsboro. The trailhead parking area is at a VFW lodge east of town. Turn right on Sullivan Street, drive 1 mile, and turn left on VFW Road, a short gravel road leading to the lodge. Park just beyond the lodge at the trailhead marked with turquoise blazes. The best overlooks begin about 7 miles north of the trailhead and continue for about 3 miles to Route 52.

Another option is to leave one car in Wurtsboro and another at the overlook parking area on the south side of Route 52, about 1.7 miles west of Cox Road near the town of Cragsmoor. You have to walk about 300 yards east along Route 52 to the trailhead (walking from the parking area, keep the guardrail and valley off your right shoulder). When you come to the end of the guardrail, look for the turquoise blazes on the right. The vistas begin after about 1.5 miles and continue for another 2 miles along the Shawangunk Ridge. If you decide to hike the full 10 miles between parking areas, pick up a map from the Catskill Hiking Shack at 169 Sullivan Street in Wurtsboro. Carrying a map is strongly recommended, as several trails intersect with the Shawangunk Ridge Trail about 1 mile north of Wurtsboro.

Where to Buy Supplies

Drive 4.2 miles north of the High Point office on Route 23, and you will come to a strip mall on the right just short of the New York border. The mall holds a grocery store, pharmacy, pizza parlor, Dunkin' Donuts, and bank. Across the road from the strip mall, you will find a gas station, McDonald's restaurant, and Dairy Queen. Continue .5 mile north on Route 23 into New York, turn left on Route 6, and drive 1.5 miles to Port Jervis. Stores are widely scattered, but the small city holds pharmacies, banks, grocery stores, delis, fast food, gas stations, a bicycle shop, and a canoe outfitter.

If you prefer to stay in New Jersey, Sussex Borough lies 8 miles south of the park office on Route 23. Here you will find grocery stores, a pharmacy, banks, restaurants, and gas stations. A bicycle shop and a sports shop specializing in cross-country skiing are located about 2 miles south of the city center. You will pass through Colesville on the way to Sussex, about 1 mile south of the High Point office. The small town is home to a pizzeria, country market, and High Point Trading Post on the left, where you can find camping supplies and renew your fishing permit.

Stokes State Forest

1 Coursen Rd.
Branchville, NJ 07826

Area. 16,067 acres.

Park office. Sussex County, 3.8 miles north of Branchville on the east side of Route 206.

Highlights. Tillman Ravine, Sunrise Mountain hawk watch, Appalachian Trail, Kittatinny Ridge, Big Flatbrook River.

Activities. Camping, hiking, fishing, boating, picnicking, swimming, mountain biking, horseback riding, birding, hunting, cross-country skiing, snowshoeing, snowmobiling, dogsledding.

Entrance fee. A fee is charged to enter the recreation area from Memorial Day weekend through Labor Day.

Park hours. Year-round, from 9 A.M. to 4 P.M.

For additional information: (973) 948-3820

At the turn of the eighteenth century, the area now known as Stokes State Forest was deemed a lost cause. It was denuded of trees, and smoldering charcoal pits left streams of smoke lingering in the air like signal fires. It's hard to imagine that the Lenni-Lenape Indians had used the land for hunting only 100 years earlier, but the arrival of Europeans brought a string of deals and royal debts that passed ownership of the area from the Dutch to King Charles II, then eventually to the Quakers in a negotiation brokered by William Penn. English and Dutch settlers followed, and both groups took part in driving the Lenape westward. Charcoal production, wood for domestic and industrial fuel, and lumber for expanding towns all contributed to the forest's demise.

During the early 1900s, what others saw as wasteland, Edward C. Stokes saw as opportunity. Governor of New Jersey from 1905 to 1908, Stokes was a practical environmentalist, establishing the Forest Park Reservation Commission in 1905 to restore and protect depleted woodlands. Stokes donated 500 acres of his estate to the cause in 1907. Later that year, the state purchased an additional 5,432 acres and dubbed it Stokes State Forest.

Today, if you're heading north and plan to stay within the borders of New Jersey, Stokes State Forest is your best bet for a wilderness experience. At 16,067 acres, the park is big enough to produce a sense of escape, and it borders the Delaware Water Gap National Recreation Area, a 50-mile stretch of land extending along the Kittatinny Ridge from Worthington State Forest in the south to High Point State Park in the north.

Stokes encompasses four campgrounds, a number of rewarding trout streams, and more than 50 miles of rugged and scenic trails along the Kittatinny Ridge. One of the biggest draws in the park is the Big Flatbrook River, a magnet for fishermen, which flows through the southern edge of Lake Ocquittunk Campground. The recreation area at Stony Lake offers all the amenities of a modern park, complete with boating, fishing, picnicking, and even a beach with a bathhouse and showers.

Camping

The four camping areas at Stokes—Lake Ocquittunk, Shotwell, Steam Mill, and Haskin's Group Campground—all lie within the shadow of the Kittatinny Ridge, bordered by the forested New Jersey Highlands. Lake Ocquittunk holds the most sought-after sites, where campers can pitch a tent on the banks of a clear mountain stream. All of the family campgrounds are open year-round with the exception of Steam Mill, which serves as an overflow area on summer weekends. Eleven log cabins ring Lake Ocquittunk, and nine wooden lean-tos are scattered throughout Shotwell. A dozen sites with wooden platforms can be found throughout the park as well. All of the campgrounds supply tables, fire rings, water, and with the exception of Steam Mill, modern restrooms.

Lake Ocquittunk Campground

Lake Ocquittunk can be crowded after Memorial Day, but many of the campsites are well spaced from one another and private. The lake is within view, and the Big Flatbrook River weaves through the southern edge of the grounds. Boats with electric motors are allowed on the lake, and some of the best trout fishing throughout New Jersey can be found in the Big Flatbrook River, although the premier trout pools are a few miles downstream. Around the campground, the river is gentle and shallow, creating just enough melody to be heard through your tent walls at night.

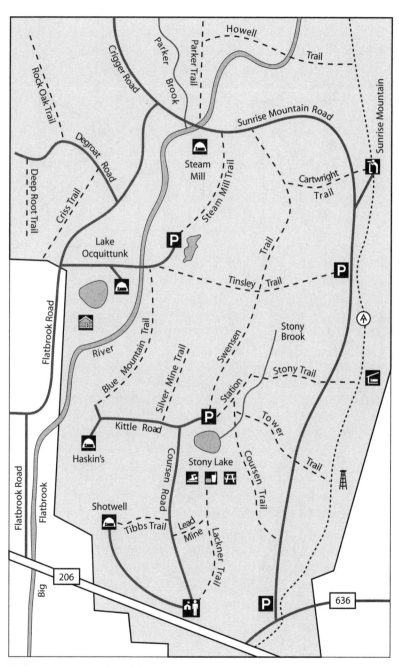

Stokes State Forest (North)

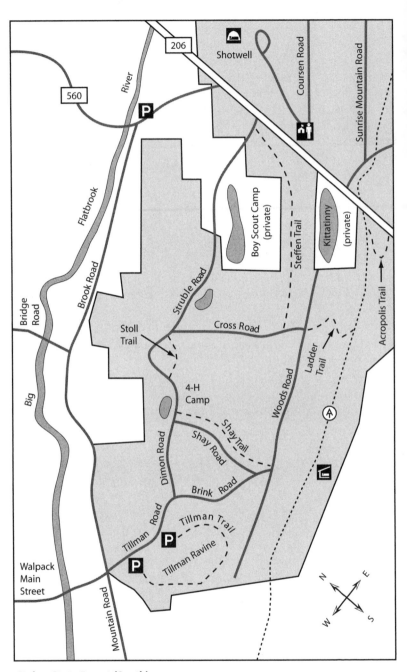

Stokes State Forest (South)

Directions. From the park office, drive north on Route 206 for 1.8 miles, and turn right just over the small bridge onto Flatbrook Road. Follow Flatbrook Road east for 2.8 miles, and turn right on the gravel road into the campground. Cabins are nearby, on the south side of Flatbrook Road about .3 mile west of Lake Ocquittunk Campground.

Sites and facilities. Ocquittunk's twenty-four campsites are each equipped with fire rings and picnic tables. Numbers 8 through 11 are designated for trailers, and 12 through 14 hold wooden platforms. The campground contains two restrooms with flush toilets, but only the one near the road offers hot showers. Water from ground pumps is within walking distance of all sites. Ocquittunk is open year-round.

Recommended sites. Don't be put off by the sites you see on the way into the campground. Keep driving past the trailer area, and turn right on the dirt road leading to numbers 13 and 14. If you like privacy, these are without doubt the most secluded spots to pitch a tent in the entire park. Anomalies, they sit by themselves down one dirt road, separated from the rest of the campground by the Big Flatbrook River. Both hold wooden platforms and lie directly on the river, although up a small embankment. Site 13 occupies a clearing at a dead end, and unless you need a restroom close at hand, it is the best option in the forest for anyone seeking seclusion.

If those two are taken, drive back to the paved road and continue southwest through the campground. The loop to the right contains four of the most sought-after sites at Lake Ocquittunk, 15 through 18, all resting on the banks of the slow-moving Big Flatbrook River. Site 16 is the best of the group, set back from the road in a forested clearing. The last two hidden spots in the campground, numbers 6 and 7, lie near the trailer area on the main road. Take the path beyond the trailers and walk 100 feet down a gradual embankment. You will come upon both sites, encircled by woodland and resting on the shore of Lake Ocquittunk.

Lake Ocquittunk Cabins

Stokes State Forest offers eleven cabins on the west shore of Lake Ocquittunk and two on the other side of Flatbrook Road about half a mile from the lake. Ten of the cabins on the lake each sleep four people, but the park allows up to six if you make arrangements in advance. The main room in each cabin holds a woodburning stove and a wooden table and chairs. You can forget the typical camping rituals while you're here, as the kitchen provides hot and cold running water, a refrigerator, and an electric stove with an oven. The bathroom contains a modern

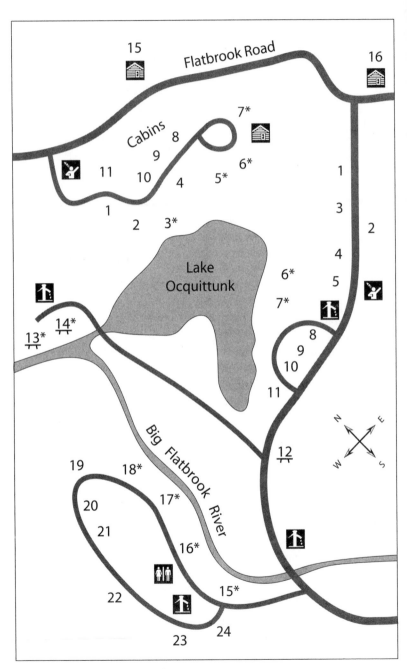

Lake Ocquittunk Campground

toilet and sink, but no showers. Community showers are in a separate building near the entrance to the cabin complex.

The remaining three cabins differ from the others in that they accommodate more people and contain their own showers (and cost more to rent). Cabins 7 and 15 each supply eight beds. Cabin 16 contains twelve beds divided between two separate bedrooms, as well as two full bathrooms with showers. Cabins 7 and 16 are equipped with fireplaces, and number 15 has a woodburning stove. Cabins 1 through 15 are available from April 1 through December 15, and cabin 16 is available from April 14 through November 30. All cabins can be reserved up to 11 months in advance. They're hard to get, so reserve as early as possible.

Directions. The entrance for cabins 1 through 11 is on the south side of Flatbrook Road, about .3 mile west of Lake Ocquittunk Campground. Cabin 15 is on the north side of Flatbrook Road, about .1 mile east of the entrance for the other cabins. Cabin 16 lies .3 mile east of the Lake Ocquittunk Campground on the north side of Grau Road.

Recommended cabins. Most of the cabins are within view of their neighbors, either on a small hill near Flatbrook Road or down a slope closer to the lake. If you're looking for privacy, cabin 3 practically touches the shore of Lake Ocquittunk and is surrounded by woodland. It's also centrally located near the shower building. Cabins 5 and 6 are farther away from the showers but still in a good location, resting about 30 yards from the shore of Lake Ocquittunk and some distance from the road. Group cabins 15 and 16 are supremely private, resting well off the road with no neighboring buildings or towns. Group cabin 7, situated in the cabin complex, is well spaced from the other cabins in a forested clearing.

Shotwell Campground

On sunny midsummer days, when the Lake Ocquittunk Campground becomes crowded, most people head for Shotwell. The campground lies near the park office but remains peaceful and quiet. Lake Ocquittunk is located 5 miles to the east, the Big Flatbrook River lies almost a mile to the north, and the recreation area is minutes away by car. Several sites will make you forget summer crowds, and a few nearby trails lead to the recreation area. Tibbs Trail, beginning at the southeast corner of the campground, provides an easy walk through forest and meadow, ending at Coursen Road. An almost 3-mile walk along Tibbs, Lead Mine, and Lackner Trails leads to the beach at Stony Lake and two popular trails climbing the Kittatinny Ridge.

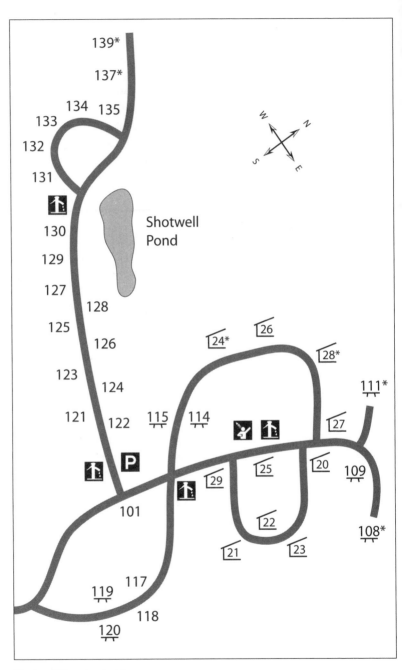

Shotwell Campground

Directions. From the park office, drive 100 yards east on Coursen Road, and turn left onto Shotwell Road just before the wooden bridge. Continue 1.2 miles north on Shotwell Road to the campground.

Sites and facilities. Shotwell's twenty-seven campsites and ten lean-tos are each equipped with fire rings and picnic tables. One restroom contains modern toilets and showers, and water pumps are within walking distance of all sites. Shotwell is open year-round.

Recommended sites. The four sites at the ends of the roads to the north and west, 108, 111, 137, and 139, are the most private spots at Shotwell, hidden by forest some distance from the road. Number 139 has a barrier of trees and brush on its border with 137. Four others, 118, 119, 120, and 135, are separated from the road and ringed by trees, but they are adjacent to other sites. The best lean-to choices are 24 and 28, withdrawn from the main path in a forested grove.

Steam Mill Campground

Steam Mill is fairly secluded, situated 5 miles from the recreation area near the border of High Point State Park. Chestnut oak and sugar maple trees surround the campground, which lies at the hub of several trails and rivers. Parker Trail follows Parker Brook into High Point State Park to the east and across the Big Flatbrook River to the west. Three trails fan out to the north, including Deep Root Trail, one of the more remote destinations in the park. Steam Mill Trail, south of the campground, is a relatively flat walk extending about .8 mile through hemlock and pitch-pine forest.

Directions. Follow the directions to Lake Ocquittunk Campground, proceed 1.9 miles past the campground entrance, and turn right on Crigger Road. Drive .2 mile and turn right into Steam Mill Campground.

Sites and facilities. Steam Mill's twenty-six campsites are each equipped with fire rings and picnic tables. One water pump is centrally located, and one restroom contains pit toilets but no showers. The campground is open only on weekends, from noon Friday to noon Monday, April 1 through October 31. No reservations are taken for this campground.

Recommended sites. Steam Mill serves as a good destination on busy weekends when Ocquittunk and Shotwell are full, and you will find several private sites scattered throughout the campground. Sites 207, 209, and 217 are fairly secluded, with a row of trees providing a border between neighbors. Number 209 is the most isolated of the three, and 207 overlooks a wooded rise. Although 225 and 226 sit near the camp-

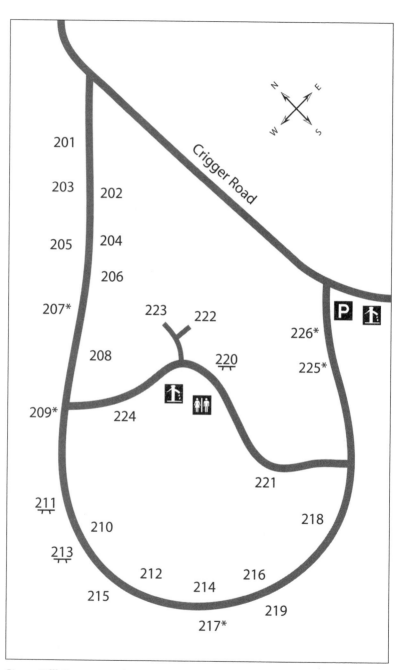

Steam Mill Campground

ground entrance, they are set apart from the surrounding sites and relatively private. The nearby parking area is rarely used. Site 215 overlooks a slight rise but lacks the tree cover elsewhere in the campground.

Haskin's Group Campground

Nine group sites, designated by letters A through I, are made up of treeless grass fields linked end to end. Site H is the only one that escapes the look of a green lawn, set in a forested clearing at the end of the road. The Big Flatbrook River lies north of the campground, and Blue Mountain Trail begins across Kittle Road. The recreation area is within walking distance, 1 mile southeast along Kittle Road. Sites A through F each accommodate thirty campers, site G holds sixty-five, H holds ten, and I holds forty-five. Each of the sites contain fire rings, picnic tables, and grills. Three restrooms with modern toilets are within walking distance of all sites. The restroom next to site I contains showers, and water pumps are scattered throughout the campground. From the park office, drive 1.8 miles northeast on Coursen Road and turn left on Kittle Road. Proceed .8 mile to the group campground on the left. Haskin's is open from April 1 through October 31.

Trails

The twenty-five marked trails throughout Stokes offer enough variety for almost any hiker. They range from easy walks along a valley or stream to more difficult ascents like the Ladder Trail, a steep climb to 1,200 feet. The Appalachian Trail represents the longest hike in Stokes, a rugged 12.5 miles blazed along the Kittatinny Ridge. The shortest trail in the valley is Tibbs, at .5 mile, connecting Shotwell Campground to Coursen Road. Totaling almost 50 miles, the trails encompass altitudes ranging from 500 feet just west of Tillman Ravine to 1,653 feet at Sunrise Mountain.

The scenic overlooks from Kittatinny Ridge make the Appalachian Trail a common destination for hikers. Seven trails climb the ridge, almost all of them rated as difficult. The Ladder Trail, on the south side of the park, is only .4 mile long and hits the Appalachian Trail at about 1,200 feet. The Acropolis Trail, near Route 206, is the steepest in Stokes, achieving overlooks of Culvers Lake and the Pocono Plateau. Other challenging hikes include Cartwright Trail, a direct climb to Sunrise Mountain; Tower Trail, a steep ascent culminating in decent views near the Normanook Lookout Tower; and Stony Trail, a climb past a few small waterfalls ending at a shelter used by Appalachian Trail hikers.

Trail Mileage and Difficulty

TRAIL	MILES	DIFFICULTY	BLAZE	USES
Acropolis Trail	1.0	D	brown/yellow	e,h,m
Appalachian Trail	12.5	M	white	h
Blue Mountain Trail	1.4	E	brown/green	b,d,e,h,m,s,x
Cartwright Trail	0.9	D	brown/red	e,h,m
Coursen Trail	1.3	E	blue	b,d,e,h,m,s,x
Criss Trail	2.0	M	gray/green	e,h,m
Deep Root Trail	1.0	E	red/yellow	e,h,m
Howell Trail	1.6	M	gray	e,h,m
Lackner Trail	2.0	E	black	b,d,e,h,m,s,x
Ladder Trail	0.4	M	blue/gray	e,h,m
Lead Mine Trail	1.0	E	blue/gray	e,h,m
Parker Trail	2.4	M	green	b,d,e,h,m,s,x
Rock Oak Trail	1.5	M	blue/yellow	e,h,m
Shay Trail	0.6	E	brown/yellow	e,h,m
Silver Mine Trail	1.0	E–M	red	e,h,m
Station Trail	0.9	M	green	e,h,m
Steam Mill Trail	0.8	E	blue	e,h,m
Steffen Trail	1.8	E	black/gray	e,h,m,s,x
Stoll Trail	0.7	M	blue/gray	e,h,m
Stony Trail	0.7	M	brown	e,h,m
Swensen Trail	3.8	M	red	b,d,e,h,m,s,x
Tibbs Trail	0.5	M	blue/green	e,h,m
Tillman Trail	0.6	E	no blaze	h
Tinsley Trail	2.8	D	yellow	b,d,e,h,m,s,x
Tower Trail	1.0	D	green	e,h,m

Three parking areas give easy access to the Appalachian Trail, all located on Sunrise Mountain Road. The one at the top of Sunrise Mountain is the most popular and may seem a bit unfair to some of the hikers who make the climb. The parking area 1 mile to the west affords more privacy and gives access to both the Kittatinny Ridge and Tinsley Trail, which heads north into the forest. The third access point is just south of the park office on the corner of Sunrise Mountain Road and Route 636 (Mattison School Road). It is possible to park on Sunrise Mountain Road at the Tower Trail or Stony Trail crossing, although space is limited and the areas are not designated for parking.

The trails around the recreation area will accommodate hikers interested in easier walks. Silver Mine Trail, although rated as moderate, is wheelchair accessible up to the waterfall. Blue Mountain Trail is a bit easier, stretching 1.4 miles through undulating countryside and thick hardwood forest to the Lake Ocquittunk Campground. Another easy hike, Lackner Trail, begins at Stony Lake and extends through a varied forest of red maple, white pine, and eastern hemlock, passing several sandstone deposits along the way. Tibbs Trail, a gentle and constant incline from Shotwell Campground to Coursen Road, provides a short walk past an unnamed pond and serves as a shortcut to Coursen Road. Farther afield, try the Shay or Deep Root Trails if you like seclusion.

Activities

Choose an activity and you will be impressed by Stokes State Forest. The views from Kittatinny Ridge will always attract the most interest, but many of the flatter trails along the valley provide excellent terrain for mountain biking and horseback riding. Most anglers are inspired by the pristine beauty and excellent catches of the Flatbrook River, where trout are stocked by the thousands every year. The recreation area at Stony Lake offers swimming off a sandy beach, and two picnic areas cater to visitors throughout the summer. Tillman Ravine and the hawk watch at Sunrise Mountain are unique to Stokes, both deserving of at least an afternoon. Even the colder months are popular here, when winter travelers will find miles of trails and roads reserved for cross-country skiing, snowmobiling, and dogsledding.

Tillman Ravine

The red shale of Tillman Ravine, recently deemed one of the ten most beautiful wild places in New Jersey, gives way to spring-fed Tillman Brook, where meandering waterfalls spill down the rock in a series of cascades. At certain points, small pools form against a backdrop of hemlock and white pine. An area known as the Teacup is the most dramatic section, accessed by a short but steep walk down to the water. On hot August days, Tillman Brook acts as a natural refrigerator—the ravine stays about 10 degrees cooler than the surrounding area. Several well-beaten paths are proof of Tillman's popularity, but oppressive crowds are rare, even during the peak of summer. Two parking areas along Tillman Road give access to the ravine. Both areas offer restrooms with pit toilets. Drive .3 mile north of the park office on Route 206, and turn left on Struble Road. Proceed 4.3 miles to the second Tillman Ravine parking area on the left, where you will find a .1-mile trail leading to the Teacup. Tillman visitors should consider a detour to Buttermilk Falls 2 miles to the south; see the Surrounding Points of Interest section for details.

Sunrise Mountain Hawk Watch

Some of the premier sites in the United States for observing the fall hawk migration are in New Jersey. Sunrise Mountain's hawk watch is the most popular, and one of the best in the state. The fall migration takes place between August and December, and peak activity occurs during September and October. Dozens of species are counted every day, including common sightings of eagles, falcons, kestrels, and a diverse assortment of hawks. Northern harriers, merlins, Cooper's hawks, gyrfalcons, Swainson's hawks, and others fly through regularly. The greatest numbers occur from early to midmorning, one or two days after a cold front has moved through the area. A pavilion at the top of Sunrise Mountain provides the best viewpoint.

Fishing

If only one area could be chosen where each park shines on a state or regional scale, fishing in the Big Flatbrook River would win the award for Stokes State Forest. The river rivals many of the premier trout streams in the northeastern United States, and up to 30,000 trout are stocked during the season. The middle portion of the river, between Route 206 and Little Flatbrook River, produces the best results. A designated fly-fishing area runs from Route 206 about 4 miles downstream to Mountain Road and receives well-deserved praise from anglers. Drive 1.1 miles north of the park office on Route 206, and turn left on Route 560 (Dingmans Road). Proceed .6 mile to the parking area on the corner of Brook Road, a thin dirt road paralleling the river. The section of the river along Brook Road is prime trout territory, but parking is a creative endeavor if you travel any farther west.

All of the remaining lakes and streams throughout Stokes allow fishing, and many are stocked several times throughout the spring and summer. Small boats with electric motors are allowed on Lake Ocquittunk, which is stocked with 1,000 trout each spring. Largemouth bass, catfish, and sunfish are also abundant, with pickerel and yellow perch found in smaller numbers. Stony Lake is stocked with trout three times in April and May, and fishing is good during stocking. Largemouth bass, smallmouth bass, pickerel, catfish, and sunfish are also found in the lake but not in abundance. Stony and Parker Brooks are designated wild trout streams, subject to different restrictions, such as no live bait and catch-and-release during certain parts of the season. Check the latest regulations for annual changes.

Boating

Boating within Stokes is limited to 8-acre Lake Ocquittunk. The lake does not offer a boat ramp, but you can launch small boats with electric motors from the shore. The surrounding Culvers, Owassa, and Kemah Lakes are all private, but you are within a short drive of the wild and scenic upper Delaware River, a popular canoe and kayak destination. See the Worthington State Forest chapter for more information.

Swimming and Picnicking

A short footpath leads to the beach, where you will find picnic tables and grills lining the shore, a playground, and modern restrooms with showers. A small, cordoned-off area of Stony Lake is overseen by a lifeguard from Memorial Day weekend through Labor Day. You will find a second picnic area north of the lake across from a large activity field know as Kittle Field, where a small footbridge leads to about thirty private tables and grills in a wooded grove. Groups of twenty or more can reserve the Kittle Field picnic area, but you must make reservations at least five days in advance.

Mountain Biking

Mountain biking is officially allowed on all of the trails except Tillman Ravine and the Appalachian Trail. The most sought-after views lie at the end of several steep trails climbing the ridge, all of them better suited for a pair of hiking boots, but many of the trails lining the valley run along quiet streams and the rolling foothills of the Kittatinny Mountains. Blue Mountain Trail is relatively flat but still a challenging ride, crossing several streams and fallen trees in its 1.4-mile course from Kittle Road to Lake Ocquittunk. Howell, Lackner, Station, Swensen, Tinsley, and Parker Trails are all popular biking routes. You can combine the trails with many of the country roads that bisect the forest. Struble Road extends an undulating 4 miles through hardwood forest and past three lakes to Tillman Ravine, rising and falling about 400 feet in the process. See the Trails section for destinations and distances.

Horseback Riding

Horseback riding is allowed on all of the trails in the park except Tillman Ravine and the Appalachian Trail, but the steeper trails climbing the ridge are not suited for horses. See the Mountain Biking section for trails and roads that stretch through the flatter sections of Stokes.

Birding

Between Stokes State Forest and the surrounding wildlife management areas, habitat ranges from low-lying marshland to ridgetop pines. The hawk watch at Sunrise Mountain is a well-known birding spot at Stokes, but the forest also supports breeding and migrating warblers in spring. Check the areas surrounding Grau Road, Lake Ocquittunk, Kittle Road, and Steam Mill Campground for hooded, golden-winged, and blackburnian warblers. A Sutton's warbler, which is a rare hybrid between a yellow-throated warbler and a northern parula, has been seen in the spruce groves along Grau Road in recent years. Parker Brook and the Big Flatbrook River create a small maze of streams just south of Steam Mill Campground on Crigger Road, an area known for flycatchers, warblers, kingbirds, and vireos. Herons sometimes fish at Lake Ocquittunk Campground, where the Flatbrook River creates a marshy area around sites 15 through 19. See the Sunrise Mountain Hawk Watch section for information about the annual hawk migration.

Hunting

Almost 94 percent of the park's 15,996 acres is open to the hunting of deer, small game, waterfowl, and wild turkeys. The area is popular with hunters during wild turkey season, which occurs in Stokes from mid-April through May (turkey hunting areas 1 and 2). The forest is also a challenging deer-hunting area because of the mountainous terrain. The majority of Stokes falls within deer management zone 1. Times and regulations vary, so check the current information for annual changes.

Winter Activities

The forest's northern latitude and high elevation make Stokes a popular destination for winter trail activities. When snowfall exceeds 8 inches, several areas of the park are opened up to snowmobilers and dogsledders, including Lackner, Coursen, Swensen, Blue Mountain, Tinsley, and Parker Trails. Several roads allow snowmobiles throughout the winter, regardless of snow depth, including Sunrise Mountain, Degroat, Grau, and Crigger Roads. There are also sixteen trails and roads encompassing almost 25 miles open to cross-country skiing and snowshoeing, including those open to snowmobiles as well as Brink, Cross, Dimon, Shay, and Woods Roads and Steffen Trail. The Cross Country Ski Center at nearby High Point State Park offers groomed trails, rentals, and repairs.

Flora and Fauna

Habitat within Stokes ranges from high-altitude lakes and the Kittatinny Mountains to deeply cut ravines and the meandering Flatbrook River. A diverse blend of hardwood trees covers the area, including red oak, black oak, sugar maple, and American beech. Pitch pine and black birch inhabit the high cliffs of the Kittatinny Ridge, and eastern hemlock and white pine can be found in the low-lying areas of Tillman Ravine. Examples of scarlet oak, shagbark hickory, red pine, black gum, and eastern red cedar are present throughout the landscape.

Black bears, eastern coyotes, red foxes, beavers, and other wildlife inhabit the mixed hardwood forest, but Stokes is also home to two extremely rare, endangered species. Only a handful of healthy dwarf wedge mussel colonies are known in the world, and one of them is found in the cool, clean waters of the pristine Flatbrook River. The tiny mollusk, thought to be extinct in New Jersey until 1998, is a global, federal, and state endangered species. The almost extinct small whorled pogonia is found in Stokes as well, a yellow-green orchid known to stay underground and dormant for many years before flowering. Hundreds of bird species can also be seen in the park, and rarities are counted throughout the fall at Sunrise Mountain's hawk watch.

Surrounding Points of Interest

The Flatbrook River flows south from Stokes into the Flatbrook-Roy Wildlife Management Area, an excellent destination for fly fishing. Buttermilk Falls near Tillman Ravine plunges 90 feet within view of the road and is usually quiet and devoid of travelers during the week. High Point State Park borders Stokes to the north, and Swartswood State Park offers great boating and fishing only 10 miles to the south. Almost any destination within the Delaware Water Gap National Recreation Area deserves attention, many of them covered in the Worthington State Forest chapter.

Flatbrook-Roy Wildlife Management Area

The Little Flatbrook and Big Flatbrook Rivers meet in the 2,090-acre Flatbrook-Roy Wildlife Management Area. Fishing is similar to that on the Big Flatbrook River near Stokes and well worth the drive. Wild turkey, ruffed grouse, pheasant, deer, and two shooting ranges also make this a popular hunting destination. Flatbrook-Roy is an easily accessible wildlife management area, with nine parking areas scattered throughout the forest. You will find parking areas giving access to the Big Flatbrook River on the corner of Brook Road and Route 560, along Brook Road, and along Route 615 (Ennis Road).

Reaching the Flatbrook-Roy office and access to the Little Flatbrook River requires a short trip. Drive 1.1 miles north of the park office on Route 206, and turn left on Route 560 (Dingmans Road). Proceed .9 mile and turn left on Route 615 (Ennis Road). Continue .9 mile to a bridge over the Little Flatbrook River and a parking area on the right. This is a quiet spot, but the bridge was closed at last check. If you cannot proceed, return to Route 560 (Dingmans Road) and turn left. Drive 2.8 miles, always bearing left, to arrive on the other side of the bridge. Continue .4 mile beyond the bridge and bear left on Kuhn Road. Proceed .5 mile to the Flatbrook-Roy office entrance on the left. A dirt path leaves from behind the office and heads .2 mile to the river. For parking near the confluence of the Big Flatbrook and Little Flatbrook Rivers, turn left out of the office, drive .7 mile, and bear left on Bridge Road. Continue 50 yards to a grassy area on the left side of the road. A thin dirt trail leads to a spot about 100 yards downstream of the joining of the two Flatbrook Rivers.

Buttermilk Falls

One of New Jersey's most accessible waterfalls, this 90-foot cascade lies directly on Mountain Road only 2 miles south of Tillman Ravine. Adjacent to the 387-acre Walpack Wildlife Management Area, it is a vista that surprises first-time visitors with its size and beauty. Ribbonlike bands of white water drop down a vertical rock face of red shale to form a pool below. A winding staircase leads to the top, with a series of viewing platforms spaced out along the climb. The blue-blazed Buttermilk Falls Trail leads into the forest along a source branch of the Flatbrook River and climbs 1.9 miles to the Appalachian Trail. Follow the directions for Tillman Ravine, and drive west from the Teacup parking area for .5 mile to Mountain Road. Turn left on Mountain Road (Walpack Cemetery marks the turn), and proceed 1.9 miles to the Buttermilk Falls parking area on the right.

Where to Buy Supplies

Although Newton is 12 miles south on Route 206, the city offers almost anything a traveler needs, including banks, pharmacies, sporting goods, grocery stores, gas stations, car repair, and restaurants. The town of Branchville is 3.8 miles south of the park office on Route 206 and contains a deli, bakery, and country market. Stokes Sport Shop is .4 mile south of the park office on the west side of Route 206; here you will find fishing tackle and other sporting goods. A few restaurants lie closer to Stokes, scattered along Route 206 between the park office and Branchville. Jumboland Diner is 1.6 miles south of the park office on the left, and a bagel shop and pizza and pasta restaurant sit next to each other about 2.2 miles south of the park office on the east side of Route 206.

Worthington State Forest

HC 62, Box 2
Columbia, NJ 07832

Area. Worthington State Forest, 6,584 acres. Delaware Water Gap National Recreation Area, 70,000 acres.

Park office. Warren County, 2.9 miles east of I-80 on the north side of Old Mine Road.

Highlights. Sunfish Pond Natural Area, Appalachian Trail, Mount Tammany, Delaware River, Delaware Water Gap National Recreation Area.

Activities. Worthington State Forest: camping, hiking, fishing, boating, picnicking, birding, hunting. Delaware Water Gap National Recreation Area: hiking, fishing, boating, picnicking, swimming, mountain biking, horseback riding, birding, rock climbing, scuba diving, hunting, ice fishing, cross-country skiing, snowshoeing.

Entrance fee. No fee is charged to enter Worthington. A fee is required to enter Watergate Recreation Site and Smithfield Beach in the Delaware Water Gap National Recreation Area.

Park hours. Year-round, from dawn to dusk.

For additional information: (908) 841-9575

Worthington State Forest supports so many natural landmarks that it's hard to believe the entire area barely dodged the fate of being buried under billions of gallons of water. The construction project was called the Tocks Island Dam, and it took an act of Congress to stop it. In 1978, as a result of unending pressure from environmentalists and local residents, the Upper Delaware was protected under the federal Wild and Scenic Rivers Act to be preserved in its natural state forever. Anyone who has gazed at the horizon from an overlook along the Appalachian Trail can't help but be grateful for the preservation of this inspiring land and what it holds.

From the day the Tocks Island Dam was proposed in 1955, conservationists began viewing the area along the Delaware River with a new appreciation. The dam project was officially scrapped in 1992, and today Worthington's borders represent a park within a park. At 6,584 acres, the state forest makes up a small part of the 70,000-acre Delaware Water

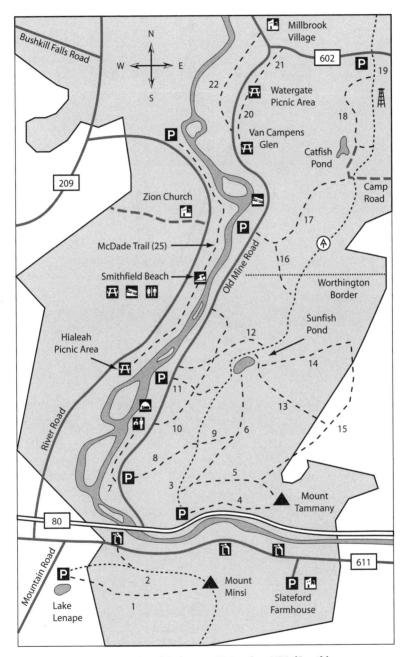

Worthington State Forest and Delaware Water Gap NRA (South)

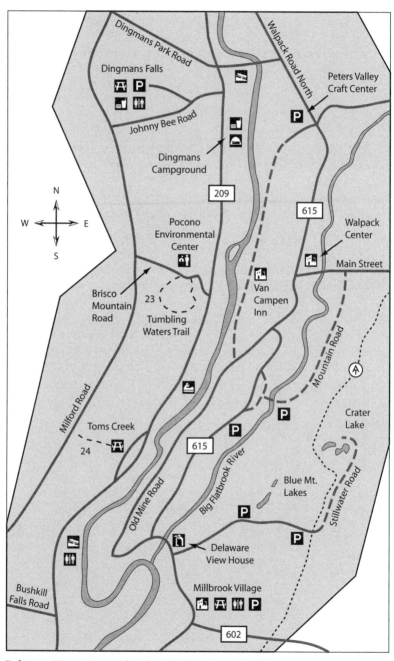

Delaware Water Gap National Recreation Area (North)

Gap National Recreation Area (DWG) extending from Mount Minsi in the south almost to the New York border. It is an area that sees more visitors each year than national parks such as Yellowstone, Yosemite, and the Grand Canyon. Industrialist Charles Campbell Worthington would have been pleased to see what became of his original 8,000-acre estate. The forested land is bordered by the Kittatinny Ridge and the Delaware Valley, where visitors will find secluded campsites, 70 miles of trails, and outdoor pursuits ranging from rock climbing to exploring the shores of a high-altitude glacial lake known as Sunfish Pond.

Camping

Worthington offers only one family camping area, but it receives more visitors each year than any other public campground in the state. The park benefits from modest development, so campers don't have to contend with the activity of swimming beaches, concession stands, or central recreation areas. Tent and trailer sites stretch for 2 miles along the Delaware River, a handful resting close enough to the riverbank for the running water to relax you at night. Some are perched on an overlook surveying the scene. Many of the campsites are large enough to accommodate trailers, and three group sites near the park entrance hold up to thirty-five campers. The Kittatinny Ridge rises 1 mile to the south, topped by the Appalachian Trail and viewpoints of the panoramic Delaware Valley. A number of trails begin climbing the ridge directly from the campground, and a boat ramp next to the park office means campers don't have to drive very far to access the river.

Family Campground

Worthington's campground is so popular that choosing the right site is crucial if you want a modicum of privacy. It is also wise to reserve ahead, because options near the water disappear quickly on sunny days throughout the spring and summer. Many of the sites border the Delaware River in small and isolated clearings, so the campground maintains a wilderness feel and sense of privacy despite its popularity. Tent sites 1 through 23 are situated at a dead end, private enough to insulate you from the bulk of the activity in the park. A few of them are so close to the water that you can watch kayakers lazily float past your evening campfire. If you find yourself pitching a tent at one of the prime waterside sites, Worthington provides views of the Delaware that can easily occupy an entire weekend.

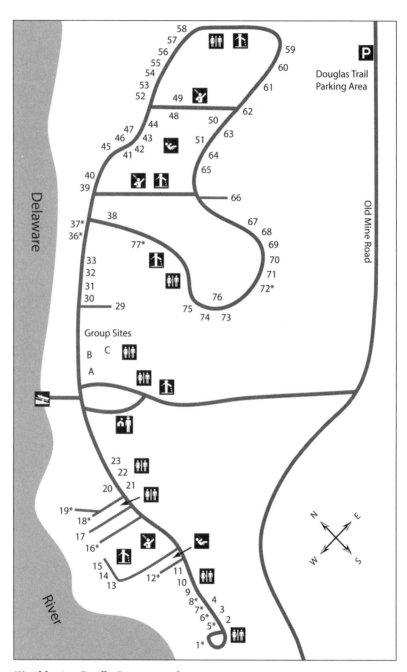

Worthington Family Campground

Directions. Campsites begin at the park office and line the Delaware River to the east and west.

Sites and facilities. Worthington holds sixty-nine tent and trailer sites; numbers 1 through 23 are reserved for tents only. All of the amenities of a developed park are close at hand, including hot showers, modern restrooms, and drinking water from well pumps. Each site holds a fire ring and picnic table. Three of the fifteen restrooms are equipped with hot showers, one to the west of the park office and two to the east. Two small playgrounds sit on opposite sides of the park, and a boat launch accessing the Delaware lies next to campsite 23. The campground is open from April 1 through December 31.

Recommended sites. The best of tent sites 1 through 23 also hold the best views anywhere in the campground. The spot that receives no competition for privacy, beauty, and scenery is site number 1, standing alone at the far west end of the campground and close enough to the Delaware to reflect your campfire at night. Next best on the water for privacy is 16, facing a sweeping scene of the river about 30 yards from the road. Number 19 is a short drive away from the road, secluded, and on the banks of the Delaware, and 18 is set on a 100-foot rise overlooking the water. Numbers 5 through 8 and 12 come next for aesthetic appeal, all on the river but a bit open to the road. The remaining tent sites are close to the road, close together, or near park activity, although good backup choices directly on the water include 9 through 11, 13 through 15, and 20.

Sites 29 through 77, east of the park office, allow tents and trailers, and most of them are spaced out over an open lawn. Numbers 36 through 58 line the Delaware, but the view is blocked by a row of trees and hedges. Sites 36 and 37 offer the best scenery, an obscured glimpse of the Delaware through a row of trees. A few worthy options away from the water include 77, a private spot bordered by trees, and 72, which is set back from the road and surrounded by hedges. Sites 59 through 65 will serve those who like to combine sunshine with a modicum of privacy, as they are separated from the rest of the campground by a treeless field.

Group Campground

Three group sites, A, B, and C, are situated next to the park office in the center of the family campground. Site C provides the most cover, a modest border of trees between the road and camping area. Site A consists of a grass lawn adjacent to the road, and site B is a tiny clearing bounded by a few trees. An obscured view of the Delaware River lies across the road. Each site holds thirty-five campers and is equipped with drinking water, fire rings, picnic tables, and modern restrooms. Showers are available at the family campground, a short drive to the east or west. Group camping is available from April 1 through December 31.

Trails

Worthington's thirteen marked trails total 28.5 miles, ranging from quiet walks along river valleys to mountain ascents that end at stunning overlooks of the Delaware Valley. Four trails leave from the immensely popular Dunnfield Creek parking area on I-80, including a well-traveled section of the Appalachian Trail (AT). At only 6.5 miles, this part of the AT receives so many visitors during sunny weekends that the overflow-parking area is often full, and you will find cars parked on the grass along Old Mine Road. One reason for such interest is easy access to one of the most beautiful and picturesque sections of the Kittatinny Ridge within Worthington. You can find the parking area and avoid I-80 by taking Old Mine Road south from the park office for 3.7 miles, passing the I-80 entrance ramp and Kittatinny Point Visitor Center. Follow the U-turn to the left where the sign points toward I-80 west. Dunnfield Creek parking area is immediately on the right after the U-turn. Don't miss it or you will end up on the interstate.

The quickest way to gratification from the Dunnfield Creek parking area is to take the Mount Tammany Trail or the Blue-Blazed Trail, both difficult climbs leading to the top of 1,527-foot Mount Tammany and spectacular overlooks of the Delaware River. If you're wondering where all those magazine cover photographs of the Delaware Valley come from, this is it. The Appalachian Trail leaving from the same parking area is almost as popular, a moderate 3.8-mile hike rising 800 feet to Sunfish Pond. About 2.4 miles beyond the southwest corner of Sunfish Pond, the AT rises to Raccoon Ridge and 1,500-foot lookouts to the east and west. If you're pining for solitude, try the Dunnfield Creek Trail, a serene hike along a wild trout stream with options to climb up to the AT along the route. Bears sometimes linger at spots along this trail, as hikers tend to avoid the valley.

Many of the remaining trails in Worthington climb the ridge to meet the AT, and the shortest routes begin at the parking areas along Old Mine Road. Garvey Springs Trail leaves from the Douglas parking area (1 mile north of the park office on Old Mine Road) and is the most direct hike

Trail Mileage and Difficulty

TRAIL	MILES	DIFFICULTY	BLAZE	USES
1. Mount Minsi Fire Road	1.5	D	no blaze	h
2. AT to Mount Minsi	1.5	D	white	h
3. AT to Sunfish Pond	3.8	M	white	h
4. Mount Tammany Trail	1.3	D	red	h
5. Blue-Blazed Trail	1.5	D	blue	h
6. Dunnfield Creek Trail	3.5	E	green	h
7. Karamac Trail	1.2	E	no blaze	h
8. Farview Trail	1.3	D	yellow	h
9. Holly Springs Trail	0.4	D	red	h
10. Rockcores Trail	2.7	E	green	h
11. Douglas Trail	2.5	D	blue	h
12. Garvey Springs Trail	1.2	D	orange	h
13. Turquoise Trail	1.1	D	turquoise	h
14. Sunfish Pond Fire Road	1.6	M	no blaze	h
15. Mount Tammany Fire Road	3.1	M	no blaze	h
16. Kaiser Trail	2.0	D	blue	h
17. Coppermine Trail	1.8	D	red	h
18. Rattlesnake Swamp Trail	4.0	M	orange	h
19. AT to Catfish Fire Tower	1.0	M	white	h
20. Van Campens Glen Trail	1.5	E	yellow	h
21. Millbrook-Watergate Trail	0.5	E	no blaze	h
22. Hamilton Ridge Trail	2.5	E	no blaze	h
23. Tumbling Waters Trail	3.0	M	orange	h
24. Toms Creek Trail	1.0	E	no blaze	h
25. McDade Trail	5.0	E	no blaze	h,m,x

to Sunfish Pond, encompassing a steep climb from 400 to 1,200 feet in its 1.1-mile course to the lake. Douglas Trail begins across Old Mine Road near the same parking area, but it weaves around a bit to join the AT a short distance from the pond. Farview and Holly Springs Trails combine to form a 1.7-mile hike to the ridge, beginning about 1.9 miles west of the park office at the Farview parking area on Old Mine Road.

A few easier trails running through flat and quiet valleys can allow you to avoid crowds as well. The Karamac Trail is a quiet, little-traveled trail that makes use of an abandoned railroad bed as it follows the Delaware River from the Karamac parking area on Old Mine Road to the campground. Rockcores Trail rises 300 feet along the ridge and offers interpretive placards at trailside. Several trails that receive less foot traffic leave from the Coppermine parking area, Mount Minsi, and Millbrook Village. See those subjects in the Surrounding Points of Interest section for details. All of the trails within Worthington and the vast majority within the DWG allow hiking only.

Activities

The possibilities in and around Worthington vary as greatly as the altitude, from scuba diving, fishing, and canoeing in the Delaware River to rock climbing on 1,463-foot Mount Minsi. Most of the trails are limited to hiking, but it hardly seems to matter once you have climbed to the top of the nearest overlook and surveyed the scene. Hiking boots produce more than their share of rewards at Worthington. The Delaware Water Gap National Recreation Area picks up where Worthington falls short. An easy drive to the north will take you to swimming beaches, recreation areas with picnic tables, dirt tracks and roads open to mountain biking, and even a hawk watch atop Raccoon Ridge.

Sunfish Pond Natural Area

It's worth the trek, but go on a weekday if you want to avoid peak activity. A 3.8-mile hike along the Appalachian Trail leads to Sunfish Pond, a high-altitude glacial lake that glistens like glitter at sunset. The pond basin was carved out by receding glaciers at the end of the last ice age, and the acidic water that remains supports only a few species of fish, including the pumpkinseed sunfish. A 1.5-mile trail circles the lake, passing through stands of chestnut oak to an overlook on the east shore. The Appalachian, Farview, Douglas, and Garvey Springs Trails all lead to the pond.

Fishing

You can't go wrong casting a line in the Delaware River if you are looking for excellent catches and proximity to the Worthington campground. The Delaware is responsible for more records than any other body of water in the state, including a 29-pound tiger muskellunge, a 13-pound, 10-ounce walleye, and a 42-pound, 1-ounce carp landed in 1987. Huge American shad run in May, and the boat ramp area at Eshback is known as a local shad hot spot. Smallmouth bass, muskellunge, walleye, and catfish are all common, and fly fishing is popular for trout. A boat ramp next to the park office gives easy access to the river. If you want to explore other areas of Worthington State Forest, Dunnfield Creek is one of the few streams remaining in New Jersey that supports native brook trout, and it is subject to wild trout regulations. Fishing is also allowed in Sunfish Pond but is poor, even for sunfish.

Many rivers and ponds throughout the DWG support a variety of fish, including rainbow trout, brown trout, smallmouth bass, and pickerel. The Flatbrook River is an advisable destination, especially for fly fishing. The shallow, picturesque stream rivals some of the premier trout streams in the northeastern United States, both for pristine beauty and excellent catches. As many as 30,000 trout are stocked in the spring, creating a huge draw for fishermen. See the Walpack Wildlife Management Area section below for recommended trout-fishing spots along the Flatbrook River. Other notable destinations outside of Worthington include Van Campens Brook and Toms Creek for rainbow trout and Catfish Pond for pickerel. See Surrounding Points of Interest for details.

Boating

Six boat launches line both sides of the Delaware between I-80 and Milford. The river is wide and slow along this 30-mile stretch, which makes it perfect for easy canoeing. Walpack Ridge and Walpack Bend provide scenic distractions, where many of the deserted islands support breeding birds, archaeological sites, and native plants. More than 100 primitive campsites have been set up on some of the islands and along the banks of the Delaware River, available to canoeists for one-night stays with no fee required. Maps of the river campsites can be found at many canoe liveries, the Kittatinny Point Visitor Center, or online at the National Park Service website.

Dozens of liveries in the area rent canoes for one- and two-day trips. The closest one to Worthington is Pack Shack Adventures, just over the bridge in Delaware Water Gap, Pennsylvania. Kittatinny Canoes in Dingmans Ferry, Pennsylvania, is the oldest livery on the river and sponsors the annual Delaware River Clean-Up, responsible for removing more than 180 tons of trash from the river over the past decade.

Other liveries nearby, those closest to Worthington listed first, and all in Pennsylvania, include Chamberlain Canoes (Minisink Hills, 1 mile north of I-80 on River Road), Shawnee River Adventures (based out of the Shawnee Inn in Shawnee), Adventure Sports (Marshalls Creek), and Dingmans Campground (Dingmans Ferry).

Picnicking

Put on your hiking shoes or rent a canoe and find a quiet spot—the opportunities are endless if you don't require a table. If you would rather stay near the campground, one small picnic area lies next to the Delaware River near the Worthington office. Other traditional picnic areas are available throughout the DWG at areas such as Watergate Recreation Site, Hialeah, Smithfield Beach, and Toms Creek. See the Surrounding Points of Interest section for details. You are in bear country, so take the appropriate precautions.

Swimming

One beach within a short drive of Worthington gives access to the Delaware River. Smithfield Beach in Pennsylvania is located 5.6 miles north of I-80 on the east side of River Road. The surrounding recreation area offers picnic tables, modern restrooms, an activity field, and fishing spots along the river. You will also find a concrete boat ramp and access to McDade Trail, the only trail in the park open to mountain bikers.

Mountain Biking

McDade Trail, discussed in the Surrounding Points of Interest section, is a relatively flat 5-mile ride and the only trail within Worthington or the DWG that allows bikes. Another interesting ride if you're searching for seclusion is to follow Old Mine Road where it forks to the west past Van Campen Inn. Although flat, the route is rarely traveled by cars, and you will find yourself cycling across small one-lane bridges with woods and farmland to the east and the Delaware River 50 feet below to the west. The road is so potholed that mountain bikes probably make better time than cars along the route.

Stop at Van Campen Inn along the way, or park at the inn and start your ride from there. The 1746 gray brick structure accommodated guests such as John Adams and can be viewed from the outside any day of the week. You can see the inside on Sundays during the summer (hours vary) or on Van Campen Day, usually the second or third Sunday in October. A small parking area barely fits five cars, but you will rarely see any other visitors. If you want to park at the inn, drive 8.4 miles north of the park office on Old Mine Road and turn left toward Millbrook to stay on Old Mine Road. Proceed 2 miles to Route 615 and turn left to continue on Old Mine Road. Drive another 5.3 miles and turn left on the grated dirt road (still Old Mine Road). Drive 2.1 miles to Van Campen Inn on the right.

Horseback Riding

Mountain bikers can at least claim one trail in the Worthington area. Horseback riders are not so fortunate, but the suggested route for mountain bikers also applies to horseback riders. The road near Van Campen Inn is flat, rarely traveled by cars, and made of packed dirt or gravel.

Birding

If part of the idea of birding is to experience the environment, then the Delaware Water Gap National Recreation Area will accommodate any birder willing to hike, paddle, or climb. More than 260 bird species have been recorded in the park, including 30 types of warblers during spring migration. One main event in the fall is the annual raptor migration and hawk watch at Raccoon Ridge, where the naturalists chalk up about 15,000 sightings of rare hawks and eagles every year. The DWG is also home to about 20 wintering bald eagles, arriving in early December to take advantage of the Delaware's open water during the coldest months of the year. Warblers nest on vacant islands in the channel, and the Kittatinny cliffs support nesting peregrine falcons in spring. More than 70,000 acres of protected habitat stretching from Worthington to the New York border provide a variety of opportunities for any birder willing to explore.

Rock Climbing

The Kittatinny Ridge, especially the rock cliffs facing the Delaware, offer some of the most rewarding rock and ice climbs in New Jersey. More than 200 rock-climbing routes have been established throughout the park, and frozen waterfalls produce dozens of possible ice climbs. Mountains and ridges throughout the DWG are popular for climbing, rappeling, and bouldering. The middle cliffs of Mounts Tammany and Minsi draw the most attention from climbers. The steepest and longest routes with the cleanest rock faces are at Point of Gap Overlook on Route 611 in Pennsylvania and a ledge known as Ricks Rock, where the Appalachian Trail crosses Route 602 in New Jersey.

Scuba Diving

Diving is permitted along the length of the Delaware River within the DWG. Walpack Bend and Point of Gap are two well-known dive spots. There's an old boxcar in the river about 7 feet down and 20 feet offshore near the Point of Gap parking area—look for the yellow railroad tie onshore and bear straight across the river for 20 feet to the wreck. The main channel gets rather dark at a maximum depth of 50 feet, and the current flows swiftly in the middle of the river. You may come up with a few old bottles, and the scenery can include tires, bicycle frames, lawn mowers, sofabeds, and kitchen sinks. Divers might consider volunteering in July for the annual On and Under the Delaware Clean-Up, when groups scour the river to collect and haul away tons of trash. Believe it or not, the project has a waiting list for volunteers. Contact Kittatinny Canoes in Dingmans Ferry, Pennsylvania.

Hunting

Almost 90 percent of Worthington's 6,584 acres is open to the hunting of deer, small game, waterfowl, and wild turkeys. Most of the Delaware Water Gap National Recreation Area is open to hunting as well. Recreation areas, historical sites, environmental centers, and other populated areas are off limits as usual. The area is popular with physically fit hunters, who need to be in good shape to negotiate Worthington's terrain. Deer and wild turkey are the main attraction. Worthington and the DWG fall in deer management zone 4, the waterfowl north zone, and turkey-hunting areas 1, 2, and 3.

Winter Activities

Camping ends at Worthington when January begins, but the trails remain open to hikers throughout the winter. Cross-country skiing and snowshoeing are allowed in a few places throughout the DWG, including McDade Trail. Ten miles of ski trails weave through the secluded Blue Mountain Lakes, beginning at the parking area on Blue Mountain Road just north of Millbrook. Slateford Farmhouse near Mount Minsi offers ski routes through rolling hills and hardwood forest, including a 1-mile beginners' trail, a 1.5-mile intermediate trail, and a 3-mile advanced trail. Ice climbing is prized in the park as well, especially on the cliffs of Mounts Tammany and Minsi facing the Delaware. The cliffs also harbor some of New Jersey's few wintering bald eagles, with several pairs remaining throughout the year to fish the Delaware's ice-free waters.

Flora and Fauna

Worthington State Forest and the surrounding DWG are defined by a wide variation in habitat. The 70,000-acre area encompasses the Delaware River, high-altitude ridges, lowland ponds, mountain streams, freshwater marshes, hardwood forest, reclaimed farmland in various stages of succession, and even cactus barrens populated with prickly pears. You stand a good chance of finding almost any animal native to northern New Jersey within the Delaware Water Gap National Recreation Area. The number of freshwater mussels alone that inhabit the park total 297 species, a diversity found nowhere else in the world. Add 60 species of fish, 260 species of birds, and elusive mammals such as black bears, bobcats, beavers, and coyotes. Even the diversity of plant life seems endless, exemplified by the 70 species of ferns that make a home in the park.

The list of rare and endangered inhabitants is a long one, including 48 plant species and 89 animals considered endangered, threatened, or species of concern. The first pair of nesting peregrine falcons in the area since the 1950s recently took up residence on the cliffs of Mount Minsi. The timber rattlesnake and blue-spotted salamander are protected species, as are the dwarf wedge mussel and five other bivalves found in the tributaries of the Delaware River. Countless unusual plants inhabit the park, including a butterfly-shaped flower known as Dutchman's breeches, resembling a set of white pants hung upside down on a clothesline. Black bears, once reduced to less than 100 individuals throughout the state, are also making a strong resurgence all along the Kittatinny Ridge and are now estimated at more than 1,100.

Surrounding Points of Interest

The Delaware Water Gap National Recreation Area extends 40 miles along the Delaware River, encompassing more than 100 trails and 200 miles of roads, and receiving 5 million visits each year. The 70,000-acre area is hardly one destination, but a variety of destinations. The AT heads north of Worthington along the Kittatinny Ridge toward Stokes State Forest, while Old Mine Road passes a number of natural sites that just begin to cover the Delaware Water Gap's recreation areas, historical villages, mountain trails, and even destinations on the Pennsylvania side. If that's not enough to keep an explorer busy for months, Worthington is surrounded by four wildlife management areas, one state park, one state forest, the islands and waterways of the Delaware

River, and more of the same across the border in Pennsylvania. A few of the many possible destinations are covered in the 45-mile driving tour outlined below. Take along a packed lunch and some water; the tour could occupy a full day, depending on how much time you spend at each site.

The driving tour begins at the Coppermine parking area. Drive north on Old Mine Road from the Worthington park office for 4.3 miles, and you will arrive at the Coppermine parking area on the left, a good place to access the Appalachian Trail. The abandoned Pahaquarry Copper Mines lie across the road, begun in 1750 and mined in stages over the next 168 years. Two trails leave from across Old Mine Road. The 1.8-mile Coppermine Trail, marked in red, climbs 700 feet along a small stream and past an abandoned mine to the Appalachian Trail at Camp Road. The 2-mile Kaiser Trail, marked with blue blazes, veers off from the Coppermine Trail to climb the ridge and meet the AT at an altitude of 1,400 feet.

Van Campens Glen and Watergate Recreation Sites

Driving north of the Coppermine parking area for .2 mile along Old Mine Road brings you past the Poxono Access on the left, one of six boat launches between Worthington and the New York border. Head north another 1.7 miles to Van Campens Glen Recreation Site on the right, a popular picnic area on Van Campens Brook. About 1.7 miles farther north lies the Watergate Recreation Site on the right, offering an open-air concert area, fifty picnic tables, parking, restrooms, and trails, all situated around a small lake. The yellow-blazed Van Campens Glen Trail stretches between the two recreation areas, following Van Campens Brook past one waterfall and a small footbridge. Watergate Recreation Site charges an entrance fee throughout the summer.

Millbrook Village

Drive .4 mile north of the Watergate Recreation Site, turn left at the intersection, and then turn right into the Millbrook Village parking area. The restored buildings create an image of the nineteenth-century village that once stood at the site, where settler Abram Garris first built a gristmill in 1832. A self-guided walking tour takes you past an 1840 schoolhouse, the original 1850 boardinghouse, and about twenty other structures either reconstructed or original to the village.

A few worthy trails lie near the village or within a short drive. The Millbrook-Watergate Trail is a dirt track that begins at the village church and leads to Van Campens Glen Trail, past a waterfall, and on to the Van Campens Glen parking area 2 miles south. The orange-blazed Rattlesnake Swamp Trail leaves from a parking area on Millbrook Road (about 1.1 miles south of the village) and heads 4 miles past Rattlesnake Swamp to end at Catfish Pond. Walk south on the AT for about 1 mile from the same parking area, and you will come to some incredible views from Catfish Fire Tower. At 1,565 feet, the base of the tower offers a sweeping 360-degree overlook of the Delaware Valley to the north and west and the Kittatinny foothills to the south and east.

Walpack Wildlife Management Area

Turn right out of the Millbrook parking area, drive 1.4 miles north, and turn right into the Delaware View House. The 1837 former inn now acts as a general store, and you will sometimes see Appalachian Trail hikers kicking back on the wide porch. The namesake view is a huge curve in the course of the Delaware River known as Walpack Bend, best seen after the trees have dropped their leaves in fall.

Continue another .6 mile from Delaware View House, across the Big Flatbrook River bridge, to Route 615. You will turn right, but both roads merge back together about 5 miles to the north, and both are scenic drives. The left road follows Old Mine Road along the Delaware River, and turning right takes you north on Walpack Road, paralleling the Big Flatbrook River through Walpack Wildlife Management Area.

Turn right, and drive 3 miles to a parking area on the right leading to the Big Flatbrook River. This is the first parking spot in the Walpack Wildlife Management Area, a 387-acre preserve known mainly for its excellent trout fishing. For the best access to the river and a very secluded fishing spot, drive another 50 yards north to Haney's Mill Road (an unmarked dirt road) and turn right. Drive .25 mile east on Haney's Mill Road to the first parking area on the right, which provides good access to the Big Flatbrook River. Continue another 100 yards and turn right on Mountain Road, cross the Big Flatbrook River after about 50 feet, and then park on the right beyond the bridge. Unpack your fishing gear and enjoy the isolation; trout are abundant near the parking area and from the bridge.

Walpack

Continue along Haney's Mill Road, and you will rejoin Walpack Road about .2 mile north of the Mountain Road bridge. Proceed north on Walpack Road for 2.1 miles to the Walpack Inn on the right, where prime rib and rack of lamb are served in a warm dining room polished to a deep mahogany brown. The country view from the inn's double windows is serene, but the restaurant is open only on weekend evenings.

Another .4 mile brings you to Main Street and Walpack Center on the right, a tiny village looking much as it did in the nineteenth century. The 1850 former storekeeper's quarters is now home to the Walpack Historical Society. All eleven buildings in the village date from as far back as 1830, including Walpack Methodist Church, erected in 1872. Visit the Walpack Historical Society office and sign the register before heading back to Walpack Road (the main road where you came in). Turn right, then follow the directions for Dingmans Falls, one of the premier sights in the DWG.

Dingmans Falls

From Walpack Center, drive north on Walpack Road for 3.1 miles to a four-way intersection. The main road turns right, but drive straight across the intersection, bearing slightly left onto Walpack Road North. Parking for Peters Valley Craft Center, where artists from around the country demonstrate their skills during the summer, is immediately on the left. Proceed 1.8 miles from the intersection to Dingmans Park Road and turn sharp left. Drive .1 mile and cross the bridge into Pennsylvania. A popular parking area is on the left just beyond the bridge. Here you will find a boat launch, parking, and restrooms. Continue west on Dingmans Park Road for another .5 mile to Route 209 and turn left. Proceed .2 mile and turn right at the Dingmans Falls Visitor Center sign (Johnny Bee Road, but it's not marked). Drive .4 mile to a fork in the road and bear right. Dingmans Falls parking is .6 mile beyond the fork.

The falls have been a tourist attraction since the late 1800s, when a gristmill and a cider mill stood at the base of the cliff. Dingmans Creek tumbles toward the Delaware through sharply cut cliffs and a forest of eastern hemlock. A .5-mile boardwalk leads past Silver Thread Falls, at 80 feet, merely a foreshadowing of what lies at the trail's end. Dingmans Falls is one of the tallest waterfalls in the DWG, at 130 feet, and its graceful flow makes it one of the most beautiful. Foaming white water sprays over angled brown cliffs, flanked by green hemlocks and the tumbling echo of the falls. You can make a steep climb of 240 steps to the top of the cascade and a view of the boardwalk below. Picnic tables, restrooms, and a bookstore surround the visitors center and parking area.

Pocono Environmental Education Center

From Dingmans Falls, retrace your drive back to Route 209 and turn right, heading south along the Delaware and back toward the Worthington campground. Dingmans Campground is .6 mile along on the left, home to a small general store and organized canoe trips on the Delaware. Drive another 3.9 miles south on Route 209 to Brisco Mountain Road and turn right. Continue .8 mile to the top of the hill and the Pocono Environmental Education Center on the right. Six well-marked trails surround the center, totaling 13 miles and ranging from .3 to 5 miles long. Marked with orange blazes, the Tumbling Waters Trail starts across the road from the environmental center office and runs 3 miles through a hemlock ravine, passing a scenic overlook of the Delaware Valley and two waterfalls along the way. On days when the Dingmans Falls parking area is full, the Tumbling Waters Trail offers a quiet and peaceful alternative. You will find trail maps at the office along with a very knowledgeable staff.

Toms Creek Picnic Area

Drive back to Route 209 and continue south. You will pass the Eshback canoe launch on the left after 1.8 miles, where vistas of the Delaware Valley dominate the west beyond cultivated farm fields and woodland. Toms Creek Picnic Area is situated off a side road that veers to the right at 3 miles (TR 306, but it's not marked). The picnic area was once the site of Egypt Mills village, a busy crossroads with a mill serving to grind local grain before Route 209 was moved eastward to follow its present course. This is a quiet picnic spot but not much traveled, probably because it lacks the larger waterfalls and overlooks of the tourist attractions to the north and south. Yet the beauty and serenity of the river make it worth a visit. An easy 1-mile trail begins at the west end of the picnic area. Rolling hills border the trail to the north, where a few feeder creeks tumble down the ridge from Egypt Mills Pond. Toms Creek runs through a small gorge to the south, forming a mile-long series of cascades along the trail. Fishing is allowed in the creek, where trout are the main catch.

Bushkill Falls

Turn right out of the picnic area and rejoin Route 209 after .6 mile. Turn right on Route 209. After 1 mile, you pass Bushkill boat ramp on the left, one of the lesser-traveled boat ramps on the Delaware complete with a concrete ramp, restrooms, and a telephone. Bushkill Falls Road is 1 mile south of the boat ramp on the right. Turn right on Bushkill Falls Road and drive 1.7 miles to the entrance of the falls on the left. Described as the Niagara of Pennsylvania, Bushkill Falls is encircled by four gift shops, an ice cream parlor, snack shops, a bookstore, and restrooms. An entrance fee gets you through the gate to three short trails leading around the falls. The red trail offers the best view and usually leaves the large groups behind. The falls are open from 9 A.M. to 6 P.M. throughout the spring, summer, and fall.

Smithfield Beach

Drive back to Route 209 from Bushkill Falls and turn right. Proceed 1.6 miles south on Route 209 and turn left on River Road. The next 3.6 miles on River Road takes you along the Delaware River to Zion Evangelical Lutheran Church. The church sits on Zion Church Road, a dirt road on the right, about 100 yards from the corner of River Road. The innocuous brick building was built in 1851 and makes for a peaceful rest stop, as you will probably be the only one in the parking area. Headstones in the cemetery across the road date from the early nineteenth century.

Continue about 1 mile south of the church on River Road to the entrance of Smithfield Beach on the left. This is a popular recreation site, mainly because it the only spot along the Delaware that allows swimming, and there is an entrance fee during the summer. It also holds one of the best boat ramps in the DWG, a concrete ramp wide enough to hold two boats side by side. Restrooms, a bathhouse, and picnic tables line the shores of the Delaware. Smithfield Beach also provides access to the 5-mile McDade Trail, the only trail in the DWG that allows mountain biking, cross-country skiing, and snowshoeing. The trail cuts through the center of the recreation area, heading north from the boat launch along the Delaware and south from the beach to Hialeah Picnic Area.

McDade Trail

About 1.9 miles south of Smithfield Beach on River Road lie Hialeah Picnic Area and the southern end of McDade Trail. This is the only trail in the DWG open to mountain bikes, running 5 of a planned 32 miles along the Delaware from Hialeah northward. Cutting mainly through flat farmland, the trail passes Smithfield Beach to end at a parking area on River Road. Apart from a hill at each end, McDade is an easy bike or hike, alternating between farmland, new-growth forest, and an occasional glimpse of the Delaware. Centuries-old farmhouses and cottages that once occupied the land on either side of the trail were demolished in the 1950s to make way for the Tocks Island Dam, a project that was decommissioned in 1978 in the face of mounting opposition. An example of the kind of buildings lost to demolition can be seen in the 1740 Newcomb House, still standing on River Road just south of the Hialeah Picnic Area exit.

Hialeah Picnic Area

Forget grass lawns and tables strung end to end—Hialeah Picnic Area is a simple and serene spot to unpack a lunch. Each table comes with its own parking spot, and the entire site is bordered by forest to the west and the Delaware River to the east. Tables at the north end offer the best views of the river and are nearer McDade Trail. There's a modern restroom, but Hialeah is not overdeveloped, as evidenced by an absence of grills. Enjoy the scenery, pause for lunch, or hike part of McDade Trail before heading back to the Worthington campground. Turn left out of the Hialeah exit, passing through the town of Shawnee at 1.5 miles, where you will find a general store and the Shawnee Inn. Continue another 2.5 miles, turn left on Route 611, and drive .1 mile to the I-80 east on-ramp on the right. Take I-80 east to the first exit in New Jersey (this is Exit 1, but it's merely marked "Exit") and head back to the Worthington campground along Old Mine Road.

Mount Minsi

Mount Minsi, across the Delaware, is the most traveled destination in the DWG after Mount Tammany and Sunfish Pond. Overlooks from Mount Minsi rival those on the New Jersey side, but you have to work to get there. Trails to the top are steep and difficult. The Lake Lenape parking area off Mountain Road is the best place to begin. Take I-80 west from Worthington to Pennsylvania Exit 310, the first exit over the river. Follow the off-ramp for Delaware Water Gap and Route 611 South. Turn right at the bottom of the off-ramp and drive .3 mile to the Route 611 traffic light; then turn left on Route 611 south. Proceed .4 mile and turn right on Mountain Road, a small road on the right next to the Deerhead Inn. Drive .1 mile, then turn left on the first side road into the Lake Lenape parking area.

Two trails leave from the parking area and climb to the top of 1,463-foot Mount Minsi, both ending at overlooks of the Delaware Water Gap and Delaware River. The white-blazed AT arches 1.5 miles and 1,060 feet to the top of the mountain, passing some great vistas along the way. About 1 mile into the hike, a short side trail, marked with a sign printed "View," leads to a sweeping scene of the Delaware River bending around Mount Tammany and the Kittatinny Ridge to the east. Lookouts from the top are even better, showing the Delaware River far below, snaking through the forested Delaware Valley. Mount Minsi Fire Road also leaves from Lake Lenape, extending 1.5 miles and climbing 1,060 feet to the top of the mountain. You can form a 3-mile loop by taking the AT to the top of Mount Minsi and the fire road back to the parking area. Beware, though—the fire road is a road in name only, and you will find it no easier than the Appalachian Trail.

If you drive south from the Lake Lenape parking area along Route 611, you will come to three scenic overlooks bordering the road. The first is Resort Point Overlook, about .3 mile south of Mountain Road on the left. This was once the site of the Kittatinny Hotel, the first Delaware Water Gap resort opened in 1832. A short side trail begins across Route 611 and climbs to meet the AT, which heads north to Lake Lenape and south to Mount Minsi. Point of Gap Overlook is 1.4 miles farther south along Route 611 on the right, followed by Arrow Island Overlook on the right. All of the overlooks face scenes of Mount Tammany and soaring raptors along the cliffs.

Where to Buy Supplies

The closest supplies are in the tiny, slow-paced town of Delaware Water Gap in Pennsylvania. Follow the directions above for Mount Minsi, and you will find yourself in a small town stretching along two main roads. The pizza parlor on the corner of Broad Street and Route 611 is quick and popular with local residents. The diner on Broad Street offers a varied menu and good service, and two gas stations near I-80 each hold convenience stores. The Deerhead Inn on Main Street (Route 611) serves dinner at reasonable prices, has outdoor tables on the veranda, and features live jazz Thursday and Friday evenings. Continue west on I-80 for more substantive supplies. Exit 308 in Pennsylvania takes you to East Stroudsburg, and Exit 307 leads to Stroudsburg. Both cities offer a variety of conveniences, including banks, pharmacies, car repair, grocery stores, sporting goods, and a variety of restaurants.

Swartswood State Park

P.O. Box 123
Swartswood, NJ 07877

Area. 2,472 acres.

Park office. Warren County, 5.3 miles west of Newton on the west side
of Route 619.

Highlights. Swartswood Lake.

Activities. Camping, hiking, fishing, boating, picnicking, swimming, mountain biking, horseback riding, birding, hunting, ice fishing, cross-country
skiing, snowshoeing, ice skating.

Entrance fee. A fee is charged to enter the recreation area from Memorial
Day weekend through Labor Day.

Park hours. Year-round, from dawn to dusk.

For additional information: (973) 383-5230

The land around Swartswood State Park has been farmed since Capt.
Anthony Swartwout and his family settled on the northern end of
the lake in the 1750s. Captain Swartwout's experiences reveal an earlier Lenni-Lenape Indian presence: He and his family were slain by local
tribes in retribution for his involvement in the French and Indian War.
Keen's Grist Mill on the southwest edge of the park occupies a spot that
has been milling grain since the American colonies declared independ-
ence, and the park itself is one of the oldest in New Jersey. The original 1914 land donation was a mere 12.5 acres, now the site of Emmans
Grove Picnic Area.

The two lakes garner the majority of attention today, much as they
did in Captain Swartwout's time. At 494 acres, Swartswood Lake sits
next to Little Swartswood Lake in a tandem that draws boaters, anglers,
and swimmers during the summer months. A single family campground rests near the shore, where tent and trailer sites remain open
year-round. From the developed recreation area, you are never far from
a sandy beach, modern restrooms, food concession, and two boat
ramps. Almost 6 miles of trails crisscross the eastern end of the park,
and avid hikers can escape summer crowds on two nearby rail trails

totaling 48 miles. Birding, canoeing, camping, and hiking give access to the natural areas of Swartswood, and those interested in a relaxing afternoon need venture no farther than the picnic tables near the beach.

Camping

One family campground borders Swartswood Lake, and three group sites occupy a separate campground near the park entrance. Most of the sites are large enough to accommodate trailers, and Swartswood's paved roads make access easy for almost any vehicle. You will not be caught in the wilderness here, as both campgrounds are within a few hundred yards of the recreation area and its public beach, telephones, and food concession. Portable radios can be a common sight during peak season, but you stand a good chance of finding a deserted campground and two serene lakes throughout the quiet days of fall and winter.

Family Campground

Swartswood's campground is highly developed, perfectly suited for a family outing or group event. Tent and trailer sites string end to end along the access road near Swartswood Lake, some set on green lawns and others surrounded by hardwood forest on the northern edge of the campground. Six yurts rest in a peaceful area about 150 yards from Swartswood Lake. You will find a boat launch reserved exclusively for campers next to site 65, and modern amenities such as hot showers and laundry facilities are close at hand. Consider reserving ahead—the campground is very busy during the summer.

Directions. Drive inside the Swartswood entrance, turn right at the park office, and proceed .2 mile to the campground.

Sites and facilities. Swartswood's sixty-five family sites and six yurts, each equipped with fire rings and picnic tables, are within walking distance of modern restrooms, hot showers, and drinking water. The yurts are round canvas tents, each furnished with two double-deck bunks. A boat launch, laundry room, playground, and trailer sanitary station are situated throughout the campground. The park allows camping year-round.

Recommended sites. With two lakes totaling 569 acres, it's a bit disappointing that none of Swartswood's campsites rest directly on the water. Numbers 1 through 21 occupy a grass lawn, and about half of them are large enough to accommodate trailers. An area of woodland begins beyond campsite 22, where small niches in the forest line the

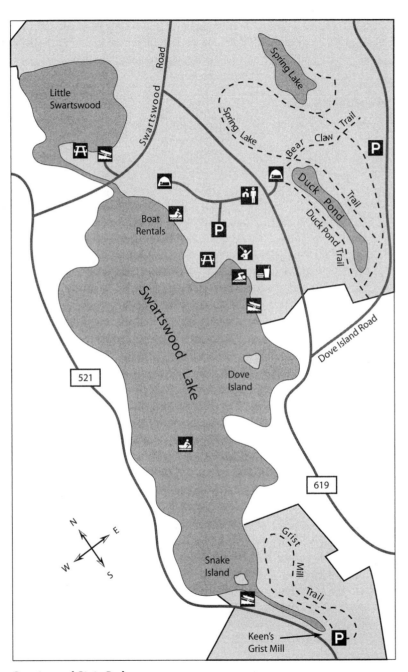

Little
Swartswood

Swartswood Road

Spring Lake

Spring Lake

Bear Claw Trail

Duck Pond

Duck Pond Trail

P

Boat
Rentals

P

Swartswood Lake

521

Dove
Island

Dove Island Road

619

N
E
W
S

Snake
Island

Grist Mill Trail

Keen's
Grist Mill

P

Swartswood State Park

paved access road. Site 62 is encircled by a thin barrier of trees, and 38, 39, 58, and 59 are set back from the road slightly more than their neighbors. Yurts 1 and 5 are the best options for privacy, situated some distance from the others in forested clearings.

Group Campground

Three group sites, labeled A, B, and C, are located directly across from the park entrance on Route 619. They each occupy secluded clearings near Duck Pond, well removed from the activity of Swartswood's recreation area and far enough from the highway to produce a sense of escape. Site C is supremely private, set on the shore of Duck Pond and encircled by bushes. Site B is a better option for avoiding insects, as it lies a short distance from the pond, and site A borders the campground access road. Each site accommodates twenty campers and holds a fire ring, grill, and picnic tables. Chemical toilets and water from one ground pump are close at hand, but the campground has no showers. Group camping is available from April 1 through October 31.

Trails

Swartswood offers four marked trails totaling 5.7 miles. Three of them are interconnected near Duck Pond, essentially creating one long trail. Duck Pond Trail, .6 mile of pavement beginning near the group campground, is open to hiking, biking, roller blading, and skateboarding. Spring Lake Trail is open to mountain bikers as well, and it is the only option in the park for horseback riders. The trail begins at the end of Duck Pond Trail and continues 2.8 miles through eastern hemlock and red maple to Spring Lake, a serene pond on the eastern edge of the park. The .8-mile Bear Claw Trail also veers off from Duck Pond Trail, heading back to the group campground to form a loop. Grist Mill Trail, located on the southwest end of the park, is the most challenging trail at Swartswood, stretching 1.5 miles along the shore of Mill Pond, past the 1838 Keen's Grist Mill, then along a ridge overlooking Swartswood Lake. The Bear Claw and Grist Mill Trails are open exclusively to hikers.

The park also lies near two of New Jersey's long-distance rail trails. The Paulinskill Valley Trail begins near Warbasse and extends 27 miles southwest, passing Swartswood State Park on its way to the Columbia Lake Wildlife Management Area near the Delaware River. Along the trail, relics of the New York-Susquehanna and Western Railroad remain from when the line ceased operation in 1962. Remnants of old railroad

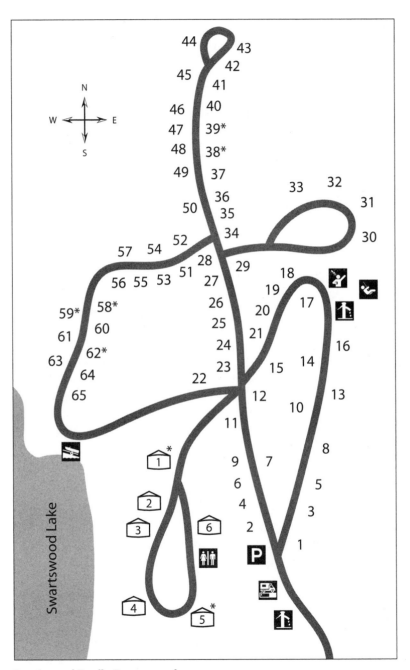

Swartswood Family Campground

Trail Mileage and Difficulty

TRAIL	MILES	DIFFICULTY	BLAZE	USES
Bear Claw Trail	0.8	E	yellow	h
Dove Island Road	1.7	E	no blaze	h,m
Duck Pond Trail	0.6	E	no blaze	h,m,s,x
Grist Mill Trail	1.5	M	no blaze	h
Spring Lake Trail	2.8	E	white	e,h,m,s,x

bridges, whistle stop markers, and junction depots can still be seen along the route. A good place to start the trail is at its closest approach to Swartswood near the east shore of Paulinskill Lake. Turn left out of the park office, drive .6 mile, and turn right on Route 622 (Newton Swartswood Road). Proceed 1.6 miles to the parking area on the right.

If you bike the Paulinskill Valley Trail 5 miles north of the parking area into Warbasse, you can pick up the 21.2-mile Sussex Branch Trail heading south. This second rail trail weaves through farmland and forest, revealing some of those natural spaces that are never apparent from roadways. The trail stretches south to Newton, then continues through Kittatinny Valley State Park and Allamuchy State Park, about 2 and 8 miles south of the city. Newton causes a break in the Sussex Branch Trail, so you have to travel through the city using local roads. A base made of cinder or crushed rock on both rail trails results in easy going for mountain biking, horseback riding, and cross-country skiing.

Activities

Swartswood State Park combines a developed recreation area with the boating and fishing opportunities of two easily accessible lakes. The sandy beach is surrounded by all the amenities of a modern park, from a bathhouse with hot showers to picnic tables and grills. Two boat ramps give access to Swartswood Lake and Little Swartswood Lake, where anglers will find an abundance and variety of fish that rival most lakes in northern New Jersey. Renting a canoe or making use of one of the two nearby rail trails are good ways to find a serene patch of forest, but mountain biking, horseback riding, and cross-country skiing are all welcome at Swartswood. Birders will not regret a visit during spring and fall migrations, and cold winters bring anglers looking for perch, pickerel, walleye, and trout through the ice.

Fishing

The number of different game fish and sheer quantity of each species make Swartswood a premier fishing destination. Swartswood Lake is one of the best walleye spots in the state, mainly because more than 200,000 walleye have been stocked in Swartswood Lake since 1992. The big lake is also known for its good largemouth and smallmouth bass fishing, and trout are stocked at a rate of about 4,000 per year. At a maximum depth of 52 feet, the lake is deep enough to maintain a fair holdover population, so fishing for trout is available year-round. Pickerel, yellow perch, and catfish are abundant as well, and thousands of channel catfish have been stocked in recent years. You will even find crappie in the big lake, although they are not as common as Swartswood's other species. A boat ramp next to the recreation area provides easy access to the lake, and the boat livery sells live bait.

Little Swartswood Lake and Spring Lake offer excellent fishing as well. Trout are stocked in Little Swartswood at a rate of about 1,500 per year, along with a few hundred tiger muskellunge and channel catfish. Aside from bluegill, the most abundant species in Little Swartswood, fishing is good for largemouth bass, pickerel, yellow perch, and catfish. Smallmouth bass can be found in lesser numbers, and a few carp inhabit the shallow water. A boat ramp on the south shore provides access to the lake. Fishing is also allowed from the shore of Spring Lake, an often overlooked option at Swartswood, where you will find a good population of largemouth bass, pickerel, catfish, and sunfish.

Boating

At a combined 569 acres, the two lakes at Swartswood are among the largest and most accessible natural lakes in New Jersey, home to a boat livery, two public boat ramps, one floating dock, paved access roads, and more than 7 miles of shoreline. The waters have been the subject of extensive conservation and reclamation efforts, and as a result, only electric motors are allowed in the lakes. Swartswood Lake Boat Rentals, next to the beach, offers rowboats, canoes, kayaks, pedal boats, and small sailboats. You will find one concrete boat ramp on the south side of Swartswood Lake's recreation area and another on the south shore of Little Swartswood Lake off Swartswood Road. A floating dock, where you can launch canoes or small boats, is located on the southwest corner of Swartswood Lake off Route 521.

Strong winds across Swartswood Lake make it a popular destination for sailors, and the big lake is an easy paddle aside from occasional high winds in the north. The western section of the lake adjoins parkland, where a small island and several sheltered coves keep wind to a minimum. Much of the shoreline to the west is residential, but the houses are far enough inland to leave a buffer of trees for scenery. Paddlers can avoid the busy recreation area by putting in at the floating dock on the southwest end of Swartswood Lake. A small cove leads from the dock to Keen's Grist Mill, once used to produce cornmeal. The boat concession is open from May through September, and the boat ramps require no extra fee.

Picnicking

The main picnic area at Swartswood surrounds the beach and recreation area. Many of the fifty tables north of the beach occupy a wooded grove on Swartswood Lake, although a few sit behind a row of trees blocking any view of the water. You will find more tables and a covered pavilion south of the beach, most of them on a manicured green lawn overlooking Swartswood Lake. Grills, water, restrooms, a playground, and a food concession are nearby. A separate picnic area on the south shore of Little Swartswood Lake serves as a refreshing variation, with three lonely tables and grills overlooking the quiet water. All three tables are usually deserted, even though they offer a view of the bald eagle nest on the opposite shore. One chemical toilet sits in the parking area, but the site has no water or other facilities.

Swimming

Thousands of visitors arrive at Swartswood's beach throughout the summer. A thin strip of sand about 35 yards wide is backed by a grass lawn and picnic tables, where a cordoned-off area of Swartswood Lake allows swimming from Memorial Day through Labor Day. The nearby bathhouse holds modern restrooms with showers and a first-aid station, and the parking area accommodates about 200 cars. Playgrounds, a boat livery, and a volleyball net encircle the beach, and the food concession sells items ranging from hot dogs to sunscreen.

Mountain Biking

Spring Lake and Duck Pond Trails are open to mountain bikes. Duck Pond Trail is paved, but Spring Lake Trail travels along a gently sloping dirt track, through a forest of pin, chestnut, red, and black oak trees and along the shores of two quiet ponds. You can combine Spring Lake Trail with Dove Island Road if you ride through a parking area situated on the east end of the trail. Although paved, Dove Island Road provides a scenic 1.7-mile ride past farm silos and open fields ending at Ridge Road. You can either turn around at the end or turn right on Ridge Road and cycle along the west bank of Paulinskill Lake. See the Trails section for information about the Paulinskill Valley and Sussex Branch Trails, two long-distance trails converted from abandoned railroad tracks.

Horseback Riding

Spring Lake Trail allows horses, and you will find parking on Dove Island Road near Duck Pond. Turn right out of the park office, drive .8 mile, and turn left on Dove Island Road. Proceed 1.2 miles to the parking area marked "Equestrian Trail" on the left. You will find a few gentle hills and some rocky sections, but no great technical challenges. The nearby Paulinskill Valley Trail is open to horses as well, but parking for trailers is a creative endeavor near Swartswood. See the section on the Paulinskill River Wildlife Management Area below for possible parking areas.

Birding

Swartswood Lake has few rivals when it comes to viewing waterfowl on New Jersey's inland lakes. Fallouts occur regularly, when huge flocks of migrating birds are forced to land because of weather conditions. More than 500 common mergansers splashed into the lake on a single March day in 1995. Other separate fallouts in past years have brought 200 ruddy ducks, 150 green-winged teals, 200 ring-necked ducks, and 160 common loons. Many of the more common waterbirds are found at Swartswood throughout the spring and summer, including buffleheads, canvasbacks, gadwalls, and greater and lesser scaups. During migration, black scoters, surf scoters, goldeneyes, hooded mergansers, and horned, pied-billed, and red-necked grebes gather on the lake. Look for waterfowl from the swimming beach, all three boat launches, Grist Mill Trail, Spring Lake Trail, and the bird blind on Duck Pond Trail. Swartswood's pair of nesting bald eagles can be seen from the boat launch area on Little Swartswood Lake.

Hunting

The hunting of deer, small game, wild turkeys, and waterfowl is allowed on a 900-acre section of the park located east of Route 619. It is not a popular hunting destination, but hikers should take note during open season. Bear Claw, Duck Pond, and Spring Lake Trails run through the hunting area. Swartswood falls within deer management zone 5.

Winter Activities

A number of activities continue throughout the year at Swartswood. The number of park visitors in January and February slows to a handful, so camping during the winter almost guarantees an escape from crowds. Sites 1 through 21 remain available year-round. Duck Pond and Spring Lake Trails are open to cross-country skiing and snowshoeing, and ice skating is allowed on the lakes given safe conditions. Both lakes support ice fishing during the colder months, when perch, pickerel, walleye, and trout are the main catches. Little Swartswood is one of only four lakes in Sussex County targeted for winter stocking, receiving up to 1,000 trout each November. The lakes don't freeze every year, so ensure that ice conditions are safe before venturing out.

Flora and Fauna

Cultivated farmland and fields in various stages of succession dominate the area around Swartswood Lake. The younger fields support eastern red cedar, eastern hemlock, and a variety of maples, then pines appear as the fields develop, and finally oaks and other hardwoods take hold in the older areas. The variety of plant life inhabiting Swartswood is heartening, given the amount of suburban development around the two lakes. The park is home to five varieties of oaks, six types of maple trees, and more than 200 herbs, sedges, grasses, and ferns. Swartswood Lake itself is the subject of a variety of conservation efforts targeted at curbing the growth of algae and other invasive plants. Plans include linking Swartswood State Park with nearby Paulinskill River Wildlife Management Area through land acquisition, eventually connecting the two areas as a buffer against development. Taken as a whole, the conservation area makes up the Paulinskill Watershed, crucial habitat for state endangered animals such as the long-tailed salamander. The globally endangered dwarf wedge mussel relies on the region as well, as do breeding birds and a wide array of rare and migratory waterfowl.

Surrounding Points of Interest

Anyone desiring an escape into the wild need only travel 10 miles west. The Delaware Water Gap National Recreation Area stretches 50 miles from High Point State Park in the north to Worthington State Forest in the south. Along the way, it encompasses two state forests, one state park, the Appalachian Trail, the Delaware River, and the Kittatinny Ridge. See the chapters covering Worthington State Forest, Stokes State Forest, and High Point State Park for more information about the Delaware Water Gap and many other wildlife areas throughout the region.

Paulinskill River Wildlife Management Area

The Paulinskill River flows through this 2,000-acre protected area of red maple, black birch, and American elm. Above the dam at Route 614, the river widens into Paulinskill Lake, a picturesque canoeing destination surrounded by meadows and rolling hills. The river and lake are stocked with about 30,000 trout each spring, so the wildlife management area is a popular destination for anglers during stocking. Hunting is also allowed for deer, small game, and waterfowl.

One of the best ways to access the area is along the Paulinskill Valley Trail. Turn left out of the park office, drive .6 mile, and turn right on Route 622 (Newton Swartswood Road). Proceed 1.6 miles to the main parking area on the right, a good place to start if you want to head south along the trail. Several parking areas also line Junction Road, which begins across the highway from the main parking area. If you want to hike north along Paulinskill Valley Trail, drive .9 mile north on Junction Road and turn left on Parsons Road. Proceed 70 yards to the parking area on the right. Anglers and paddlers should continue on Parsons Road for another .4 mile and cross a small bridge to the parking area on the left, where a dirt ramp gives easy access to Paulinskill Lake.

Whittingham Wildlife Management Area

The headwaters of the Pequest River run through Whittingham's 1,930 acres, home to a freshwater marsh, hardwood forest, and rolling fields. The upper reaches of the Pequest River are stocked with about 2,000 trout, but the area is more popular with hunters than anglers. The Rockport Pheasant Farm releases thousands of pheasant and quail into the fields every year, and a dog-training area is located near the northern border. Proving a diverse array of visitors, butterfly-watchers mark this as a productive park for species such as orange sulphur, eastern tailed blue, and pearl crescent. The park is wild and undeveloped, with unmarked trails open to hikers, cross-country skiers, and horseback riders (a permit is required for horseback riding, available from the Division of Fish and Wildlife). The Whittingham office is on Fredon Springdale Road about .1 mile south of Route 618 near Springdale. One parking area lies .2 mile south of the office on the left, and three parking areas line Route 611 south of Springdale.

Where to Buy Supplies

The tiny town of Swartswood offers a country store and a pizzeria on Swartswood Road, about .1 mile east of Route 521 (West Shore Drive). For more substantive supplies, travel 5.3 miles east to the city of Newton. Parking can be difficult, but the city contains restaurants, grocery stores, banks, pharmacies, and gas stations. Turn left out of the park office, drive .6 mile to Route 622 (Newton Swartswood Road), and turn right. Proceed 4.3 miles to Mill Street, turn right, and continue .4 mile into Newton.

Jenny Jump State Forest

P.O. Box 150
Hope, NJ 07844

Area. 4,288 acres.

Park office. Warren County, 9.4 miles northwest of Hackettstown on the corner of Far View Road and State Park Road.

Highlights. Greenwood Observatory, Jenny Jump Mountain Range, secluded campsites.

Activities. Camping, hiking, fishing, boating, picnicking, mountain biking, birding, hunting, ice fishing, cross-country skiing, snowshoeing.

Entrance fee. None.

Park hours. Year-round, from dawn to dusk.

For additional information: (908) 459-4366

Almost 4,300 protected acres line the Jenny Jump Mountain Range, an area of rock cliffs and shallow mountains formed at the end of the Wisconsin Ice Age. Two-ton boulders, remnants of glaciers that receded 12,000 years ago, look as if they have been strewn like dice along the trails and streams lining the ridge. Six trails cross the park, some climbing above 1,000 feet through thick stands of white pine and chestnut oak. A short hike produces wide-angle views of the Great Meadows, a former lake bed carved out by retreating glaciers, and the Pequest River Valley can be seen to the east from the pinnacle of Summit Trail. The park's secluded campsites are spread out through the forest in a unique fashion, with no central campground, making Jenny Jump the perfect destination for campers seeking privacy. Hiking, hunting, fishing, and birding are all deserving endeavors at this peaceful and often-overlooked forest.

Camping

Jenny Jump's family campground, eight shelters, and two group sites go relatively unnoticed by New Jersey campers. You will sometimes find a note on the office door during the off-season urging campers to

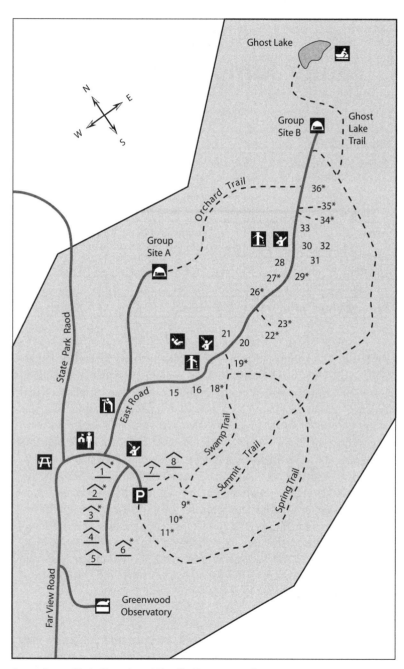

Jenny Jump State Forest and Family Campground

choose a site and slide money through the mail slot. The tranquility is no doubt due to the absence of developed recreation areas, swimming beaches, and food concessions, which makes Jenny Jump a perfect escape from the typical summer tourism scene. The remote sites are well spaced throughout a dense forest of sugar maple and red oak, some perched atop wooded hills surrounded by glacial erratics, and others recessed into the forest at the end of thin hiking trails. Travelers looking for a quiet and relaxing place to pitch a tent will find the perfect match amid the foothills of Jenny Jump Mountain.

Family Campground

Jenny Jump's twenty-two tent and trailer sites line East Road in the shadow of a forested ridge. Eight shelters lie on the west end of the campground near the park office, but the sprawling layout of the campground means you have to drive almost 1 mile to the last campsite, number 36, on the east end of the park. A few of the sites are large enough to accommodate small trailers. Most occupy secluded clearings far from the road and pressed in by trees, where the nearest chance of nighttime lights comes from the tiny town of Hope almost 3 miles to the west.

Directions. Sites 15 through 36 begin .5 mile east of the park office and line both sides of East Road for another .4 mile. The eight shelters are accessed from a parking area about .1 mile south of the park office. A set of log stairs on the east side of the parking area leads to tent sites 9 through 11.

Sites and facilities. Jenny Jump's twenty-two tent and trailer sites contain fire rings and picnic tables. Two restrooms service the sites along East Road, each equipped with chemical toilets and a shower. Water pumps are located next to both of the restrooms, and a playground lies next to site 21. The eight shelters are more like small two-room cabins, each furnished with a woodburning stove, two double-deck bunks, and a small table with benches inside, in addition to a picnic table and fire ring outside. One modern restroom next to the shelter area offers flush toilets, hot showers, and a drinking fountain. The campsites are open from April 1 through October 31, and the shelters are open year-round.

Recommended sites. The campsites at Jenny Jump will not disappoint travelers in pursuit of quiet and isolation. If you are looking for maximum privacy, drive south from the park office for about .1 mile, and park at the trailhead parking area. Climb the log stairs leading east, and you will reach sites 10 and 11 perched on top of the hill. Number 9 is about 50 yards away, sitting by itself near the Summit Trail. Jenny Jump's eight shelters are accessed from the same parking area, and numbers 1, 2, 3, and 6 are the most private, set back from the road in wooded clearings.

The remainder of the sites lie east of the park office along East Road. Numbers 18 and 19 sit 80 yards from the road near Swamp Trail, 22 and 23 are hidden from view atop a small hill, and 26, 27, and 29 are recessed into the forest. The sites at the end of the road, 34 through 36, are isolated as well, although 35 and 36 sit next to each other. Only one of the sites, number 28, is large enough to accommodate an average-size trailer, but a few sites can accommodate campers or very small trailers, including 20, 21, 26, and 29.

Group Campsites

Jenny Jump's two group campsites, designated by letters A and B, are located on opposite sides of the park. The dirt access road leading to site A begins about 100 yards east of the park office. The drive is quite scenic, past woodland and fields for about .3 mile to a clearing holding five picnic tables and a fire ring. The site is supremely private, accommodating up to twenty-five campers. You will find two pit toilets, but no showers or water. Site B holds up to forty campers and lies .9 mile east of the park office at the end of East Road. The wooded clearing contains picnic tables, a fire ring fitted with a grill grate, and two pit toilets, but no showers. Water is available about .2 mile to the west at the family campground restroom. Both sites are open from April 1 through October 31.

Trails

Jenny Jump's six trails total 8.2 miles, and all except one, the Mountain Lake Trail, are open exclusively to hikers. Three of the trails begin at the trailhead parking area .1 mile south of the park office. The blue-blazed Spring Trail heads east from the parking area and runs along a rock ledge through a maze of glacial erratics. The massive boulders, many the size of a two-story house, line both sides of the path between limited views of a small stream to the south. The 1.5-mile Summit Trail, blazed in yellow, heads east from shelter number 8 and climbs above 1,000 feet to overlooks of the Pequest River Valley to the east and the sod fields of the Great Meadows to the south. Swamp Trail, marked with red blazes, splits off from the Summit Trail about .1 mile from the trail-

Trail Mileage and Difficulty

TRAIL	MILES	DIFFICULTY	BLAZE	USES
Ghost Lake Trail	1.3	M	light blue	h,s,x
Mountain Lake Trail	3.7	M	yellow	h,m,s,x
Orchard Trail	0.7	E–M	white	h,s,x
Spring Trail	0.7	M	blue	h,s,x
Summit Trail	1.5	M	yellow	h,s,x
Swamp Trail	0.3	M	red	h,s,x

head and continues relatively flat for .3 mile along the side of Jenny Jump Mountain.

The white-blazed Orchard Trail is the easiest of the remaining three trails, extending .7 mile from group campsite A to a parking area near campsite 36. Two additional trails lie in opposite directions some distance from the park office. The blue-blazed Ghost Lake Trail begins at group campsite B and stretches 1.3 miles to Ghost Lake, ranging in altitude from 900 feet up to 1,000 feet, and back down to 600 feet, in the process. The sixth trail near Mountain Lake stretches through a disconnected patch of forest 6.6 miles southwest of the park office. It is the only trail open to mountain bikers. See the Mountain Biking section below for more information on the Mountain Lake Trail.

Activities

The absence of a central recreation area at Jenny Jump is exactly its natural appeal. Seldom will you encounter other hikers on the trails during the week, and fishing is relaxing and private at Ghost Lake. Mountain bikers head for the western section of the park, where Mountain Lake Trail rises above 1,000 feet. The Greenwood Observatory is open to the public on Saturday evenings, and during the day, one quiet picnic area caters to visitors in pursuit of solitude. Winter travelers can fish through the ice at Ghost Lake, cross-country ski along the base of Jenny Jump Mountain, or hike along the Summit Trail to views of the valley below.

Greenwood Observatory

An official title may seem pretentious for this 10-foot-square shed that stands atop Jenny Jump Mountain, but it has been used by the United

Astronomy Clubs of New Jersey (UACNJ) for more than a decade. The organization holds public classes and stargazing gatherings between 8 and 10:30 P.M. on Saturday nights from April through October. A 28-inch Newtonian reflector, tiny astronomy museum, and lecture hall are the centers of attention. The UACNJ has labeled the spot as one of the few dark sky locations left in New Jersey. Drive south of the park office on Far View Road for .5 mile, and turn left on the observatory access road. Proceed .2 mile to the observatory at the end of the road.

Fishing and Boating

Ghost Lake is only about 10 feet deep, but the fishing isn't bad for large-mouth bass and crappie. Channel catfish and bluegill are stocked certain years as well. Canoes and small boats with electric motors are allowed on the lake, but there is no boat ramp.

Jenny Jump also borders a tiny section of Mountain Lake, 7 miles southwest of the park office, but the lake was recently removed from the state's stocking program, and public access is limited. See the Mountain Biking section for directions. You will find several productive boating and fishing destinations within a reasonable drive of the Jenny Jump office. See the Stephens and Allamuchy Mountain State Parks chapter for information on Lake Hopatcong, and the Worthington State Forest chapter for a description of the Delaware River. The Pequest River is covered below.

Picnicking

Jenny Jump's only picnic area is situated across from the park office on State Park Road. A mowed grass field bounded by woodland holds about a dozen tables and grills. The site is private and quiet. Water and restrooms are available at the shelter parking area near the office.

Mountain Biking

Mountain Lake Trail, almost 7 miles southwest of the park office, is the only trail at Jenny Jump that allows mountain biking. Marked in yellow, it is the longest trail in the park, rising and falling 3.7 miles through thick stands of red maple and chestnut oak. Three climbs reach an altitude of almost 1,000 feet, followed by descents of 300 to 500 feet after each climb. A few overlooks of Mountain Lake are unobscured only after the trees drop their leaves in the fall. The altitude variation and loose rock along the path make this a moderate to difficult ride. Drive south on Far View Road for 1.7 miles and turn left on Route 611 (Hope

Road). Continue 1.5 miles and turn right on Route 617 (Mountain Lake Road). Drive 2.9 miles, bear right on Lakeside Drive North, and proceed .5 mile to the parking area on the right.

Birding

The terrain surrounding Jenny Jump includes rock cliffs and mountains, wetlands, open fields, and hardwood forest, a variety of habitats that support several migratory and nesting bird species in the spring and fall. The Spring and Summit Trails are prime warbler territory during spring. At least five pairs of worm-eating warblers nest in the area, along with cerulean and golden-winged warblers, rose-breasted grosbeaks, and wild turkeys. Travel along Shades Road between Route 611 and Ghost Lake, where migrating soras, least bitterns, and a variety of flycatchers, warblers, and vireos can be seen in the wetlands and other habitats south of the road. Northern parulas have lingered along Shades Road in recent years. Ghost Lake and the surrounding wetlands support belted kingfishers, olive-sided and Acadian flycatchers, Louisiana waterthrushes, winter wrens, and a number of warblers. Drive north of the lake toward an area of open fields and woodland, where eastern wood-pewees, scarlet tanagers, orchard orioles, and eastern kingbirds can be seen from the roadside.

Hunting

Just over half of the forest, about 2,400 acres, is open to the hunting of deer, small game, waterfowl, and wild turkeys. All of the marked trails are affected, so hikers should be aware of open seasons. Check the Division of Fish and Wildlife website for annual regulation and open season changes. Jenny Jump falls within deer management zone 5.

Winter Activities

Woodburning stoves provide heat throughout the winter at Jenny Jump's eight shelters, and you are almost guaranteed a peaceful trail during the colder months. A pleasant walk along the Summit Trail reveals views of sprawling farms to the south and the Pequest River Valley to the east, unobscured by summer's thick foliage. The best vantage point is from a rock ledge on the south side of the trail about .1 mile from the trailhead parking area. All of the trails and roads allow cross-country skiing and snowshoeing, although the Summit, Mountain Lake, and Ghost Lake Trails are more suited to hiking. Ghost Lake allows ice fishing, where perch and pickerel are the main catch.

Flora and Fauna

Jenny Jump represents a gateway to black bear country in New Jersey. Bears are relatively common at Jenny Jump State Forest and points north, yet they are a rare occurrence 15 miles to the south at Voorhees State Park. Black bears, along with deer, wild turkey, red foxes, and other wildlife, occupy an unusual mixture of rock cliffs and shallow mountains, remnants of glacial activity that ended 12,000 years ago. The ridgetop forests are part of the Pequest River Watershed, where more than 100 species of birds occur, many endangered, such as the vesper sparrow and short-eared owl. Red maple, black birch, white oak, and many other tree species join at least 250 types of herbs, vines, shrubs, ferns, and grasses to form the varied habitat throughout the park. Add the streams and valleys of the Great Meadows to the east, and the combination makes up an essential part of New Jersey's Central Highlands.

Surrounding Points of Interest

Allamuchy State Park, about 10 miles to the east, offers more than 40 miles of all-purpose trails, as well as fishing in the Musconetcong River. Beyond Allamuchy, Lake Hopatcong's recreation area and boat ramps give access to New Jersey's largest lake. Worthington State Forest and the Delaware Water Gap National Recreation Area are a mere 15 miles to the northwest, with 70,000 acres of protected land open to all sorts of pursuits. These destinations and a number of others within a twenty-minute drive of Jenny Jump are covered in the Stephens and Allamuchy Mountain State Parks and Worthington State Forest chapters.

Pequest Wildlife Management Area

The Pequest Trout Hatchery produces 600,000 brown, rainbow, and brook trout each year for distribution to the various streams and lakes throughout New Jersey. You can see the process of trout rearing in action, from egg collection to stocking, between 10 A.M. and 4 P.M. daily. Programs such as intermediate fly tying and ice fishing basics are scheduled throughout the year. From the park office, take Far View Road south for 1.7 miles and turn left on Route 611 (Hope Road). Drive south on Route 611 for 2.4 miles, and turn right on Route 46. Drive 3.1 miles west on Route 46 to the Pequest Trout Hatchery on the left.

The hatchery makes up only a part of the Pequest Wildlife Management Area, a 4,610-acre forest bordering the Pequest River. An archery range, education center, and a few trails surround the hatchery. Pheasant are stocked in the surrounding woods from the Rockport Pheasant Farm, making this a popular area for hunters seeking small game, deer, wild turkeys, and waterfowl. The Pequest River parallels Route 46 from the Pequest Wildlife Management Area to the town of Vienna, and not surprisingly, it is a common destination for trout fishers. Up to 30,000 trout are stocked from the adjacent hatchery every year.

Where to Buy Supplies

Hackettstown, 9.4 miles to the east, is the largest nearby city and the only option for substantial supplies within 10 miles. Drive 1.7 miles south on Far View Road and turn left on Route 611 (Hope Road). Proceed 2.4 miles, turn left on Route 46, and continue 5.3 miles to Hackettstown. The quickly growing city contains grocery stores, sporting goods, pharmacies, banks, auto repair, fast food, and a variety of restaurants. A few restaurants and gas stations are widely scattered within 5 miles of Jenny Jump. You will find two gas stations and a drive-in hamburger restaurant in the town of Great Meadows, about 4.1 miles to the south on Route 46. Hope, 3 miles to the west on Route 519, holds a small luncheonette, pizzeria, and bank.

Stephens and Allamuchy Mountain State Parks

800 Willow Grove St.
Hackettstown, NJ 07840

Area. Allamuchy Mountain State Park: 8,683 acres. Stephens State Park: 805 acres.

Park office. The Stephens State Park office in Warren County serves both parks and lies 1.6 miles north of Main Street in Hackettstown on the east side of Route 604.

Highlights. Waterloo Village, Allamuchy Natural Area, Musconetcong River.

Activities. Camping, hiking, fishing, boating, picnicking, mountain biking, horseback riding, birding, hunting, ice fishing, cross-country skiing, snowshoeing.

Entrance fee. None.

Park hours. Year-round, from dawn to dusk.

For additional information: (908) 852-3790

The highlands rising from the Musconetcong River were the Allamachtey, or "Place within the Hills," to the Lenni-Lenape. The land was not as pristine when the Morris Canal came through in 1831, followed by the Sussex Railroad, signaling a transition to the industrial age that can be seen today in the restored village of Waterloo east of the park. A 228-acre donation from landowners Augustus and Marsena Stephens began a wilderness revival, resulting in a 9,266-acre protected area that contains one of the most extensive trail systems in northern New Jersey.

Allamuchy Mountain State Park and Stephens State Park are essentially one entity, separated only by the Musconetcong River. Sections of the two parks still retain the feel of that hidden retreat described by the Lenni-Lenape, where a walk down the trail can make you feel apart from mechanized society. More than 40 miles of trails are open not just to hikers, but also to a wide array of activities from snowshoeing to horseback riding. At least three overlooks provide a view of four lakes,

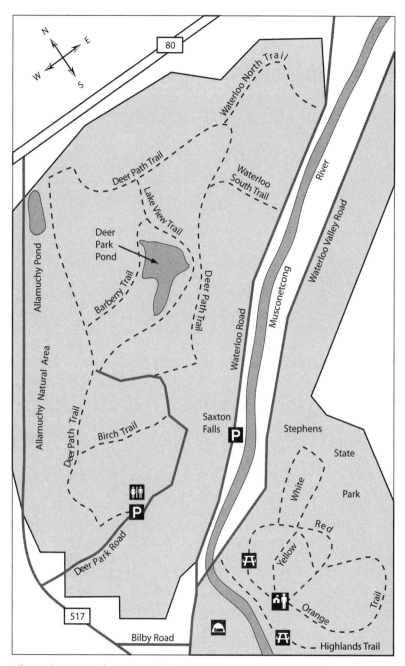

Allamuchy Mountain State Park (South) and Stephens State Park

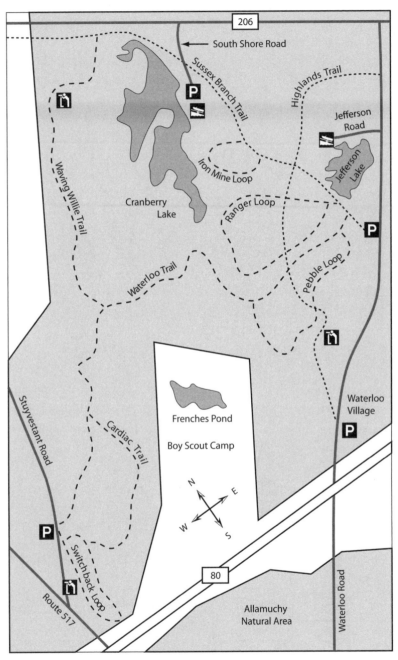

Allamuchy Mountain State Park (North)

where boating and fishing are unmatched for privacy. Camping is basic but quiet at the forty sites resting near the banks of the Musconetcong River, and two serene picnic areas line the water's edge.

Camping

Camping is uncomplicated at Stephens. One campground contains forty tent and trailer sites, but you will find no cabins, yurts, or lean-tos anywhere within the park, nor will you find a site large enough to hold groups of more than six campers. As a result, the campground is quiet and peaceful. Its location also makes it a perfect base of operations from which to explore the surrounding area. A set of wooden stairs leads from the campground, across the Musconetcong River, to the park office and two picnic areas. Allamuchy's trails begin less than 2 miles to the north, Saxton Falls lies 1 mile to the east, and Waterloo Village is within a five-minute drive.

Directions. From the park office, drive across the Musconetcong River bridge and turn right on Park Road. Proceed .3 mile to Waterloo Road and turn left. Continue .2 mile to the campground on the left. You can also walk from the park office by crossing the bridge and then climbing the stairs across Park Road.

Sites and facilities. The park's forty tent and trailer sites are each equipped with fire rings and picnic tables. One modern restroom lies at the center of the campground, but the restroom does not contain showers. Water from ground pumps and one playground are within walking distance of all sites. The campground is open from April 1 through October 31.

Recommended sites. The best option for privacy is site 33, situated 100 feet from the access road in a wooded clearing. Site 31 is ringed by trees, and numbers 12, 13, and 14 are recessed into the forest but a bit open to the road. Sites 19, 32, and 35 are wide enough to accommodate trailers, and 4, 5, 10, 20, and 22 can hold campers or very small trailers.

Trails

Five short trails totaling about 4.5 miles make their way through the forested slopes of Stephens State Park south of the Musconetcong River. A section of the Highlands Trail begins at the park office and heads along the Musconetcong River to several quiet picnic tables near the water's edge. This .8-mile section of the Highlands Trail is the only trail

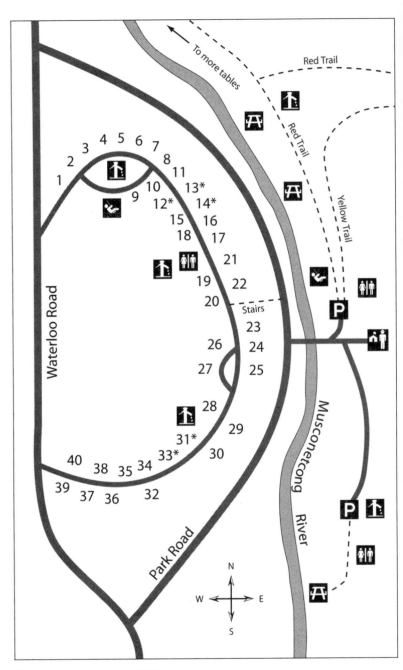

Stephens Family Campground

within Allamuchy or Stephens that is off-limits to mountain bikes and horses. Four other trails marked with colored blazes run through the forest, all of them open to horseback riding, mountain biking, and cross-country skiing. The Red and Yellow Trails both begin near the park office and extend a combined 1.5 miles along the Musconetcong River. The .9-mile White Trail begins where the Red Trail leaves off, and the 1.3-mile Orange Trail climbs 500 feet through a series of wooded hills east of the park office.

If you head north across Route 604, at least 15 miles of marked and unmarked trails crisscross the Allamuchy Natural Area between I-80 and the Musconetcong River. The trails in this area are in the process of being charted, blazed, and mapped by park personnel, so look for added routes in the coming years. Six blazed trails total 11.1 miles through an area of hardwood forest and marshland that ranges in altitude from 600 to 1,100 feet. The best place to begin is at the parking area on Deer Park Road, about 2 miles north of the Stephens office. The white-blazed Deer Path Trail begins north of the parking area and forms a 6.6-mile loop around the outer rim of the natural area. You can access any of the five shorter trails along the route. All of the trails throughout the Allamuchy Natural Area allow hiking, mountain biking, horseback riding, cross-country skiing, and snowshoeing.

At least 25 miles of marked and unmarked trails weave through the section of Allamuchy State Park north of I-80. Here you can hike or ride all day and may never see another human being. One of the easiest places to start is on the well-beaten Sussex Branch Trail, which begins at the Waterloo Road parking area by Jefferson Lake. Using the Sussex Branch Trail as a reference point, you can explore the many side trails that branch off to the east and west. Eight marked trails total 24.7 miles through an area of lakes, mountain overlooks, and hardwood forest. The white-blazed Waterloo Trail begins just north of the Sussex Branch Trail parking area, extends 5.3 miles past 1,222-foot Allamuchy Mountain, and ends at a parking area on Route 517. The other seven marked trails north of I-80 range from 1.3 to 3.4 miles, all of them open to hiking, mountain biking, horseback riding, cross-country skiing, and snowshoeing.

About 3.8 miles of the Highlands Trail and 2.7 miles of the Sussex Branch Trail cut through the area north of I-80 as well. The Highlands Trail is a long-distance route envisioned to extend 150 miles from the Hudson River to Phillipsburg when complete. This section of the Highlands Trail represents an exception, as it is one of the few areas along the trail's entire length that allows horses and mountain bikes. Look for the diamond-shaped teal blazes north of Jefferson Lake. The 21.2-mile Sussex Branch Trail begins at Waterloo Road and continues north to Branchville, following the route of the old Sussex Branch Railroad and passing through Kittatinny Valley State Park. The trail is wide and flat along its entire length and allows hiking, mountain biking, horseback riding, cross-country skiing, and snowshoeing.

Trail Mileage and Difficulty

TRAIL	MILES	DIFFICULTY	BLAZE	USES
Stephens State Park				
Highlands Trail	0.8	E	teal	h,s,x
Orange Trail	1.3	D	orange	e,h,m,s,x
Red Trail	1.0	E	red	e,h,m,s,x
White Trail	0.9	E	white	e,h,m,s,x
Yellow Trail	0.5	E	yellow	e,h,m,s,x
Allamuchy State Park (South)				
Barberry Trail	0.8	E	red	e,h,m,s,x
Birch Trail	0.6	E	yellow	e,h,m,s,x
Deer Path Trail	6.6	M	white	e,h,m,s,x
Lake View Trail	1.7	E–M	blue	e,h,m,s,x
Waterloo North Trail	0.9	D	orange	e,h,m,s,x
Waterloo South Trail	0.5	D	green	e,h,m,s,x
Allamuchy State Park (North)				
Cardiac Trail	3.2	D	purple	e,h,m,s,x
Highlands Trail	3.8	D	teal	e,h,m,s,x
Iron Mine Loop	1.3	M	blue	e,h,m,s,x
Pebble Loop	3.1	M	yellow	e,h,m,s,x
Ranger Loop	2.6	D	red	e,h,m,s,x
Sussex Branch Trail	2.7	E	no blaze	e,h,m,s,x
Switchback Loop	2.0	M	orange	e,h,m,s,x
Waterloo Trail	5.3	D	white	e,h,m,s,x
Waving Willie Trail	3.4	M	green	e,h,m,s,x

Activities

The first thing that strikes many visitors to Allamuchy is the absence of a central recreation area. You will find no beach, food concession, or common gathering place other than the Stephens office and adjoining picnic tables. Parking areas throughout the forest give access to 40 miles of trails, several picnic areas, and Allamuchy's four lakes. You will not have to rely solely on a pair of hiking boots to explore this park. The trails are open to an array of uses, ranging from cross-country skiing to mountain biking. Anglers arrive to fish the surrounding lakes and Musconetcong River, one of New Jersey's premier trout streams. Waterloo Village and the Morris Canal lie just outside the borders of the park, both worthy destinations on a summer afternoon.

Waterloo Village

The impeccably restored buildings show examples of Waterloo's transformation over a period of 250 years. A village has stood on this site along the Musconetcong River since iron ore was discovered in the area around 1760, when Andover Iron Works constructed a forge and began producing bar iron for export to England. The Morris Canal came through in 1831, and Waterloo became a busy inland port supporting a gristmill, schoolhouse, inn, and tavern. The Sussex Railroad put an end to the prosperity around 1870, bypassing the village of Waterloo and signaling the demise of the Morris Canal.

Visitors can see buildings that remain from throughout the history of Waterloo Village, including a reproduced Lenni-Lenape encampment and a working gristmill, sawmill, and blacksmith's shop. More than thirty restored buildings are on display, including a 1760 stagecoach inn and tavern, the 1859 Waterloo United Methodist Church, and an 1831 general store. A restored nineteenth-century farmstead occupies the north end of the village, where you will find an 1825 log cabin and live farm animals roaming the fields. Drive north of the park office on Waterloo Road (Route 604) for 3.9 miles until you cross I-80. The Waterloo Village entrance is the first right turn past the interstate.

Saxton Falls and Morris Canal

The Morris Canal began construction in 1824 and stretched from the Delaware River to the Hudson River by the time it was completed in 1836. Saxton Falls was once a free-flowing series of cascades, but a timber dam was erected during the 1820s to provide water for the canal, later replaced by a concrete dam. The dam still stands today, producing an artificial waterfall, and the downstream section of the Musconetcong River is heavily stocked with trout. Part of the Morris Canal has been restored near the falls, and a 1-mile section of the old towpath begins at the parking area. The old canal lock and a few buildings can still be seen along the towpath. Parking for the falls is 1.3 miles north of the park office on the south side of Waterloo Road.

Fishing

The Musconetcong River receives almost 50,000 trout each year from the nearby Pequest Trout Hatchery, more than any other body of water in New Jersey save the Raritan River. If you add the trout stocked in Lakes Musconetcong and Hopatcong to the east, the number exceeds 60,000. Brown trout regularly weigh in at more than 10 pounds, and rainbow trout approaching 20 inches inhabit the eddies near Stephens State Park. Saxton Falls, although usually crowded with anglers, is the most heavily stocked point along the river. You will find parking and access points all along the Musconetcong River from Saxton Falls to the Stephens camping area.

Cranberry Lake is the best of Allamuchy's four lakes when it comes to numbers of fish and access to the shore. Up to 3,000 northern pike are released into the lake certain years, and trout are stocked at a rate of about 1,000 per year. You will find a good number of catfish and sunfish, but pickerel, largemouth and smallmouth bass, and yellow perch are almost as abundant. This 179-acre lake is the only one at Allamuchy that allows outboard motors. The boat ramp is located off Route 206 on South Shore Road.

Three other lakes within the borders of Allamuchy allow fishing and boats with electric motors, but access is limited. Deer Park Pond lies in the middle of the forest with no boat ramp, but the variety of fish is second only to Cranberry Lake. Although electric motors are allowed, you have to drive along a dirt access road, then hike to the pond from one of the three surrounding parking areas. Fishing is good for largemouth bass, pickerel, yellow perch, catfish, and sunfish. Jefferson Lake provides easy access from a parking area on Jefferson Road, but you can expect only fair fishing for largemouth bass, yellow perch, crappie, and catfish. Allamuchy Pond offers no official access points, and finding a parking area off Route 517 is a creative endeavor. The lake supports an excellent population of crappie, good fishing for largemouth bass, and fair fishing for catfish and yellow perch.

Boating

Motors of unlimited horsepower are welcome on Cranberry Lake, but boaters on Deer Park Pond, Jefferson Lake, and Allamuchy Pond are limited to electric motors. Two of the four lakes offer boat ramps. To arrive at the Cranberry Lake boat ramp, drive 2.1 miles north of Waterloo Road on Route 206 and turn left on South Shore Road. Proceed .1 mile to the boat ramp on the right. The Jefferson Lake access point is a dirt ramp meant for small boats. Drive .8 mile west of Route 206 on Waterloo Road and turn right on Jefferson Road. Proceed .3 mile and turn right at the Jefferson Lake Day Camp sign. Continue 130 yards to the boat ramp on the left.

Canoes suit the Musconetcong River when the water level is high enough, usually in early spring and during the annual release of water from Lake Hopatcong in November. Be prepared to portage, though, as the river is blocked by a great many working and obsolete dams. You can canoe year-round above the dam at Saxton Falls, where Saxton Lake extends for about a mile upstream. A privately run and very basic boat concession next to the boat ramp at Cranberry Lake rents rowboats and canoes during the spring and summer.

Picnicking

Two serene and forested picnic areas lie to the north and south of the Stephens office. An access road heads south from the office to a small parking area, where you will find a short trail leading to about ten tables overlooking the Musconetcong River. Restrooms are located along the trail, and a water pump sits at the trailhead. Another trail heads north from the office, and isolated picnic tables line the riverbank from the trailhead to a parking area on Waterloo Valley Road. Water pumps are evenly spaced along the .6-mile trail, and restrooms lie at each end. At the north end, a bridge leads across the Musconetcong River to a small island holding four quiet tables and one central grill.

Mountain Biking

Many riders rate Allamuchy as the best destination in New Jersey. Almost 4 miles of marked trails at Stephens State Park, more than 11 miles of blazed trails in the Allamuchy Natural Area, and at least 25 miles of marked and unmarked trails north of I-80 are all open to mountain biking. They range from flat and easy fire roads to thin trails with obstacles such as boulders, tree roots, and challenging ascents. They vary in altitude from 600 to over 1,000 feet. The trails north of the interstate get most of the attention from hard-core riders. This section of the park is home to the 24 Hours of Allamuchy Endurance Mountain Bike Race in August, a grueling around-the-clock event that begins at noon on Saturday and ends at noon on Sunday. The unmarked trails north of I-80 can get confusing, so it is wise to carry a topographic map. See the Where to Buy Supplies section for information about guided rides through the park.

Horseback Riding

All of Allamuchy's trails are open to horses. One of the best places to begin is at the parking area on Deer Park Road, where you will find a restroom and ample parking for trailers. A relatively flat dirt road begins next to the restrooms and extends 1.6 miles to the blue-blazed Lake View Trail leading to Deer Park Pond. Along the ride, you will pass the Birch, Deer Path, and Barberry Trails, all open to horseback riding. The Double D Guest Ranch in Blairstown offers guided rides through the park. Check doubledguestranch.com for specifics.

Birding

Allamuchy's wide-ranging habitat makes it a good place to see a variety of birds in a small area. Waterfowl and wading birds use the wetlands of the Musconetcong River Valley for breeding and wintering habitat, resulting in rare sightings such as the sandhill crane seen here in 1994. The endangered pied-billed grebe nests in the area, as does the American bittern. Deer Park Pond is warbler territory, with species seen during migration including cerulean, golden-winged, worm-eating, and mourning warblers. Check the working farms and open fields surrounding Allamuchy for migrating American pipits, vesper sparrows, and Lapland longspurs, in addition to state threatened species such as the bobolink and grasshopper and savannah sparrows. Hawks use the ridges and forests on their way south in the fall, and a local hawk watch recently recorded more than 10,000 migrating raptors over Allamuchy during a single fall migration, including rarities such as Cooper's and red-shouldered hawks, as well as bald eagles.

Hunting

About 69 percent of the land north of the Musconetcong River, most of it north of I-80, is open to the hunting of deer, small game, wild turkeys, and waterfowl. A little more than half of the land in Stephens State Park, about 473 acres, allows the hunting of deer, small game, and wild turkey. Allamuchy falls in deer management zones 6 and 8 and is popular with deer hunters from September through December.

Winter Activities

Allamuchy's trail system provides a variety of terrain for cross-country skiing or snowshoeing. Difficulty levels range from the wide and flat Sussex Branch Trail, perfect for cross-country skiing, to trails encompassing tough climbs more appropriate for a pair of hiking boots. Views from Allamuchy's overlooks are spectacular enough throughout the year, but they become even better after the trees drop their leaves in fall. The Highlands Trail takes in the Musconetcong River Valley and Waterloo Lake from about 1,000 feet, and the overlook lies less than a mile from the parking area on Waterloo Road. Given safe conditions, ice fishing is allowed on Cranberry and Jefferson Lakes and Deer Park Pond, where you will find good populations of perch and pickerel. Although camping ends in November, Allamuchy's extensive trails and rugged terrain make it a worthwhile destination throughout the year.

Flora and Fauna

Allamuchy and Stephens State Parks fall within the Musconetcong River Watershed, an area that drains into the larger Delaware River Watershed. More than 14 percent of the state's forested habitat and 40 percent of New Jersey's trout waters occur in the two watersheds, and the area is home to fourteen species of salamanders, fifteen snakes, ten turtles, and countless birds, mammals, plants, and insects. Old-growth hardwood forest at higher elevations gives way to hemlock and spruce trees, then cultivated farm fields and wetlands to the south. Traveling north, the expansive forests of New Jersey's Upper Highlands stretch from Stephens State Park to the New York border.

The rivers, ponds, and marshland provide breeding grounds for waterfowl and important habitat for other threatened and endangered wildlife. Beavers maintain a foothold at Deer Park Pond, and you can sometimes see their ongoing construction from the Lake View Trail. The state-threatened barred owl inhabits the forests of Allamuchy, and the Musconetcong River supports the state-endangered wood turtle and critically imperiled brook floater mussel. Black bears are making a comeback here as well, and the wild turkeys so common throughout the forest today were nonexistent a mere twenty-five years ago. In December 2007, sections of the Musconetcong River Watershed became protected under the federal Wild and Scenic Rivers Act, one step toward removing the many obsolete dams that disturb the river's natural flow.

Surrounding Points of Interest

Anyone dissatisfied with the rugged trails at Allamuchy can head a few miles to the east, where the unmarked trails of Hackettstown Reservoir weave through about 2,000 forested acres. Drive 10 miles farther east, and anglers will come upon New Jersey's largest lake at Hopatcong State Park. Yet more trails lie a few miles to the north at Kittatinny Valley State Park, and to south, a fish hatchery and pheasant farm reveal where some of New Jersey's wildlife truly originates.

Hackettstown Reservoir

Hikers at Stephens State Park will notice a few trails that head east into an undeveloped forest. Parcels of protected land bought through the Green Acres Program border Stephens State Park to the north and east, making up an area known as Hackettstown Reservoir. Part of the project responsible for restoring the Morris Canal, this tract of land has no roads or marked trails, but it is possible to follow a series of unmarked trails all the way to Budd Lake. This is one of the reasons why mountain bikers claim that the area, together with Stephens and Allamuchy State Parks, holds almost 100 miles of trails. The land supports several streams, one small waterfall, and large tracts of unbroken hardwood forest. It is a popular hunting destination, so hikers should check the open-season schedule before venturing out.

Kittatinny Valley State Park

The Sussex Branch Trail continues 4 miles north of Cranberry Lake into Kittatinny Valley State Park, a 3,641-acre area encompassing four lakes, limestone cliffs, picnic tables, and even a small airport. About 8 miles of trails are open to hiking, mountain biking, horseback riding, cross-country skiing, and snowshoeing. Lake Aeroflex offers a boat ramp and is stocked with more than 2,300 trout each year, but the lake is better known for its excellent largemouth bass fishing. It also holds the unusual state record of an 8-pound landlocked salmon caught here in 1951. The other three water bodies—Twin Lakes and Gardners and Whites Ponds—are peaceful, secluded hiking destinations that allow fishing as well. Aeroflex-Andover Airport, home to Andover Flight Academy, is a tiny, picturesque airport with only two short runways bordered by forested ponds and rolling woodland. Follow Waterloo Road for about 2.6 miles east of I-80 and turn left on Route 206. Proceed 6.2 miles north on Route 206 and turn right on Goodale Road. Continue 1 mile to the park office access road on the right.

Hopatcong State Park

At 9 miles long and covering 2,685 acres, Lake Hopatcong is New Jersey's largest lake, and one of the most heavily stocked bodies of water in the state. During a recent typical stocking season, the lake received more than 10,000 trout, 144,000 walleye, 25,000 hybrid striped bass, 1,400 tiger muskellunge, and 1,300 muskellunge. The Division of Fish and Wildlife added almost 900,000 walleye fry the same year. Massive fish are caught at Lake Hopatcong every day, some approaching the state-record 33.2-pound channel catfish landed here in 1978 and a 13-pound rainbow trout caught in 1988. The lake would already be one of New Jersey's finest fishing destinations if the list ended there, but you will also find excellent populations of pickerel, yellow perch, and catfish, along with a good number of largemouth and smallmouth bass, crappie, carp, and sunfish.

Basketball courts, a food concession, picnic tables, playgrounds, hot showers, and a swimming beach are just a few of the attractions beyond fishing at Hopatcong State Park. Anyone tired of motorboat restrictions has another good reason to head for Lake Hopatcong. This is one of the few lakes that allows unrestricted outboard motors, in addition to Jet Skis, sailboats, and kayaks. There's a boat ramp at the north end of the park, and private marinas rent almost anything that floats, from canoes to catamarans. The park is located about 10 miles northeast of the campground. Turn right out of the Stephens office onto Waterloo Road, drive 6.2 miles, and turn right on Route 206. Proceed .7 mile, bear left on Route 183, drive .9 mile, and then make a sharp left on Brooklyn Road. Continue 2.8 miles and turn right on Lakeside Boulevard. Proceed .1 mile to the park entrance on the left.

Hackettstown Fish Hatchery

If you have visited the Pequest Trout Hatchery near Jenny Jump State Forest, then you know where all the stocked trout in New Jersey began their existence. Hackettstown is where all the other stocked species in the state are spawned. Every year, more than 2 million fish make their way from brood stock to egg to river through the Hackettstown hatchery. The list includes channel catfish, muskellunge, tiger muskellunge, northern pike, walleye, bluegill sunfish, and largemouth, smallmouth, striped, and hybrid striped bass. The hatchery is made up of two segments, one on the east side of Hackettstown and one on the west. Visitation requires a reservation; check with the Division of Fish and Wildlife.

Rockport Pheasant Farm

An estimated 90 percent of all pheasants alive in the state today hail from the Rockport Pheasant Farm, which releases about 55,000 birds each year into wildlife management areas throughout New Jersey. The farm has been at it since 1923, and the operation is funded entirely from the sale of hunting licenses. About 2,700 hens produce 160,000 eggs from March through July. The eggs incubate for 24 days; then the chicks are moved into temperature-controlled rooms for about six weeks. The pheasants occupy range pens until early November, when they are loaded into trucks and transported to various wildlife areas. You can tour the 30 acres of range pens from 7:30 A.M. to dusk seven days a week. The farm is located on Rockport Road (Route 629) about 3.5 miles south of Hackettstown.

Where to Buy Supplies

Turn left out of the Stephens office exit onto Waterloo Road and drive 2.2 miles to Main Street in Hackettstown. The small city contains grocery stores, pharmacies, banks, sporting goods, restaurants, auto repair, and almost any other item a traveler may need. Drive 6.5 miles east of the Stephens office on Waterloo Road, turn right on Route 206, and you will find a gas station, pharmacy, convenience store, bagel shop, diner, two banks, and a pizzeria. Cycle Works, a bicycle shop offering guided tours of Allamuchy, is about .2 mile north of Waterloo Road on the west side of Route 206. On the west side of the park, a strip mall across the road from Allamuchy Pond contains a café, pharmacy, pizzeria, deli, convenience store, and bank.

Wawayanda State Park

885 Warwick Turnpike
Hewitt, NJ 07421

Area. 34,918 acres.

Park office. 1.4 miles south of the New York border on the west side of Warwick Turnpike.

Highlights. Wawayanda Swamp Natural Area, Bearfort Mountain Natural Area, Wawayanda Lake, extensive trail system.

Activities. Camping, hiking, fishing, boating, picnicking, mountain biking, horseback riding, birding, hunting, ice fishing, cross-country skiing, snowshoeing, snowmobiling, ice skating.

Entrance fee. A fee is charged to enter the recreation area from Memorial Day weekend through Labor Day.

Park hours. Year-round, from dawn to dusk.

For additional information: (973) 853-4462

Wawayanda is New Jersey's largest state park. Atlantic white cedar swamps, clear mountain lakes, remote hemlock ravines, and an altitude variation of more than 900 feet make up 34,918 acres on the northern edge of New Jersey. Most of the land sits at an elevation of 1,200 feet bordering New York State, with Bearfort Mountain rising to almost 1,500 feet in the southwest section of the park. Wawayanda offers three group campsites only, but the park is well worth a visit for anyone seeking rugged terrain and an extensive set of trails, including a 6-mile section of the Appalachian Trail. Most of the activity surrounds Wawayanda Lake, where you will find a developed recreation area with picnic tables and a swimming beach. The trails and fire roads allow a wide range of uses, from hiking to snowmobiling, and three remote wildlife areas reveal the true nature of this park—its wild and rugged interior.

Camping

Wawayanda's three group campsites lie in a forested clearing next to a clear mountain stream. Wawayanda Lake is .2 mile to the west by trail,

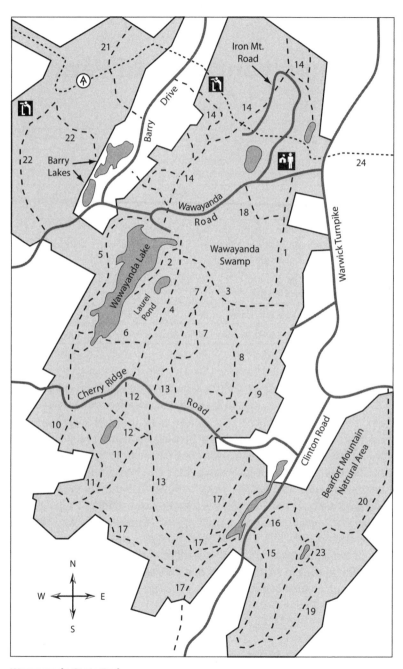

Wawayanda State Park

and the recreation area is a 1.5-mile drive. Sites 1, 2, and 3 have a
capacity of fifteen, thirty-five, and twenty-five campers, respectively,
but are for groups only, with a minimum of seven campers. All three
sites occupy open grass lawns backed by woodland and offer picnic
tables, fire rings, and grills. Number 1 is slightly more private than the
others, sitting by itself at the end of the road near a rock cliff. You will
find no showers or water pumps at the campground, but water is available at the park office and recreation area. Two chemical toilets sit near
the campground entrance. Drive west through the park entrance gate
and proceed 1 mile to the campground access road. Turn left and continue .6 mile to the campground on the left. The group sites are open
from April 1 through October 31.

Trails

Wawayanda's twenty-four trails are open to a wide array of activities,
ranging from snowmobiling to mountain biking. The trail network, one
of the park's greatest assets, forms a matrix between remote river valleys, high mountain ridges, and serene forest lakes. Many of the trails
follow dirt roads that remain from the logging era of the 1940s, when
the New Jersey Zinc Company harvested local timber to shore up its
mines. Most of the trails lie at an altitude above 1,000 feet on the
Wawayanda Plateau, but elevations reach extremes of 1,400 feet near
Bearfort Mountain and 600 feet on the Appalachian Trail. Some trails
encompass strenuous climbs along steep rock cliffs. A few run through
an Atlantic white cedar swamp, crossing log bridges and fallen trees
along the way.

Several of the more scenic trails are also the most difficult, rising and
falling up to 400 feet in the Bearfort Mountain Natural Area. The blue-
blazed Terrace Pond North Trail is the quickest route to gratification, a
1.4-mile hike offering a spectacular overlook of the surrounding plateau
and views of Terrace Pond. Terrace Pond Circular Trail hugs the shore
of the pond, which resembles a rock-cut quarry carved out of the granite cliffs. A view from the north shore takes in the clean and clear high-
altitude lake surrounded by sheer stone walls. You can take Terrace
Pond South Trail back to the trailhead, a longer hike but worthwhile for
the overlooks of Pequannock River Watershed to the south.

Although relatively flat and well traveled, the trails running through
Wawayanda Swamp Natural Area take in the quiet beauty of the park's
interior. Cedar Swamp Trail follows a makeshift boardwalk through the

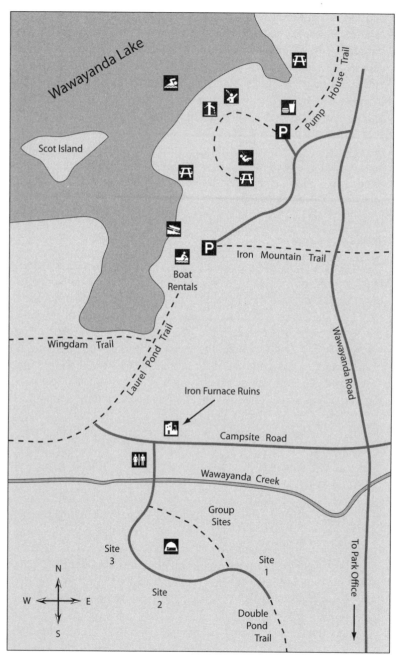

Recreation Area and Group Campground

heart of an Atlantic white cedar swamp, where northern white cedar can be seen at the southern limit of its range. William Hoeferlin Trail begins at the park office and skirts the eastern edge of the natural area, stretching through a hardwood forest filled with rhododendrons and mountain laurel. The popular Laurel Pond Trail follows a sandy road through a forest of hemlock and elm, passing sheer granite cliffs and overlooks of Wawayanda Swamp along the way. The 1846 charcoal fur-

Trail Mileage and Difficulty

TRAIL	MILES	DIFFICULTY	BLAZE	USES
1. William Hoeferlin Trail	1.8	E–M	blue	e,h,m,s,x
2. Wingdam Trail	1.1	E	blue	b,e,h,m,s,x
3. Double Pond Trail	1.7	E	yellow	b,e,h,m,s,x
4. Laurel Pond Trail	1.5	E	yellow	b,e,h,m,s,x
5. Pump House Trail	2.4	E	no blaze	h
6. South End Trail	0.5	E	no blaze	e,h,m,s,x
7. Red Dot Trail	1.1	E	red	b,e,h,m,s,x
8. Cedar Swamp Trail	1.3	E	blue	h
9. Banker Trail	1.5	E	yellow	e,h,m,s,x
10. Cabin Trail	0.5	E	no blaze	e,h,m,s,x
11. Turkey Ridge Trail	2.0	M	no blaze	e,h,m,s,x
12. Lookout Trail	1.3	M	white	e,h,m,s,x
13. Old Coal Trail	2.2	M	red	e,h,m,s,x
14. Iron Mountain Trail	2.8	D	red/white	e,h,m,s,x
15. Terrace Pond South Trail	2.4	D	yellow	h
16. Terrace Pond North Trail	1.4	D	blue	h
17. Bearfort Waters Trail	3.0	M–D	no blaze	e,h,m,s,x
18. Black Eagle Trail	0.7	E	green/white	e,h,m,s,x
19. Yellow Dot Trail	2.0	D	yellow	h
20. Terrace Pond Red Trail	1.8	D	red	h
21. Livingston East Trail	1.5	M	white	e,h,m,s,x
22. Livingston South Trail	2.5	D	no blaze	e,h,m,s,x
23. Terrace Pond Circular Trail	0.5	E	white	h
24. Appalachian Trail	6.0	M–D	white	h

nace at the northern end of Laurel Pond Trail is a remnant of the Wawayanda Ironworks, which operated until 1867.

Two of the park's easiest trails leave from Wawayanda Lake. Double Pond Trail is a good way to access some of the trails running through the Wawayanda Swamp Natural Area. It begins at the group campsites and heads east to connect with the Cedar Swamp and William Hoeferlin Trails. Double Pond is also the best trail on which to see blooming rhododendrons in late June and early July. Wingdam Trail leaves from near the boat ramp area along a wide gravel road, heading through a forest of mixed oaks and red maple to a wooden bridge spanning the dam between Laurel Pond and Wawayanda Lake. The existing dam was built by the Thomas Iron Company in 1872, raising the water level of Wawayanda Lake to supply power for the company's mining operation.

If you are searching for privacy, head for the outlying trails at the northern and southern ends of the park. Lookout Trail stretches past some massive hemlock trees to end at Lake Lookout, a peaceful destination dominated by ferns and wildflowers. Banker Trail begins at the end of Banker Road off Warwick Turnpike and leads 1.5 miles through a thick oak and hemlock forest to meet the Cedar Swamp Trail in the Wawayanda Swamp Natural Area. Old Coal Trail is usually overlooked by casual hikers, as it extends 2.2 miles through white pines and mountain laurel to the remote southern section of the park. Although not quite as private, the well-traveled Appalachian Trail leads about 2.6 miles and climbs 700 feet from the parking area on Route 94 to an overlook of New York's Shawangunk Mountains.

Activities

Wawayanda is slightly less developed than most New Jersey parks, but you will still find a typical recreation area complete with a swimming beach, picnic tables, food concession, and boat livery. The attraction for those seeking an escape lies in the park's outlying areas, the vistas and overlooks accessible by trail, and the protected natural areas within the borders of the forest. Fishing is excellent in Wawayanda Lake, and mountain biking, horseback riding, and cross-country skiing are good ways to access the park's remote interior.

Wawayanda Swamp Natural Area

The blue-blazed William Hoeferlin Trail leaves from the park office and heads into the heart of this 2,167-acre swamp dominated by Atlantic white cedar, mixed oak-hardwood forest, and thick rows of rhododendrons. The cedar swamp began forming about 15,000 years ago, and deep soil tests indicate that some sections of the swamp have remained unchanged since the last ice age. A detour on the Red Dot Trail gets you to the highest altitude in the natural area, at 1,300 feet, where you can see Wawayanda Creek passing below. This is the extreme southern range of northern white cedar, rare anywhere in New Jersey, which can be seen throughout the swamp. A branch of Wawayanda Creek feeds Laurel Pond on the western edge of the natural area, both accessed from the yellow-blazed Laurel Pond Trail, beginning at the boat ramp parking area.

Bearfort Mountain Natural Area

Several trails leave from Clinton Road on the edge of this 1,325-acre natural area, heading along the ridgeline through mountain laurel, white pine, and rhododendron. All of the trails end up at Terrace Pond, a 2.5-acre glacial lake that is one of the most picturesque spots in the park. Trails climb over rock outcroppings composed of Skunnemunk Conglomerate, or pudding stone, and offer views of Terrace Pond and the Pequannock River Watershed. The easiest access to the ridge is from the parking area on the west side of Clinton Road, about 1.7 miles south of Warwick Turnpike. Two trails begin across the road from the parking area. The blue-blazed Terrace Pond North Trail is the fastest way to Terrace Pond and offers a panoramic view of the Wawayanda Plateau about .8 mile from the trailhead.

Fishing and Boating

A concrete boat ramp gives access to Wawayanda Lake, where fishing is good for largemouth bass, pickerel, yellow perch, catfish, and sunfish. The boat ramp lies on the east end of the beach, next to a concession renting rowboats, canoes, kayaks, and small boats with electric motors. Wawayanda Lake is stocked with brown and rainbow trout, and fishing is good during stocking in April and May. About 1,000 landlocked salmon were introduced into Wawayanda Lake in May 2006, the first time any New Jersey lake has supported salmon since 1951. Plans are to continue the salmon stocking, and catches may range from 12 to 18 inches in the future.

The quality of fishing varies in Lake Lookout, Wawayanda Creek, and Laurel Pond. Lake Lookout is the only one of the three that allows boats with electric motors, but pickerel is the only abundant fish in the lake. Wawayanda Creek is stocked with about 1,500 trout each year, and you will also find fair fishing for largemouth and smallmouth bass, pickerel, and catfish. Laurel Pond is the best option if you are looking for largemouth bass, but fishing is allowed only from the shore. The pond also supports a fair population of pickerel, catfish, yellow perch, and sunfish.

Picnicking

More than fifty picnic tables and grills surround the recreation area on Wawayanda Lake. Most of them sit on a grassy hill behind the beach, but a few rest on the shore in private spots. Pine trees offer shade, and the tables cover a wide enough area to allow for some privacy. All of the recreation area's amenities are nearby, including the food concession, boat rentals, water fountains, and a playground.

Swimming

Wawayanda's beach occupies a long, thin strip of sand backed by a grass lawn and picnic tables. The view from the beach is scenic, taking in Scot Island and boats of all colors plying the water. A boat concession on the east end of the recreation area rents everything from canoes to small boats with electric motors. An immobile trailer serves as the food concession, offering a modest selection of ice cream, hamburgers, hot dogs, pizza, pretzels, and soda. One volleyball net with a sand court lies next to modern restrooms, picnic tables, a playground, and lifeguard station. Swimming is allowed from Memorial Day through Labor Day.

Mountain Biking

Wawayanda allows biking on sixteen of the twenty-four marked trails throughout the park. Many of the trails open to bikers are former logging roads created by the New Jersey Zinc Company in the 1940s and 1950s. The terrain varies from wide and dry dirt roads along the Wawayanda Plateau to thin and marshy trails near the Wawayanda Swamp Natural Area. Some are rugged and hilly, and most entail variations in altitude that resemble a roller coaster. Cherry Ridge Road cuts through the center of Wawayanda from east to west and is a good way to form a loop out of any of the interconnecting trails. See the Trails section for individual descriptions. The trails off-limits to bikes include Pump House, Cedar Swamp, Appalachian, and the five trails throughout Bearfort Mountain Natural Area.

Horseback Riding

All of the trails open to mountain bikers are also open to horseback riders. A grass field across from the recreation area is marked for trailer parking and gives access to the horse trails near Wawayanda Lake, including Iron Mountain, Wingdam, Double Pond, and Laurel Pond. Head south on Laurel Pond Trail for 1.5 miles to arrive at Cherry Ridge Road, a country road also open to horses. Iron Mountain Trail, marked with red and white blazes and beginning at the north end of the boat ramp parking area, is a bit rocky but still popular. The trail crosses an open field, then follows a gravel road to end at the Appalachian Trail about 2.8 miles north of the trailhead. See the Trails section for additional destinations and distances.

Birding

Wawayanda's high plateau supports a small number of birds throughout the year, but breeding and migration seasons can produce some unusual sightings. Spring and early summer bring nesting species such as northern waterthrushes, Acadian flycatchers, pileated woodpeckers, and barred owls. Look for migrating sandpipers and other waterbirds near the beach and boat launch area. Cedar Swamp and Double Pond Trails are productive walks to see some of the many warblers that inhabit Wawayanda, including several elusive species such as Nashville, black-throated green, blackburnian, black-throated blue, magnolia, golden-winged, Canada, and hooded warblers. Alder flycatchers, common redpolls, purple finches, and yellow-breasted chats can sometimes be seen along the park entrance road. Bearfort Mountain Natural Area, around Bearfort Waters and Terrace Pond, supports a population of eastern bluebirds, ruffed grouse, and a variety of hawks and warblers.

Hunting

Almost 95 percent of the park, about 17,300 acres, is open to the hunting of deer, small game, wild turkeys, and waterfowl. The park is especially popular with deer hunters during the six-day firearm season in early December. Wawayanda is also home to one of the check stations for New Jersey's annual controversy, the bear hunt, which began in 2003. As always, check the latest changes and regulations before heading out. The bulk of Wawayanda lies in deer management zone 2.

Winter Activities

Wawayanda's northern latitude and high altitude, an average of 1,140 feet above sea level, make it a natural attraction for anyone who loves snow. Trails are open to cross-country skiers, snowshoers, and hikers, and this is one of the few parks that allows snowmobiles on many of the dirt fire roads crisscrossing the forest. Trails open to cross-country skiing and snowshoeing are the same as those outlined in the Mountain Biking section. Trails open to snowmobiling include Wingdam, Double Pond, Laurel Pond, and Red Dot. Wawayanda Lake is a good place to catch yellow perch and pickerel through the ice, and the lake is deep enough to support a small holdover population of trout through the winter. Even ice skating is allowed, given safe conditions. The park is open from dawn to dusk throughout the year.

Flora and Fauna

The habitat at Wawayanda varies with the altitude, from Atlantic white cedar swamp in Wawayanda Swamp Natural Area to mixed oak-hardwood forest covering the high ridges of Bearfort Mountain Natural Area in the park's southeast corner. Beavers inhabit Wawayanda Creek around the cedar swamp, and they can often be seen from the bridge on Double Pond Trail. The ridges and rock cliffs of Bearfort Mountain are home to the endangered timber rattlesnake and state-threatened red-shouldered hawk. Wawayanda Hemlock Ravine, on the northern edge of the park, makes up yet a third natural area. Inaccessible even by trail, the ravine produces a 400-foot drop through hemlock and hardwood forest to meet Wawayanda Creek at 700 feet above sea level. Three endangered plant species inhabit the ravine: Dewey's sedge, white-grained mountain ricegrass, and witch hobble. The park is also a stronghold in New Jersey for black bears, with numbers on the rise every year.

Surrounding Points of Interest

The area surrounding Wawayanda could keep a hiker busy for months, encompassing three state forests, three state parks, and six wildlife management areas. Add to the list about thirty or so county parks in Passaic, Sussex, and Bergen Counties that serve to connect much of the state-owned land. Beginning at the Wawayanda office, travelers can visit five of the main parks in the area by driving less than 20 miles south on Route 511. Trail maps for several of the destinations listed are available at the Wawayanda and Ringwood park offices.

Abram S. Hewitt State Forest

This 2,001-acre forest, accessible only on foot, is attached to Wawayanda State Forest east of Bearfort Ridge. The Appalachian Trail provides the best access and great views from the ridge, heading east from Parker

Pond near the Wawayanda office and through Abram S. Hewitt State Forest before turning north to cross the New York border. The Ernest Walter Trail, marked in yellow, splits off from the Appalachian Trail to circle West Pond and Surprise Lake.

Bearfort Ridge Trail is another good access point, beginning on the corner of Warwick Turnpike and White Road, then stretching 2.4 miles to meet the Ernest Walters Trail, leading to the park's two lakes. Two other marked trails split off from the Ernest Walters Trail into a mixture of hemlock and oak forest, upland swamp, and the rock ledges of Bearfort Ridge. Hikers seeking an escape will be at home in Abram S. Hewitt State Forest, because no other activities are allowed on the trails. A trail map is available at the Wawayanda office, which serves both parks.

Long Pond Ironworks State Park

The Wanaque River and Monksville Reservoir are the main natural attractions at this small park, once the site of an ironmaking town founded in 1766. Remnants of the old stone walls and furnaces remain, and an ongoing restoration of the village focuses on a waterwheel, the old country store, and the outlying casting houses. Two boat ramps give access to the reservoir, where fishing is good for muskellunge, walleye, bass, and trout. Several trails open to mountain biking, horseback riding, and cross-country skiing lead to three abandoned mines that were active during different periods in the town's history. The renovated country store houses a museum dedicated to the town's ironworking days, where you will find a few artifacts and photographs on display. From the Wawayanda office, drive south on Warwick Turnpike for 4.6 miles, where the road name changes to Greenwood Lake Turnpike (Route 511). Continue south on Route 511 for 4.6 miles and turn right into the recreation area.

Ringwood State Park

Ringwood State Park is home to the New Jersey Botanical Garden, a 96-acre area on the edge of the Ramapo Mountains. About 15 miles of fire roads and six well-beaten trails run through the 4,044-acre park, ranging from 1.5-mile hikes to a 7.5-mile mountain bike circuit. Small but popular 74-acre Shepherd Lake sits in the center of the park, where you will find picnicking, swimming, fishing, boat rentals, and a boat ramp. Boats with electric motors are allowed on the lake, and fishing is good for largemouth bass. Sally's Pond, Bear Swamp Lake, and a number of swamps and wetlands are accessible by trail.

Two preserved country estates within the park draw visitors throughout the week. Ringwood Manor, built in 1807, was once known as the second White House as a result of the political influence of Abram S. Hewitt and other industrial barons who occupied the manor throughout the mid-nineteenth century. Skylands Manor was built in the 1920s, featuring forty-four rooms, sixteenth-century Bavarian stained glass, and a garden path through antique stone arches. From Long Pond Ironworks State Park, turn left out of the recreation area, drive .3 mile north on Route 511, and turn right on Margaret King Avenue. Proceed 2.3 miles, turn left on Sloatsburg Road, and continue .6 mile to the Ringwood State Park entrance on the left.

Ramapo Mountain State Forest

Ramapo Mountain State Forest combines with the adjacent Ramapo Mountain Reservation to the east and Ringwood State Park to the north to form a 10,457-acre area of hardwood forest, sheer cliffs, and high mountain streams. Ramapo Lake covers 120 acres at an altitude of 550 feet, its clear water supporting good fishing for largemouth bass, pickerel, yellow perch, and catfish. You won't find any boat ramps or easy access roads near Ramapo Lake; this is an undeveloped park where trail activities rule the day. More than 25 miles of marked trails weave through the forest, and most of them make you work along rock cliffs and hills.

Many of the trails are open to mountain biking, horseback riding, and cross-country skiing, but heed the signs at the trailheads. The blue-blazed MacEvoy Trail follows a brook from the main parking area on Skyline Drive to Ramapo Lake, passing several small cascades in the process. The 1.5-mile Lookout Trail, marked in red, leaves from the lake to a view of the New York City skyline, and the red-blazed Ringwood-Ramapo Trail heads 2.5 miles north into Ringwood State Park. The Ramapo Mountain State Forest parking area is .1 mile north of Route 287 (Exit 57) on the west side of Skyline Drive.

Norvin Green State Forest

This 4,982-acre forest lies next to the Wanaque Reservoir, part of a densely packed area of parks and forests that inhabit northern New Jersey between Wawayanda State Forest, Route 23, and the New York border. Norvin Green is an undeveloped park where more than 20 miles of trails open exclusively to hikers weave through the forest. The best place to begin is from the Weis Ecology Center on Snake Den Road.

Trails leave from the parking area and range from an easy 1-mile hike along Macopin Trail to a difficult climb to the top of Buck Mountain along the 5-mile Wyanokie Crest Trail. Views are panoramic from Buck Mountain, taking in Torne Mountain to the southwest and Assiniwikam Mountain to the east. The blue-blazed Hewitt-Butler Trail is a difficult 5.5-mile hike, but it leads to a remote 25-foot cascade known as Chickahokie Falls. Other trails take in the Manhattan skyline, Wanaque Reservoir, and Lake Sonoma.

From Sloatsburg Road in Ringwood State Park, drive south on Route 511 (Greenwood Lake Turnpike) for 3.2 miles, and turn right on Westbrook Road in the borough of Wanaque. Proceed 1.9 miles and turn left on Snake Den Road. Drive .3 mile, bear left at the fork, and continue .3 mile to the Weis Ecology Center on the right.

Farny State Park

Although Farny State Park is made up of almost 4,000 acres surrounding Splitrock Reservoir, it is a quiet park with very few visitors, probably because it lacks the facilities and vistas of many parks to the north. One main trail cuts through the center of the park in a series of steep climbs and descents, offering a few views of the reservoir along the way. With the exception of the well-maintained trail and one parking area, the park lacks facilities of any kind. If you're looking for privacy and enjoy a difficult hike, this park will appeal. One parking area next to the reservoir lies on the north side of Splitrock Road just east of the Splitrock Reservoir dam. The trailhead is at a second parking area, located on the northwest side of the reservoir at the end of Durham Road. The park is undeveloped, so parking areas consist of simple dirt clearings bordering the road.

Wildlife Management Areas

Six wildlife management areas (WMAs) lie within a twenty-minute drive of Wawayanda. Wanaque WMA is the closest, situated between Abram S. Hewitt State Forest and Ringwood State Park. It is known for its four parking areas providing access to Greenwood Lake and the Wanaque River. Hamburg Mountain is another popular WMA, situated about 6 miles south of Wawayanda. It is made up of almost 3,000 acres, with parking on Lake Wildwood and boating on Silver Lake, an excellent spot for largemouth bass.

The four remaining wildlife management areas form a semicircle of protected land along the Pequannock River Watershed from Hamburg

Mountain in the north to Farny State Park in the south. Sparta Mountain WMA offers boating on Ryker Lake, one of New Jersey's lunker bass lakes and a very private fishing spot. The next two parks south along the semicircle are Weldon Brook WMA, almost 1,500 acres of marshland and mountains; then Rockaway River WMA, offering parking along a 2-mile stretch of the river.

Wildcat Ridge WMA lies adjacent to Farny State Park and is known mainly for the hawk-watch platform atop the ridge. A lesser-known attraction is the bat hibernaculum at Hibernia Mine cave, the largest of its kind in New Jersey, harboring some 30,000 bats. Wildcat Ridge is also one of the more developed wildlife management areas, with an interpretive center, restrooms, and three parking areas on Upper Hibernia Road in Morris County.

Where to Buy Supplies

Warwick in New York is the closest town to Wawayanda, and you will pass several stores along the way. Drive north on Warwick Turnpike for 3 miles, turn right on Route 94, and you will immediately come upon a supermarket, pharmacy, Dunkin' Donuts, pizzeria, and bank. Continue east on Route 94 for 1.8 miles to Warwick, home to a number of restaurants, pharmacies, banks, gas stations, convenience stores, and hotels. West Milford in New Jersey is slightly smaller than Warwick, but the shops are comparable. Drive south of the Wawayanda office on Warwick Turnpike for 4.1 miles, turn right on White Road (which becomes Union Valley Road almost immediately), and proceed 1.7 miles to West Milford. The town contains banks, gas stations, pharmacies, restaurants, fast food, and grocery stores.

The Central Region:
Hunterdon, Mercer, Somerset, Middlesex, Monmouth

Destinations within central New Jersey are perfect for those wishing to stay close to civilization. Most of the parks support developed recreation areas, and you are always within a short drive of a good restaurant or city center. Still, informed travelers can find ways to beat the crowds, and a few suggestions in this section may surprise the staunchest wilderness advocates. A trip to Ken Lockwood Gorge will bring to mind a wild mountain river, and the remote campsites at Round Valley are inaccessible by car. Most travelers know about Washington Crossing State Park and the historic village of Allaire, but very few history buffs visit the nineteenth-century locktenders' houses and mills along the Delaware and Raritan Canal. Whether you're interested in the popular beaches of Sandy Hook or the quiet, little-known destinations farther inland, central New Jersey has something to offer anyone willing to explore.

Voorhees State Park

251 Route 513
Glen Gardner, NJ 08826

Area. 1,400 acres.

Park office. Hunterdon County, 2.1 miles north of High Bridge Borough on the west side of Route 513.

Highlights. Edwin E. Aldrin Astronomical Center, surrounding points of interest.

Activities. Camping, hiking, fishing, picnicking, mountain biking, birding, hunting, cross-country skiing, snowshoeing.

Entrance fee. None.

Park hours. Year-round, from dawn to dusk.

For additional information: (908) 638-6969

oster MacGowan Voorhees was one of the youngest and most progressive New Jersey governors of the age. In 1900, he teamed up with New York governor Theodore Roosevelt in an effort to preserve the cliffs and shorefront of the Palisades, and in 1929, his Hunterdon County farm was posthumously donated to the state, forming the core of Voorhees State Park. Encompassing 1,400 acres, Voorhees is one of New Jersey's smallest parks with camping facilities, offering eight marked trails, serene picnic areas along the park access road, and camping in a secluded hardwood forest miles from the nearest highway. Three small ponds and Willoughby Brook are surrounded by a hardwood forest dominated by gray birch, black oak, and large-toothed aspen. A nearby observatory and two scenic overlooks provide the main attractions, but the best aspect of this park is what lies in the surrounding hills. Voorhees makes a good jumping-off point from which to explore Round Valley Reservoir and Spruce Run Recreation Area to the south and Ken Lockwood Gorge to the east. If you are in pursuit of a quiet and slow-paced weekend, this park is a good place to begin.

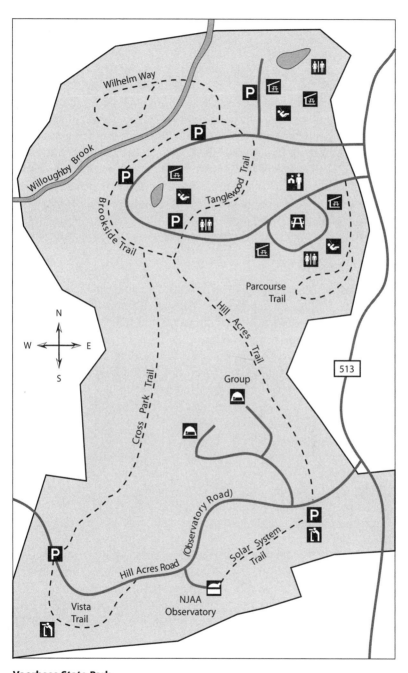

Voorhees State Park

Camping

Voorhees supports one family camping area and two group sites, both surrounded by a forest of yellow birch, shagbark hickory, and four varieties of oak. The park has no central recreation area, and the campground is situated more than a mile away from the office and the main picnic grounds, so there's no need to worry about noise associated with groups of swimmers and day visitors. With the nearest roads bearing names like Buffalo Hollow and Hill Acres, you can forget about traffic noise from major highways as well. A scenic overlook on the campground access road holds a view of Round Valley, and two trails provide short walks while you're in camp. The Solar System Trail leads from the overlook parking area to the Edwin E. Aldrin Astronomical Center, and Hill Acres Trail skirts the northeast corner of the group campsites.

Family Campground

A modest 1,400 acres means you never feel completely removed from civilization, but the campsites are well spaced throughout the forest. An access road forms two loops through dense stands of red oak and sugar maple. Campsites line both sides of the road, perched on rolling hills and gentle swales that echo the surrounding countryside. The absence of nearby highways or city lights means the campground is quiet and peaceful, yet hot showers, modern restrooms, and drinking water are close at hand. Eight of the sites are large enough to accommodate trailers, and a treeless clearing on the east side of the campground holds three shelters that are like one-room cabins, each equipped with two double-deck bunks and a woodburning stove.

Directions. Turn right out of the park office onto Route 513 (High Bridge-Califon Road). Drive south for .8 mile and turn right on Hill Acres Road (shown as Observatory Road on some maps), where a sign for the campground marks the turn. Proceed .3 mile to the campground on the right.

Sites and facilities. The park's fifty campsites and three shelters are all equipped with fire rings and picnic tables. One restroom with chemical toilets and hot showers lies near the center of the campground, and four water pumps are within walking distance of all sites. The trailer sanitary station at the campground entrance is open from April 1 through October 31. The campground is open year-round.

Recommended sites. Drive past sites 1 through 4, trailer sites that occupy an open field, and continue along the one-way road for about 300

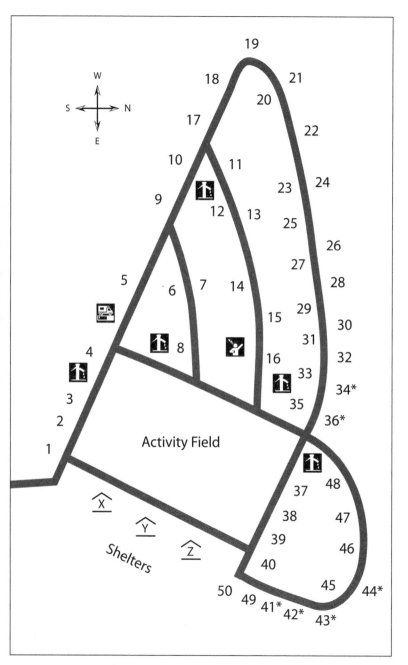

Voorhees Family Campground

yards, until you reach campsites 34 and 36. Both sites are ringed by trees and overlook a wooded rise. Continue around the access road to sites 37 through 48, and take note of the sites on the outside of the loop. In descending order of solitude, 44, 43, 42, and 41 are sheltered enough to provide a sense of escape. If you arrive with a trailer and prefer something other than a grass lawn, numbers 38 through 40 are hemmed in by forest and large enough to hold small trailers. Several options near the campground entrance make good backup choices when the park is crowded, including 5, 9, 10, 17, and 18, all well spaced and insulated from traffic.

Group Campground

Two group sites, A and B, officially accommodate fifty campers each, although anything more than twenty-five campers would probably be too cramped. Both occupy open clearings, but site B is situated at the end of the road and affords slightly more privacy. A parking area, water pump, and restroom with modern toilets and showers are within walking distance. Each site contains picnic tables and two fire rings. Follow the directions above for the family campsites, and bear right just inside the family campground entrance. The group sites are open year-round.

Trails

Eight trails run through the park, only one of them more than a mile long. At 1.3 miles, the Cross Park Trail is a self-guided walk with numbers corresponding to a park pamphlet available at the office. Aside from the Parcourse Trail, a 1-mile exercise circuit next to the office, the Cross Park Trail is the only trail designated exclusively for hikers. The others allow bikes and cross-country skiing, but that's it. Cross Park Trail is actually a small fraction of the 150-mile Highlands Trail, a route envisioned to extend from Storm King Mountain in New York to Phillipsburg, New Jersey, when complete.

The remaining trails at Voorhees represent short walks through black birch, American beech, and black, chestnut, and red oaks. Hill Acres Trail begins across the road from the Round Valley overlook and extends about 1 mile to the park access road near the office. Vista Trail, beginning .9 mile west of the campground on Hill Acres Road, provides a view of Spruce Run Reservoir only after the trees have dropped their leaves for winter. Brookside and Tanglewood Trails combine to form a 1-mile hike alongside the park access road. The .8-mile Wilhelm Trail

Trail Mileage and Difficulty

TRAIL	MILES	DIFFICULTY	BLAZE	USES
Brookside Trail	0.5	E	orange	h,m,s,x
Cross Park Trail	1.3	E	white	h
Hill Acres Trail	1.0	E	blue	h,m,s,x
Parcourse Trail	1.0	E	red/yellow	h
Solar System Trail	0.5	E	red	h,m,s,x
Tanglewood Trail	0.5	E	green	h,m,s,x
Vista Trail	0.8	E	pink	h,m,s,x
Wilhelm Way	0.8	E	yellow	h,m,s,x

is a bit more interesting, following Willoughby Brook past a small pond, and Solar System Trail provides a worthwhile distraction while you're in camp, stretching .5 mile from the scenic overlook to the observatory.

Activities

Because of the park's limited size, you might want to combine Voorhees State Park with nearby Round Valley Reservoir and Spruce Run Recreation Area in a three-park tour. (You can also add Ken Lockwood Gorge, especially if you're passionate about fly fishing.) The area provides enough distractions to occupy several weekends for anyone willing to make short side trips from Voorhees. In addition to activities inside the park, several destinations within a ten-minute drive of Voorhees are included below.

Edwin E. Aldrin Astronomical Center

The main attraction of this small complex is the Paul Robinson Observatory, home to a 26-inch Newtonian telescope. The observatory sits a mere 200 yards down the road from the family campground, the highest elevation in the park, at 840 feet above sea level. The New Jersey Astronomical Association runs Saturday evening and Sunday afternoon programs from Memorial Day through October 31. The center holds a lecture hall, library, and several smaller telescopes, and newcomers are always welcome. Even when the center is closed, it's still worthwhile to combine the Solar System Trail with a walk around the outside of the observatory. The trail begins at the overlook parking area and stretches .5 mile to the astronomical center.

Fishing

Willoughby Brook is a wild trout stream, subject to specific regulations such as catch-and-release during part of the season and no live bait. Two ponds near the park access road are meant for children and produce bluegill and an occasional bass. Several excellent fishing destinations lie within 10 miles of Voorhees as well. The Musconetcong River is second only to the Raritan when it comes to stocked trout, with almost 50,000 fish released every year. Fly fishing is popular along the entire length, although the northern section receives more praise from anglers. A number of informal access points in Hunterdon County lie within a short drive of Voorhees, including many of the side roads off Musconetcong River Road. Each of the four bridges that cross the river north of Hampton Borough makes a productive fishing spot, as they are all stocking points. Three other advisable destinations for anglers—Ken Lockwood Gorge, Round Valley Reservoir, and Spruce Run Reservoir— are covered in the Surrounding Points of Interest section below.

Boating

Spruce Run and Round Valley Recreation Areas combine to form 3,660 acres of surface water open to canoes, sailboats, and motorboats. The Musconetcong River, mentioned in the Fishing Section, makes for difficult canoeing precisely because it is heavily managed for fishing, with dams and fishways up and down its course. See the Surrounding Points of Interest section for information about the reservoirs.

Picnicking

Picnic tables begin at the park office and line both sides of the park access road. Some of them are grouped together in designated areas, but many tables sit by themselves in isolated clearings. About .4 mile north of the park office, you will find a particularly serene area with tables and grills lining a grassy hill on the edge of a small pond. Two group picnic areas, A and B, occupy the corner of the park access road and Route 513. Each accommodates up to 100 people, but area A is better suited for groups over 50. Area B is more private, situated away from the road and bounded by woodland. Groups must make reservations at least five days in advance. Three modern restrooms service all of the picnic areas, and at least one of them is always within walking distance.

Swimming

Voorhees does not offer swimming, but campers can use the beach at Spruce Run Recreation Area, provided the beach is not filled to capacity. Simply show your camping permit at the entrance gate. The Spruce Run beach is open from Memorial Day weekend through Labor Day. See the Surrounding Points of Interest section for directions.

Mountain Biking

All but the Cross Park and Parcourse Trails are open to mountain biking, but none of them are more than a mile long. You can combine Hill Acres Trail with the quiet and seldom-traveled Hill Acres Road, which produces a relatively easy ride over rolling hills. Another option is to head for Ken Lockwood Gorge Wildlife Management Area. A 1.6-mile dirt road leading through the gorge, although flat and easy, still makes you feel as if you have left New Jersey for the Appalachian Mountains. Columbia Trail crosses over Ken Lockwood Gorge atop a railroad bridge about .6 mile from the northern border of the wildlife management area. Access the trail by climbing up to the top of the train trestle from the bottom of the gorge (a tough climb carrying a mountain bike) or from the trailhead in High Bridge, about .1 mile west of the corner of Church and Mill Streets. See Ken Lockwood Gorge Wildlife Management Area below for more information.

Birding

Voorhees is known for its migrating warblers in spring. Naturalists have recorded more than twenty species in a single day, including a pair of nesting Kentucky warblers near the campground. Willoughby Brook attracts flycatchers near Brookside Trail and Wilhelm Way, but the best warbler areas are along Hill Acres Trail. Park at the Round Valley overlook and walk about 100 yards along Hill Acres Trail until you reach the clearing cut for the power lines. When you return to the woods on the other side, you are in prime warbler territory. Take a minute to listen for the Kentucky warbler; this is where one pair has nested in the past. Also check out the nearby reservoirs for migrating waterfowl and shorebirds.

Hunting

About 770 of the park's 1,400 acres are open to the hunting of deer, small game, and wild turkeys, but Voorhees is not a prime area for hunting. The entire east side of the park near the Voorhees access road is off-limits, as are the areas surrounding the campground, observatory, maintenance area, and parking areas.

Winter Activities

Voorhees lies in the middle of Hunterdon County's rolling countryside, and you will never regret a visit in November when the leaves are in transition. A view of Hill Acres Road arched over by autumn trees made the short list for this guidebook's cover photograph. Three shelters on the east end of the campground offer woodburning stoves during the winter, and the park is open year-round for camping, hiking, and cross-country skiing. The observatory runs a few winter programs; check the New Jersey Astronomical Association website for a current schedule.

Flora and Fauna

Voorhees should not be judged by its size. Sugar maple, white ash, shagbark hickory, American beech, and black, chestnut, red, and white oaks dominate the older areas of the forest, accompanied by an understory of shrubs and vines including striped wintergreen, witch-hazel, spicebush, Japanese barberry, and staghorn sumac. The surrounding area, New Jersey's Central Highlands, supports three federal-endangered or threatened, eight state-endangered, and eleven state-threatened species, as well as seventy species listed by biologists as animals of special concern. The federal-endangered bog turtle, the state-endangered red-shouldered hawk, and the state-threatened barred owl are just a few rare animals found in and around Voorhees State Park. Some of the more elusive warblers are migratory inhabitants in the spring, and you may spot a bald eagle, as a pair has nested at nearby Round Valley every spring for the past decade. Although black bears are still an unusual sight this far south, they become more common with each passing year.

Surrounding Points of Interest

Campers at Voorhees are in a perfect position to explore the surrounding area. Two state recreation areas and one of New Jersey's most beautiful wildlife management areas are within a 10-mile drive, all worthy of a day trip or even a few hours on a sunny afternoon. Brief descriptions of the recreation areas are included below, but check the separate chapters covering Round Valley and Spruce Run for more detailed information.

Ken Lockwood Gorge Wildlife Management Area

More than a few fly-fishing streams have been compared to the Norman Maclean novel *A River Runs Through It*, and Ken Lockwood Gorge is one such example. Receiving 60,000 trout annually, the Raritan River as a whole is the most heavily stocked trout stream in New Jersey, and the section running through Ken Lockwood gets its share at about 30,000 trout. Environmentalist Ken Lockwood spent countless hours away from his desk at the *Newark Evening News* fly-fishing the Elbow, a trout hot spot just downstream from the railroad bridge.

You don't have to be an angler to be inspired by Ken Lockwood Gorge. This is one of New Jersey's most scenic wildlife management areas, where white water cuts through cliffs more reminiscent of the Colorado River than the Raritan. Hiking up to the train trestle puts you on the Columbia Trail, which stretches 7 miles from High Bridge to Valley Brook Road on the border of Morris County. The Columbia Trail rises about 100 feet above the riverbed and provides the best view of the gorge. You can also hike along the dirt access road paralleling the river. Drivers should beware, though—the road has claimed a few muffler systems.

Follow Route 513 south from the park office for 1.4 miles and turn left on Cregar Road, which is not marked at the turn. Follow this road, which turns into Cokesbury Road, for 1 mile to the Raritan River. Cross over the river and turn left at the end of the bridge onto Raritan River Road, also not marked at the turn. Drive north on Raritan River Road for .1 mile to enter the wildlife management area. Proceed along the potholed access road with care. Follow the river north for another 1.4 miles to the railroad bridge and a small parking area.

Spruce Run Recreation Area

Spruce Run's 11-billion-gallon reservoir is its main attraction. Boating, fishing, and birding are all popular, and the camping is convenient if you're coming from Voorhees. No need for a long hike in pursuit of a campsite; the spots are directly on the water with parking close at hand. Turn right out of the Voorhees office onto Route 513 (High Bridge-Califon Road), drive south for 1.4 miles, and turn right on Cregar Road. Continue 1.3 miles and turn right on Route 31. Proceed .2 mile, turn left on Van Syckels Road, and continue 1.5 miles to the Spruce Run entrance on the left.

Round Valley Recreation Area

Similar to Spruce Run, Round Valley's 55-billion-gallon reservoir is the biggest draw for boaters, anglers, and birders. The campground at Round Valley, the only wilderness campground in New Jersey outside of Wharton State Forest, is accessible by foot, boat, or mountain bike alone. The reservoir holds the state records for smallmouth bass, freshwater eel, and brown and lake trout—more records than any other body of water in New Jersey save the Delaware River. In the spring and fall, migratory birds and waterfowl are attracted to the reservoir. Follow Route 31 south to I-78 east. Proceed east on I-78 for .3 mile and bear right at the first exit (Exit 18, Route 22 east). Follow the long off-ramp for .2 mile to Route 22 east. Drive east on Route 22 for 1.3 miles and turn right on Round Valley Access Road. Follow the access road for 1.5 miles to the recreation area entrance on the left.

Hacklebarney State Park

Hacklebarney is a relatively small park that often goes unnoticed, partly because it lies beyond several unmarked dirt roads and is difficult to find. At 978 acres, the area supports shallow streams that cut through a glacial valley surrounded by eastern hemlock and chestnut oak. About 5 miles of manicured paths cross over the Black River along wooden bridges. Leave the well-beaten paths behind and walk along the stream for a bit more privacy. Picnic tables are common fixtures, but several large boulders in the river make better resting spots. Fishing is good in the Black River for brown, brook, and rainbow trout. No bikes are allowed on the paths.

Follow Route 513 (High Bridge-Califon Road) north from the park office for 3.1 miles and turn right on Route 512 (Main Street) in Califon. Drive east on Route 512 for 4.4 miles (the road changes names along the way, first to Academy Street and then to Fairmount Road West); then turn left on Old Turnpike Road. Drive 1.1 miles, turn right on Parker Road, and continue .2 mile to Black River Road. Turn right on Black River Road, drive 1 mile, and bear left on Hacklebarney Road. Drive .4 mile; then turn right to stay on Hacklebarney Road. Proceed .7 mile to the park entrance on the right.

Where to Buy Supplies

High Bridge is only 1.3 miles south of the campground (or 2.1 miles south of the park office) on Route 513. Main Street holds a pizzeria, several restaurants, and two auto repair garages. Hilltop Deli on Fairview Avenue serves quick subs and sandwiches, and Gronsky's Milk House offers ten picnic tables facing the Raritan River. If you head north on Route 31 from Main Street in High Bridge and drive about 1.3 miles, you will come to Skyline Bait and Tackle on the east side of Route 31 near Van Syckels Road. Drive south on Route 31 from Main Street in High Bridge for more substantial supplies. A strip mall on the northeast corner of Route 31 and Main Street holds a bagel shop, pharmacy, bank, and pizzeria. Continue south about 1.5 miles to Clinton for almost anything else a traveler needs, including sporting goods, pharmacies, banks, grocery stores, restaurants, and car repair.

Spruce Run Recreation Area

68 Van Syckels Rd.
Clinton, NJ 08809

Area. 2,012 acres.

Park office. Hunterdon County, 2.6 miles north of Clinton on the south side of Van Syckels Road.

Highlights. Spruce Run Reservoir.

Activities. Camping, hiking, fishing, boating, picnicking, swimming, bicycling, birding, hunting, ice fishing, cross-country skiing, snowshoeing, ice boating.

Entrance fee. An entrance fee is charged from Memorial Day weekend through Labor Day.

Park hours. Year-round, from dawn to dusk.

For additional information: (908) 638-8572

Spruce Run's 11-billion-gallon reservoir was once the site of the first ironworks established in the American colonies. Union Furnace ironworks opened its doors in 1742, becoming the second-oldest business in North America after the Hudson's Bay Company of Canada. The foundry cast cannonballs for the Continental Army during the Revolutionary War, and the outlying buildings doubled as a detention camp for Loyalist prisoners. Spruce Run Creek was dammed in 1963 to supply water for a growing population, and the original location of Union Furnace became engulfed by the reservoir.

Encompassing 15 miles of shoreline, Spruce Run's 1,290 acres of surface water represent almost two-thirds of the entire protected area within the park. Several of the campsites lie a stone's throw from the shore, and a developed recreation area is surrounded by a sandy beach, picnic tables, and a boat livery. Thirty species of fish inhabit the reservoir, including game fish such as hybrid striped bass, rainbow trout, and massive northern pike approaching 31 pounds. Migratory birds gather on the open water in the spring and fall, many of them rarely seen elsewhere in New Jersey. Two adjacent natural areas, the Clinton Wildlife Management Area and Union Furnace Nature Preserve, add

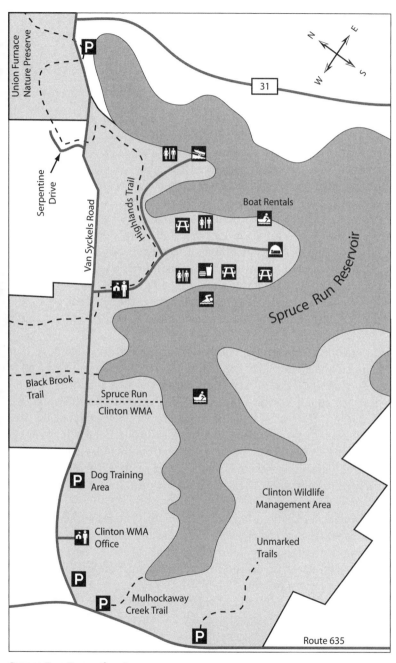

Spruce Run Recreation Area

1,934 acres to the total protected land surrounding Spruce Run. The Highlands Trail links them all together, swerving through the recreation area on its way to Voorhees State Park.

Camping

Spruce Run's sole family campground lies at the end of a wide peninsula that juts nearly a mile into the reservoir. Thirteen of the campsites sit next to the shoreline or hold a view of the water, and most of the sites are large enough to accommodate trailers. The highly developed campground provides an ideal setting if you want to dispense with the preparation necessary for a stay in the wilderness, with items like hot showers and a food concession close at hand. You will find no group sites, cabins, or lean-tos at the park, but three shelters occupy the western edge of the campground. The shelters are small, one-room cabins each containing two double-deck bunks, a wooden table and benches, and a woodburning stove. The recreation area, swimming beach, and boat livery are within walking distance of the campground. Reserve ahead; the park's one camping area is usually busy on summer weekends.

Directions. Turn right out of the park office and drive .8 mile to the campground at the end of the peninsula.

Sites and facilities. Spruce Run's sixty-seven sites and three shelters are each equipped with fire rings, picnic tables, and stand-up grills. About fifty of the sites are large enough to accommodate trailers. The campground's two restrooms contain flush toilets and hot showers. A picnic shelter, two playgrounds, and water from ground pumps are scattered throughout the grounds, and a trailer sanitary station lies at the campground entrance. The campground is open from April 1 through October 31.

Recommended sites. You will find more waterfront campsites at Spruce Run than at any other New Jersey state park. Thirteen sites offer a clear view of the water and the Cushetunk Mountains beyond. Numbers 16 and 17 rest on the shore in a private corner of the campground, where the nearest neighbor is out of sight beyond a row of shrubs and trees. Numbers 19, 20, and 25 hold views of the reservoir and are fairly private despite their position near the restroom and parking area. The remaining sites on the water—11, 13, 15, 23, 28, 37, 39, and 41—are worthy backup choices, all facing the reservoir but a bit exposed to the road. A less obvious option entails camping at one of the sites to the

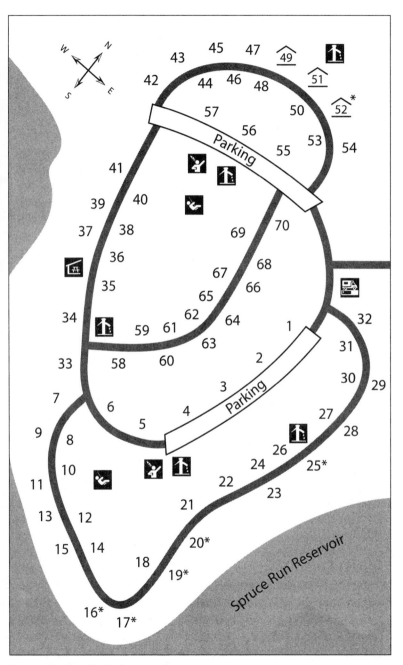

Spruce Run Family Campground

west, numbers 42 through 57. Although they sit on an open grass lawn far from the water, they are usually empty and quiet. The best of the three shelters is number 52, bordered by one other shelter to the west and trees to the north and east.

Trails

Hikers face a limited choice between the Highlands Trail, the only marked trail at Spruce Run, or one of the unmarked trails at nearby Clinton Wildlife Management Area. The Highlands Trail is envisioned to stretch from the Hudson River to Phillipsburg when complete, connecting all of the parks within the New York and New Jersey Highlands in the process. The section near Spruce Run extends from Voorhees State Park through Union Furnace Nature Preserve and on to the recreation area, before reaching Clinton Wildlife Management Area to the west.

A good place to begin the Highlands Trail is where it enters Union Furnace Nature Preserve, about 200 yards west of Route 31 on the north side of Van Syckels Road. The trail runs .9 mile through the preserve, emerging at the end of a paved cul-de-sac called Serpentine Drive. Follow Serpentine Drive for .3 mile to Van Syckels Road, turn left and walk about 100 yards, and then turn right into a small parking area. From the parking area, the trail stretches 1.3 miles through Spruce Run Recreation Area to the park office. Beware, though—the section along the reservoir cuts through tall grass and is prime tick territory.

If you want to continue into the Clinton Wildlife Management Area, turn left out of the park entrance and walk about 100 yards along Van Syckels Road to pick up the Highlands Trail again on the north side of the road. A gravel road beyond a wooden gate marks the trail entrance. This section of the Highlands Trail was only recently completed and extends a mere 1.5 miles north to the end of the line at Black Brook Road. The new section is a bit difficult to follow as well, so watch for the teal blazes as they bend along several dirt roads and narrow footpaths through Clinton Wildlife Management Area. The Highlands Trail allows hiking, cross-country skiing, and snowshoeing, but no bikes or horses.

Activities

For most visitors, the 722 acres of dry land within Spruce Run Recreation Area serve merely as a means to reach the water. The park rents everything from motorboats to kayaks, and consistent wind across the reservoir creates good conditions for sailors throughout the spring and summer. Anglers use the reservoir 365 days a year, as Spruce Run is one of the most heavily stocked bodies of water in New Jersey when it comes to variety of fish. Even the recreation area borders the water, where a sandy beach and food concession attract swimmers after Memorial Day. Birders arrive in fall, when thousands of migrating shorebirds stop to rest and feed at the reservoir on their journey along the Atlantic Flyway.

Fishing

Thirty species of fish inhabit the waters of Spruce Run. Largemouth and smallmouth bass, yellow perch, black crappie, and American eels spawn in the reservoir, and more than 5,000 brown, rainbow, and brook trout are stocked almost every year. The reservoir has received more northern pike from the state's stocking program than any other lake in New Jersey, as many as 9,000 in a single year. The state-record northern pike was caught here in 1977, weighing in at 30 pounds, 2 ounces. Hybrid striped bass, channel catfish, largemouth bass, and tiger muskellunge have been stocked over the years as well. Hybrid striped bass were first produced in the 1960s by crossing a male striped bass with a female white bass. Introduced to Spruce Run in 1990, the hybrids are known for their strength and speed. These join a variety of other game fish, such as carp, rock bass, bluegill sunfish, and three varieties of catfish. Spruce Run's many species of fish are abundant. Fishing is excellent for hybrid striped bass, northern pike, catfish, carp, and sunfish, and fair for largemouth and smallmouth bass, pickerel, and crappie.

Boating

Motors up to 10 horsepower are allowed in the lake, but on sunny days, you will see almost anything that floats. Spruce Run Boat Rental, near the campground, supplies sailboats, kayaks, canoes, sailboards, and motorboats. Sailing is popular at Spruce Run because a constant wind sweeps across the reservoir, but there's a 25-foot size limit on sailboats. This is the home base for the Hunterdon Sailing Club, which runs races and regattas throughout the year. The boat ramp is some distance from the main activity, about 1.1 miles east of the park office, where you will find three side-by-side concrete ramps and a restroom. The boat ramp access road begins .1 mile south of the park office on the east side of the park entrance road.

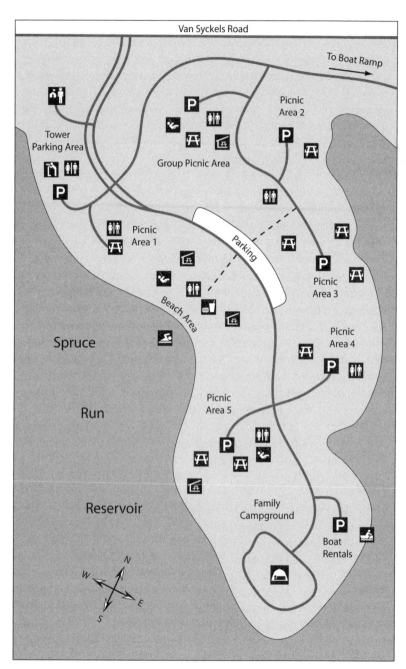

Van Syckels Road

To Boat Ramp

Picnic
Area 2

Tower
Parking Area

Group Picnic Area

Picnic
Area 1

Parking

Beach Area

Picnic
Area 3

Spruce

Picnic
Area 4

Run

Picnic
Area 5

Reservoir

Family
Campground

Boat
Rentals

N
W   E
S

Beach and Picnic Areas

Picnicking

Five picnic areas and one group site stretch out along the Spruce Run peninsula. Area 3 offers tables directly on the shore and restrooms nearby, but this site is normally closed during the off-season. When it is closed, move to area 5, where about thirty tables overlook the reservoir and restrooms are within walking distance. Area 1 lies near the beach complex and is usually busy, but it holds a nice view of the reservoir from the Tower Parking Area. Picnic area 4 offers tables on a grass lawn far from the water. Area 2 has not been open in recent years; it's used mainly for dry-dock boat storage during the winter. The group picnic area on the north end of the peninsula accommodates up to 225 people, with grills, a restroom, playground, and water nearby. Reserve the group area at least five days in advance.

Swimming

Spruce Run's central recreation area is what many people envision when they picture a classic sandy beach. The wide swimming area slopes gradually to the shore, backed by a concession stand and stone deck holding several picnic tables. Covered pavilions flank a lifeguard station, and the food concession serves everything from nachos to ice cream. Modern restrooms, a playground, and parking for about 100 cars service the beach. Spruce Run allows swimming from Memorial Day weekend through Labor Day.

Mountain Biking

If you don't want to travel, the roads around the reservoir will have to suffice, as the Highlands Trail does not allow bikes. You can try the boat launch access road, only 1.1 miles long but a quiet and peaceful ride along a road bounded by bushes and trees. If you turn right at picnic areas 2 and 3, a concrete path leads out to the main access road south of the beach. Clinton Wildlife Management Area, covered below, encompasses several short and unmarked trails, but most of them are squeezed thin by brush and tough going for a mountain bike. A few mountain-biking trails in the area include Ken Lockwood Gorge Wildlife Management Area near Voorhees State Park and Cushetunk Trail and Capoolong Trail near Round Valley Recreation Area.

Birding

Spruce Run attracts shorebirds and waterfowl by the thousands during spring and fall migration. Sandpipers, plovers, diving ducks, gulls, loons, and grebes arrive in numbers every year. On a single spring day in 2000, more than 130 common loons were spotted on the waters of Spruce Run and Round Valley. Other individual days have brought 100 common mergansers, 1,100 ring-billed gulls, 150 American wigeons, 40 greater scaups, along with American coots, buffleheads, horned grebes, and almost any other migratory waterbird found away from the coast in New Jersey. The list of rarities is a long one. Red-throated and Pacific loons, snow geese, American golden and black-bellied plovers, red phalaropes, buff-breasted and pectoral sandpipers, cattle egrets, tricolored herons, lesser black-backed and Bonaparte's gulls, red-necked grebes, greater and lesser scaups . . . the list goes on.

Fall migration is the best time for birding the reservoir, although you can often see migrants throughout the winter. Look near the outlet of all the creeks—Spruce Run, Mulhockaway, and Black Brook—as well as at the boat launch, the point of land south of the campground, and even the main parking lot for songbirds such as snow buntings. Buffleheads and other diving ducks sometimes linger around the swimming beach. Don't limit your search to the reservoir, though—Spruce Run supports a variety of migratory and nesting warblers, raptors, and songbirds as well. A few rarities that occur at the recreation area and at Clinton Wildlife Management Area include nesting yellow-breasted chats and migratory Lincoln's sparrows, northern shrikes, and Philadelphia vireos. Several good birding trails lead to the reservoir from Clinton Wildlife Management Area as well; check the Surrounding Points of Interest section for details.

Hunting

About 65 percent of the recreation area is open to the hunting of waterfowl. A variety of permits apply for various birds. Designated portions of Spruce Run are open to deer hunting certain years as well, but the times and dates vary. The New Jersey Division of Fish and Wildlife maintains a detailed and updated website for hunters, where all current regulations are posted on a seasonal basis. Spruce Run is in the waterfowl hunting area known as the north zone. The Clinton Wildlife Management Area is an advisable destination for hunters, especially if you're interested in deer. Union Furnace Nature Preserve is also open to deer hunting, although you need a hunting access permit from Hunterdon County in addition to the usual permits, among them the New Jersey Waterfowl Stamp and the Federal Migratory Bird Hunting and Conservation Stamp.

Winter Activities

Fishing is allowed year-round and continues to be a main attraction throughout the winter. A variety of fish are caught in the reservoir after November, most notably northern pike, yellow perch, and largemouth bass. The reservoir freezes solid only during very cold winters, so ice fishing is a rare opportunity. When conditions are right, you will sometimes see a few intrepid souls practicing the rare sport of ice boating, skidding across the ice on a sailboat fitted with runners. Birders enjoy warm winters at Spruce Run, as many migratory birds linger until driven south by ice. The Highlands Trail allows cross-country skiing and snowshoeing, although the section near Spruce Run is rarely used during the colder months. Hunting is allowed for certain waterfowl through December; check the open-season schedule for the latest regulations.

Flora and Fauna

Spruce Run is part of a fragmented forest system that extends from the headwaters of the Musconetcong River to the South Branch of the Raritan River, an area known as the Central Highlands. The rolling countryside and sculpted valleys support fields, marshes, and meadows, where red maple, pin oak, American elm, and other trees form pockets of forested land mixed with areas of suburban development. State endangered and threatened species maintain a foothold near the reservoirs. The American bittern, northern harrier, upland sandpiper, and short-eared owl are state-endangered. The bobolink, barred owl, Cooper's hawk, and red-headed woodpecker are state-threatened, and dozens of species that make use of the reservoirs are considered of special concern, including many raptors, reptiles, waterbirds, and amphibians. The reservoir holds 30 species of fish and provides habitat for nearly 200 species of migratory and nesting birds. Spruce Run is an important piece of the Central Highlands, serving to link several wildlife areas in central New Jersey.

Surrounding Points of Interest

Clinton Wildlife Management Area and Union Furnace Nature Preserve add 2,051 acres to the total protected land surrounding Spruce Run Reservoir. The recreation area also lies within 10 miles of Voorhees State Park to the north and Round Valley Recreation Area to the east. Check those chapters for additional destinations within a short drive of Spruce Run.

Clinton Wildlife Management Area

Clinton Wildlife Management Area encircles the western half of Spruce Run Reservoir. At 1,954 acres, it is a popular destination for hunting deer, small game, wild turkeys, and waterfowl. One shooting range is located off Route 173 to the south, and the management area office is 1.5 miles west of the Spruce Run entrance on the south side of Van Syckels Road. Several unmarked trails crisscross the wildlife area, many of them advisable birding destinations, although hikers should be aware of open hunting seasons. Hike to the mudflats at the end of Mulhockaway Creek Trail or along Black Brook just west of the Spruce Run entrance for shorebirds. The mudflats attract migratory sandpipers and plovers when the water levels are low. If you turn left out of the Spruce Run office, a number of trails begin west of the Spruce Run entrance on the north and south side of Van Syckels Road and the east side of Route 635. The trails are relatively flat and easy to follow, but none are marked.

Union Furnace Nature Preserve

This 97-acre natural area managed by Hunterdon County lies on the north side of Van Syckels Road, about 1.4 miles east of the Spruce Run entrance. The Highlands Trail runs .9 mile through chestnut oak and Japanese barberry emerging at the north end of Serpentine Drive near the park office. You can hunt deer with a Hunterdon County permit in addition to the usual state permits. The original Union Furnace, a site now buried by the reservoir, was one of the first established businesses in North America, operating from 1742 through 1781. The ironworks produced military hardware for Washington's army during the Revolutionary War.

Where to Buy Supplies

Skyline Bait and Tackle is on the east side of Route 31, about .1 mile north of Van Syckels Road. Drive south on Route 31 for .7 mile, turn right on Route 513 (Halstead Street), and continue south for .8 mile to Clinton. The small city offers almost anything a camper needs, including grocery stores, pharmacies, banks, car repair, and a variety of restaurants. Clinton Canoe and Kayak is located at 44 Main Street, and Clinton Bicycle Shop is at 51 Main Street. A Wal-Mart plaza on Route 513 just south of I-78 also holds a supermarket and sporting-goods store.

Round Valley
Recreation Area

1220 Lebanon-Stanton Rd.
Lebanon, NJ 08833

Area. 3,684 acres.

Park office. Hunterdon County, 1.5 miles south of Lebanon Borough on the east side of Route 629.

Highlights. Round Valley Reservoir, Cushetunk Trail, wilderness camping.

Activities. Camping, hiking, fishing, boating, picnicking, swimming, mountain biking, horseback riding, birding, scuba diving, hunting, ice fishing, cross-country skiing, snowshoeing.

Entrance fee. An entrance fee is charged from Memorial Day weekend through Labor Day.

Park hours. The grounds are open 8 A.M. to 8 P.M. from Memorial Day through Labor Day and 8 A.M. to 4:30 P.M. the remainder of the year.

For additional information: (908) 236-6355

At 55 billion gallons and 180 feet deep, Round Valley is New Jersey's largest reservoir and deepest lake, drawing campers, anglers, birders, and boaters from the entire region. The 3,684 protected acres hold a remote campground that is inaccessible to cars, yet a developed beach complex provides swimming off a sandy shore, picnic tables, and a food concession. The cool waters, pumped into the valley from the South Branch of the Raritan River, have produced the state records for smallmouth bass, American eel, and brown and lake trout, with new records approached every year. Migratory birds and waterfowl are attracted to the reservoir in the spring and fall. During the summer, visitors take advantage of Round Valley's two boat launches, five trails hugging the shore, and even a shallow cove open to scuba diving.

Camping

Round Valley is unique for campers in several ways. It holds New Jersey's only wilderness campground outside of Wharton State Forest, and

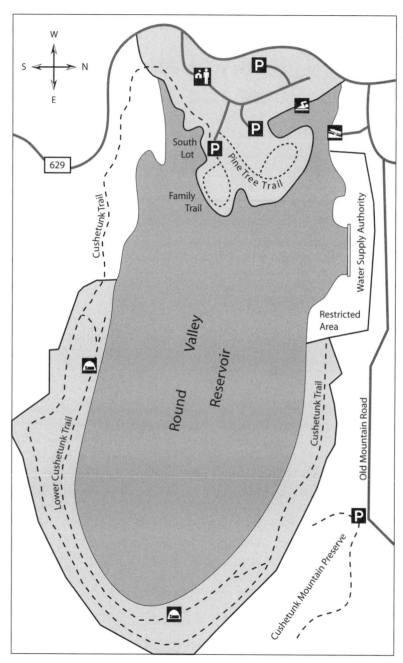

Round Valley Recreation Area

it offers the only boat launch in New Jersey reserved solely for campers and scuba divers. The wilderness camping is a bit of an anomaly, considering that the park lies only 35 miles from Newark and another 10 miles from New York City. Round Valley's campground is accessible only by foot, boat, or mountain bike. Campsites begin 3 miles from the trailhead and stretch for another 3 miles around the south shore of the reservoir. Because of the long hike, campers are required to register at the office by 4:30 P.M. before setting out.

The eighty-five campsites are perfect for anyone seeking seclusion. Options range from sites perched on a wooded hillside overlooking the reservoir to landlocked sites near Lower Cushetunk Trail. Many lie directly on the shore, and some occupy open clearings in the woods. All are spaced far from their neighbors. About forty of the sites each offer a path down to the water, a place to land small boats, and markers onshore for boaters who arrive from across the reservoir. Overnight parking is allowed at the South Lot, where you will find the campers' boat launch and a trail leading to the campsites.

Directions. Boaters can simply head east across the reservoir from the South Lot boat ramp and look for the forty placards marking sites near the water. If you're hiking or biking, take the red-blazed Cushetunk Trail on the north side of the parking lot (behind you as you face the reservoir). Hike 3 miles along the Cushetunk Trail, until you come to the yellow-blazed Lower Cushetunk Trail descending left into the campground. At last check, the Lower Cushetunk Trail was not marked at the turn. You will find site number 1 at the bottom of the hill. The campground is 3 miles long, so you must hike a total of 6 miles to reach the last campsite.

Sites and facilities. Round Valley's seventy-seven tent sites accommodate up to seven campers, and eight group sites (numbers 1 through 8) accommodate up to twenty-five campers. Most sites have fire rings, with the exception of numbers 27, 29, 84, and 85. Ten pit toilets and ten ground pumps are evenly spaced along the 3-mile Lower Cushetunk Trail and within walking distance of all sites. A covered pavilion with three picnic tables and a fire ring is located in the center of the campground between sites 47 and 48. You will also find a public telephone and gated access road for emergency vehicles between sites 47 and 48. The campground is open from April 1 through October 31.

Recommended sites. If you are seeking seclusion, it's hard to go wrong with any of Round Valley's campsites. A few rest directly onshore, many overlook the reservoir, and others lie inland near Lower

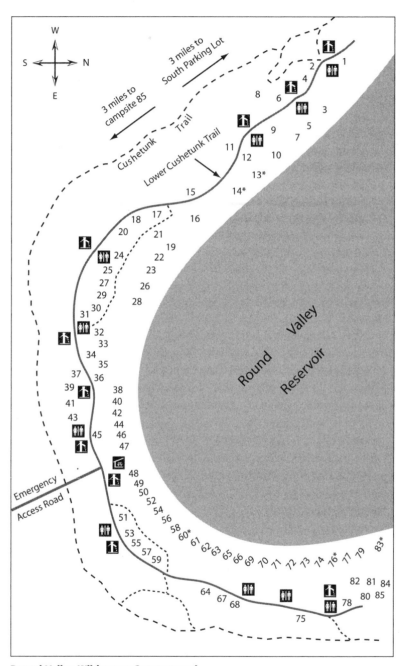

Round Valley Wilderness Campground

Cushetunk Trail. The best sites for both privacy and access to the water are located on the north side of the trail. Number 83 is one of the most secluded sites in the park and well worth the hike. It holds a clear view of the reservoir from a forested hill overlooking the scene. Number 76 lies directly onshore, where you will find a small cove for boats and a nice fire ring. Other excellent sites that border the water include 13, 14, and 60. All of these sites have a spot to land small boats and a marker facing the reservoir.

Several of Round Valley's sites are not directly onshore, but they offer vistas of the reservoir and paths down to a boat landing area. Number 70 overlooks the water from a wooded rise, 69 holds a view of the reservoir through trees, and 72 has good boat access and lies near the shore. Number 50 is isolated from its neighbors, far from the main path, and level, and 79 overlooks the reservoir behind a thin row of trees. Others with varying views include 9, 19, 22, 26, 40, 71, and 74. Another twenty-four sites offer access to the water and boat landings but limited views. See the accompanying map for a depiction of all forty-one sites near the water.

Trails

Of the five trails at Round Valley, the 9-mile Cushetunk Trail attracts the most attention from hardened hikers. Marked with red blazes, the Cushetunk Trail is open to mountain biking, horseback riding, cross-country skiing, and snowshoeing. It begins from the South Lot and stretches about halfway around the reservoir to the wilderness camping area. The trail dead-ends at the restricted New Jersey Water Supply Authority, so you have to walk back the way you came, making the hike an 18-mile round-trip. The trek is hilly and rugged, alternating between packed dirt and loose gravel, but you will find plenty of solitude and unbroken forest along the way. A 3-mile access road known as the Lower Cushetunk Trail, marked with yellow blazes, splits off from the Cushetunk Trail about 3 miles from the South Lot and heads through the campground.

Three other trails begin from the South Lot as well, only one of them more than a mile long. The 1.5-mile Water Trail begins at the bottom of the campers' boat ramp and hugs the shore of the reservoir, skirting some hilly terrain covered with pines. The green-blazed Pine Tree Trail begins across the South Lot access road, forming a quiet 1-mile loop through rolling pineland. The Family Hike and Bike Trail begins across the road

Trail Mileage and Difficulty

TRAIL	MILES	DIFFICULTY	BLAZE	USES
Cushetunk Trail	9.0	M	red	e,h,m,s,x
Family Hike and Bike Trail	0.5	E	white	h,m,s,x
Lower Cushetunk Trail	3.0	E	yellow	h,m,s,x
Pine Tree Trail	1.0	E	green	h,s,x
Water Trail	1.5	E	blue	h,s,x

as well, forming a .5-mile loop open to biking, cross-country skiing, and snowshoeing. Alas, there are no trails that completely circle the reservoir.

Activities

Much of the activity at Round Valley revolves around water—more than 2,000 acres of it. The developed beach complex attracts swimmers during the summer, and four picnic areas cater to visitors throughout the year. A concrete boat ramp on the west shore gives access to all sorts of watercraft, from motorboats to kayaks. Almost twenty species of fish have been identified at the reservoir, and most anglers are familiar with Round Valley's many freshwater fishing records. Thousands of migratory birds use the reservoir as a rest stop on their journey along the Atlantic Flyway, and birders arrive in the spring and fall to watch them. Terrestrial pursuits are not overlooked here either, as the Cushetunk Trail forms a challenging route open to mountain biking, horseback riding, cross-country skiing, and snowshoeing.

Fishing

Round Valley has produced more state records than any body of water in New Jersey save the Delaware River. Deep water and secluded coves produce the best fishing in the entire state if you're looking for huge trout. A 32-pound, 8-ounce lake trout was caught here, along with record brown trout (21-pound, 6-ounce), smallmouth bass (7-pound, 2-ounce), and an American eel weighing in at 6-pound, 13-ounce. Rainbow, brook, and brown trout are stocked at a rate of 9,000 per year, and another sixteen species inhabit the reservoir, including catfish, yellow perch, pickerel, and sunfish. Round Valley is also one of New Jersey's premier spots for largemouth bass, which are sought after second only to the trout and weigh in at up to 10 pounds. A boat launch .8 mile

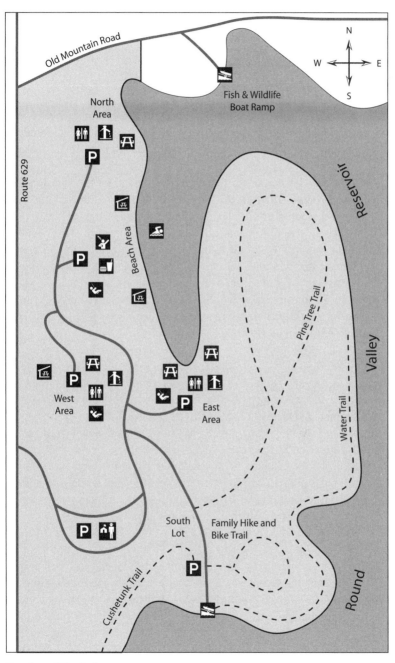

Beach and Picnic Areas

north of the park entrance has concrete ramps, but fishing from the shore anywhere along the Water Trail is almost as productive. The reservoir is a trophy trout lake subject to special restrictions, so check the latest regulations before venturing out.

Boating

Canoes, kayaks, sailboats, and motorboats are allowed on the reservoir. Paddlers tend to stick to the wooded coastline on summer weekends, because the water can get crowded with powerboats during warm weather. The boat launch at the South Lot is for campers and divers only, so boaters have to use the ramp maintained by the Division of Fish and Wildlife. Drive .8 mile north of the park entrance and turn right on Old Mountain Road. The boat ramp is immediately on the right. Unfortunately, this also means another fee—you need to show a Boat Ramp Maintenance Permit or a copy of your fishing or hunting license in your car's rear window. The closest place for a permit is the Lebanon Field Office, about .1 mile east of the boat ramp on the north side of Old Mountain Road. Motors up to 10 horsepower are allowed on the lake, and flashing lights on both dams warn boaters to come ashore when wind exceeds 25 miles per hour.

Picnicking

Four picnic areas at Round Valley offer serene spots for an afternoon if you arrive on a weekday or during the off-season. They are usually busy on summer weekends. The North Area is surrounded by relaxing scenery, with tables sitting directly at the water's edge and in private, wooded groves. The East Area offers views of the reservoir and a trail along the shore leading to the beach. Tables along the beach are popular during the summer, so the West Area sees the least activity, as it lies some distance from the water. Restrooms, grills, drinking water, and covered pavilions are available at all of the sites.

Swimming

Round Valley's swimming area is modern, developed, and extremely popular during the summer. A wide, sandy beach is open to swimmers from Memorial Day weekend through Labor Day. Picnic tables and a concession building are backed by a flagstone deck that overlooks the reservoir. The restrooms offer hot showers, a changing area, and wheelchair access. Two playgrounds and a volleyball net flank the beach, where a paved path leads to the east and north picnic grounds.

Mountain Biking

The red-blazed Cushetunk Trail is a rough 18 miles if you ride all the way to the New Jersey Water Supply Authority at the end of the trail and back. Steep inclines, fallen trees, boulders, and rocky areas will test the fitness of most riders. Bear left on the yellow-blazed Lower Cushetunk Trail 3 miles into the ride for a detour through the camp-ground, where you will find water, pit toilets, and a telephone. Another turn into the campground occurs at 6 miles, and a number of unmarked trails head north toward the Cushetunk Mountain Nature Preserve. Aside from the Family Hiking and Biking Trail, none of the other trails at Round Valley allow mountain bikes. The nearby Capoolong Trail is another out-and-back ride that overlooks Capoolong Creek and crosses several railroad bridges. See the Surrounding Points of Interest section for more information.

Horseback Riding

Horseback riding is allowed on the 9-mile Cushetunk Trail, and you will find sufficient space for trailers at the South Lot. See the Trails and Mountain Biking sections for details.

Birding

Similar to nearby Spruce Run, Round Valley is known for its population of migrating shorebirds and waterfowl in the spring and fall. Gulls, teals, mergansers, herons, loons, and grebes are all common, among others. Some of the rarer migrants include long-tailed and ring-necked ducks, great cormorants, surf scoters, red phalaropes, red-necked grebes, spotted sandpipers, and passerines such as snow buntings, American pipits, and yellow-bellied sapsuckers. Lesser black-backed, glaucous, and Bonaparte's gulls arrive in late fall.

Many visitors hope to spot the pair of bald eagles that has been nest-ing in the valley since 1995. You can sometimes see them fishing over the scuba-diving cove at the south parking lot. Other rarities seen from the same parking area include Lapland longspurs and red crossbills in the pines near the cove, and white-winged scoters, ruddy ducks, and lesser scaups in the cove itself.

The north side of the reservoir is another good birding area, harbor-ing red-headed woodpeckers and northern shrikes. Herons can be seen in the marshes bordering the east picnic area. Look near the north pic-nic area and swimming beach for loons, ducks, and gulls.

Scuba Diving

Round Valley Recreation Area is one of the few New Jersey parks where you can don a scuba tank and dive in. The diving area is accessed from the South Lot, where a pebble beach lies beyond a short, grassy slope. A small cove, where the depth is no more than 85 feet, holds an underwater training platform and sparse vegetation, but that's about it for scenery. Elsewhere on the reservoir, the bottom gradually descends to a maximum depth of 180 feet as you head toward the center of the lake. Visibility is excellent, and the water temperature exceeds 70 degrees in the summer. Diving is allowed from April 1 through October 31, and you must check in with the office before and after each dive. Your certification card, a dive buddy, and dive flag are required. The nearest dive shop is Whitehouse Aquatic Center on Route 22 west, about 3.7 miles east of Lebanon Borough.

Hunting

Round Valley allows deer hunting by special permit, and about 64 percent of the recreation area is open to the hunting of waterfowl. A variety of permits apply for various birds, among them the New Jersey Waterfowl Stamp and the Federal Migratory Bird Hunting and Conservation Stamp. Round Valley is in deer management zone 12 and the waterfowl-hunting area known as the north zone. Cushetunk Mountain Nature Preserve on the northeast side of the reservoir allows deer hunting as well, but it's county land subject to a variety of additional restrictions. For one, you need a county Hunting Access Permit. Check the Hunterdon County website for the latest regulations.

Winter Activities

Winter travelers have the right idea when it comes to finding solitude at New Jersey's more popular parks. Places where portable radios were a common sight during the summer become quiet paths along deserted picnic areas when a chill hits the air. Many migratory birds remain on the reservoir until ice forces them south, and all of Round Valley's trails are open to cross-country skiing and snowshoeing. Although Cushetunk Trail is a challenging and hilly trip, it is rarely used in the winter and makes for a great escape into the wilderness. The reservoir supports a self-sustaining population of lake trout, which means fishing is productive year-round. True ice-fishing opportunities are limited, though, as safe ice conditions rarely occur on the reservoir.

Flora and Fauna

Round Valley Reservoir is a part of New Jersey's Central Highlands, an area stretching from the Musconetcong River headwaters to the south branch of the Raritan and Lamington Rivers. Dozens of endangered, threatened, and special-concern species inhabit the area, including American bitterns, northern harriers, and red-shouldered hawks. More than 200 species of migratory birds and 19 species of fish rely on Round Valley's habitat. Plant life is similar to that at Spruce Run, with the exception of the mountainous north side of the reservoir, where tulip, beech, and hickory trees receive less sunlight than in the open valley. A variety of pines ring sections of the park, part of a 1966 reforestation project that planted 6,000 trees. Flowering dogwood, honeysuckle, and raspberry add their colors to the valley in late spring.

Surrounding Points of Interest

Voorhees State Park, Spruce Run Recreation Area, Cushetunk Mountain Nature Preserve, and Capoolong Creek Wildlife Management Area all lie within a twenty-minute drive of Round Valley. Taken together, they offer a number of hiking, fishing, and boating opportunities that make a short trip worthwhile. The Great Swamp National Wildlife Refuge is a longer drive, perhaps best saved for a separate journey. Here you will find an interesting series of boardwalks stretching through central New Jersey's only national wildlife refuge.

Cushetunk Mountain Nature Preserve

This preserve is attached to Round Valley on the northeast side of the reservoir, and most visitors won't even recognize the area as a separate park. About 380 protected acres surround Cushetunk Mountain, an area of rolling hills dominated by chestnut oak and hickory. A parking area on the north side of the reservoir gives easy access to the preserve. Drive .8 mile north on Route 629 and turn right on Old Mountain Road. Proceed 1.3 miles and turn right to stay on Old Mountain Road. Continue 1.6 miles east to the parking area on the right, just before Old Mountain Road crosses the railroad tracks. Two trails leave from the parking area. One heads directly into the preserve and stretches .5 mile to the Round Valley Recreation Area border. This trail is closed between January 1 and August 1 to protect a pair of bald eagles that returns each year to nest. The second trail follows a set of power lines and then turns south about

.5 mile from the trailhead. Both trails allow hiking and mountain biking. The trails are marked at the trailhead, but not along the trail.

Capoolong Creek Wildlife Management Area

An often-overlooked trout stream and a rail trail are the highlights of this 58-acre wildlife management area. Stretching from the hills west of Pittstown to the South Branch of the Raritan River, Capoolong Creek is stocked five times each year with a total of 3,400 trout. The rocky bottom and cool water make it a popular destination for fly fishing. An easy and scenic 3.2-mile trail follows the creek along the abandoned Lehigh Valley Railroad from Sidney to Pittstown, crossing three railroad bridges in the process. The trailhead is at the corner of Route 617 (Sidney Road) and Landsdown Road. Hikers, cross-country skiers, and mountain bikers are welcome.

Great Swamp National Wildlife Refuge

Occupying land once targeted for a 10,000-acre metropolitan airport, the Great Swamp exists in one of the most densely populated areas of central New Jersey. The 7,600-acre refuge harbors wildlife considered rare anywhere in the United States, including 244 species of birds, 29 species of fish, and 600 varieties of plants and wildflowers. Fields, forests, swamps, rivers, springs, and floodplains support endangered species such as the blue-spotted salamander. Open fields throughout the swamp are home to the largest population of nesting eastern bluebirds in New Jersey.

A set of boardwalks hovers above the swamp, beginning at Lord Stirling Environmental Education Center on the west end of the refuge. Most hikers linger around a small lake near the office, but it usually gets lonely about half a mile farther along the trail. Pick up a map at the information center and follow the intertwined trails to Boondocks Boardwalk, deep within the swamp. At times the vegetation forms a tunnel around the boardwalk as you forge ahead. Follow the Red Trail near the western edge of the refuge on the way back, past Woodpecker Swamp and an immense old oak tree nicknamed the Great Swamp Oak. The complete loop is about 3 miles.

The refuge is a bit of a drive, about 20 miles, but it's worth the detour to see one of New Jersey's few national preserves. Drive east on I-78 for 13.7 miles to exit 33 (Route 525 north toward Bernardsville). Proceed north on Route 525 for 1.7 miles and turn right on Lyons Road. Continue east on Lyons Road for 1.8 miles and turn right on Cross Road.

Drive .6 mile to the end of Cross Road and turn left on Maple Avenue. Drive .5 mile, turn right on Lord Stirling Road, and proceed 1 mile to the environmental center on the left.

Where to Buy Supplies

Kings Plaza lies 5 miles east on Route 22 east in Whitehouse Station, where you will find a bagel shop, pharmacy, grocery store, and bank. Lebanon Borough, bordering the north side of the recreation area, is a small town equipped with a few basic services along Main Street and Route 22. On Main Street, you will find a deli, general store, and pizzeria. If you head east on Route 22, you will come to a deli and Dunkin' Donuts on the right in less than a mile. Lebanon Bait and Sport Shop is on Route 22 west near the east end of Main Street. Head west on Route 22 from Lebanon Borough and you will come to a bagel shop, pizzeria, and a few auto repair garages all within 2 miles. Continue west for about 1.5 miles to Clinton (Exit 15) for almost anything a camper needs, including grocery stores, pharmacies, banks, sporting goods, restaurants, and car repair.

Delaware and Raritan Canal State Park (Bull's Island)

Delaware and Raritan Canal State Park
145 Mapleton Rd.
Princeton, NJ 08540
Bull's Island
2185 Daniel Bray Highway
Stockton, NJ 08559

Area. Delaware and Raritan Canal State Park: 5,379 acres.
Bull's Island: 80 acres.

Park office. The Bull's Island office is located in Hunterdon County, 3.3 miles north of Stockton Borough on the west side of Route 29.

Highlights. Delaware River, Delaware and Raritan Canal, canal towpath, numerous historical points of interest.

Activities. Camping, hiking, fishing, boating, picnicking, mountain biking, horseback riding, birding, cross-country skiing.

Entrance fee. None.

Park hours. Year-round, from dawn to dusk.

For additional information:
Delaware and Raritan Canal State Park (609) 924-5705
Bull's Island (609) 397-2949

During the early 1800s, the only practical way to transport freight over long distances was by water. Construction began in 1830 on the Delaware and Raritan Canal, a waterway meant to solve the transportation gap between the growing cities of New York and Philadelphia. Much of the canal was dug by hand at the expense of Irish immigrants, who suffered disease, malnutrition, and sometimes death in the process. It became one of America's busiest canals, surpassing the total tonnage transported on the Erie Canal by 1871. Steam power supplanted mules in the 1840s, and the Belvidere Delaware Railroad signaled the canal's demise around 1892, when the waterway recorded its last profitable year. The state took charge of the failing canal in 1932 for use as a water supply, and the land was dedicated as a state park in 1974.

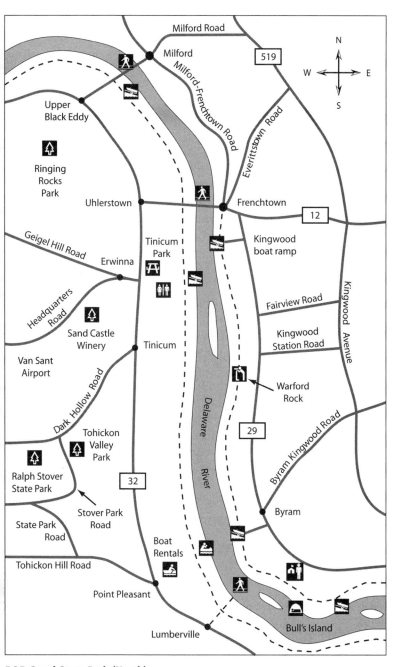

D&R Canal State Park (North)

Delaware and Raritan Canal State Park is no more than 300 yards wide, a thin ribbon of land clinging to the banks of a 70-mile-long canal. The canal runs along the east bank of the Delaware River from Bull's Island to Trenton and then curves inland and northward to meet the Raritan River near New Brunswick. A towpath once used by mules to pull barges of freight extends a total of 65.3 miles alongside the canal. Six bridges crossing the Delaware River connect the towpath on the New Jersey side to a 60-mile towpath on the Pennsylvania side, resulting in one of the most extensive trail systems in the area. Covered bridges, canal locks, and eighteenth-century inns line both sides of the Delaware, providing endless sources of exploration for paddlers, cyclists, hikers, and joggers. The park's only campground is encircled by water on Bull's Island, one of about a dozen main islands along the canal, where visitors will find a picnic area, two boat launches, and access to more than 100 miles of unbroken trail.

Camping

Campsites rest in forested clearings overlooking the water on Bull's Island, an 80-acre strip of land encircled by the Delaware River and the adjacent canal. The island is attached by footbridge to both Pennsylvania and New Jersey, so anyone pitching a tent along the riverbank will own a view of two states and the Delaware River. A few of the campsites are large enough to hold small trailers, but the park accommodates those seeking an escape from motorized vehicles as well. The northwest corner of the island is off-limits to cars, and the sound of flowing water seeps through tent walls at night.

Directions. The campground lies about 100 yards north of the park office.

Sites and facilities. The park's sixty-nine tent and trailer sites are each equipped with a fire ring and picnic table. Modern restrooms with hot showers, water from ground pumps, a playground, and a trailer sanitary station are scattered throughout the campground. One canoe launch lies next to the park office, and you will find a boat ramp on the south side of the island. The campground is open from April 1 through October 31.

Recommended sites. The river view from sites 64 through 69 is relaxing, a serenity multiplied by the fact that this section of the campground is not accessible by car. Sites 56 through 63 also lie on the quiet north side of the campground, where the Delaware and Raritan Canal is

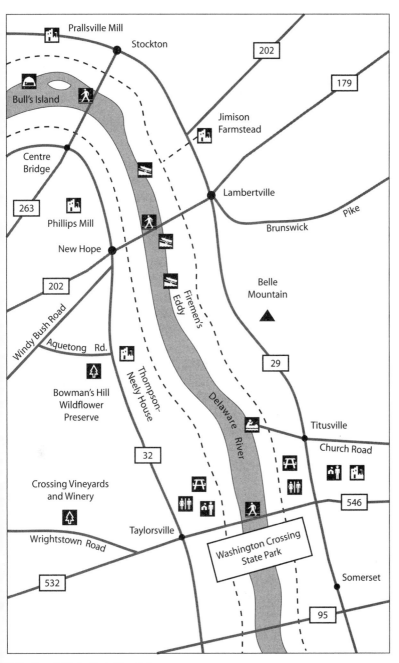

D&R Canal State Park (South)

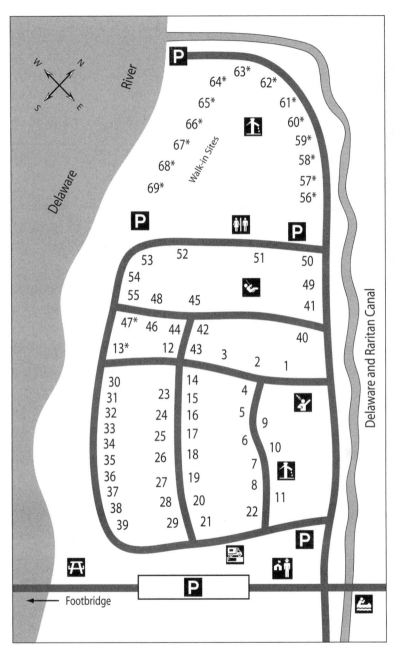

Bull's Island Family Campground

barely visible beyond the campground access road. A number of wooded and spacious sites hold views of the Delaware River but are not directly onshore, including numbers 13, 30 through 39, and 47. The remaining sites on the island are well spaced and private, separated from one another by silver maple, red cedar, and bayberry.

Trails

The two canal towpaths paralleling the Delaware River combine to form 91.4 miles of unbroken trail—31.4 miles on the New Jersey side, from Frenchtown to Trenton, and 60 miles on the Pennsylvania side, from Easton to Bristol. If you include the section of the towpath that heads toward the Raritan River from Trenton to New Brunswick, you can add another 33.9 miles. Sections of the flat trails are surfaced with asphalt or gravel, so the attraction is not taking a challenging mountain bike ride or achieving a mountain pass, but what can be found along the trail.

The towpath stretches past covered bridges, stone locktender cabins, and secluded picnic areas. Many points along the way provide an opportunity to stop for food in a quiet café, climb to the top of a scenic cliff, or admire an eighteenth-century country inn. By using the six bridges that cross the Delaware between Trenton and Milford, you can form a loop long or short enough to satisfy almost any schedule. Parking is available at several areas along the towpath. See the Surrounding Points of Interest section for detailed accounts of the routes, attractions, and facilities to the north and south of Bull's Island.

Activities

The main pursuits at Bull's Island surround the towpath, Delaware River, and adjacent canal. A tour of the surrounding towns, cafés, and historical sites will always be popular with visitors, whether by car or by bicycle along the towpath. Paddling a canoe down the Delaware and Raritan Canal is a serene and natural alternative, avoiding the pedestrians that sometimes gather around tourist towns like Lambertville and New Hope. Fishing is excellent in the Delaware, which has produced more state records than any other body of water in New Jersey, and a green strip of forested land following the canal provides areas for birding, picnicking, and biking.

New Jersey Towpath Mileage

Destinations North of Bull's Island

TOWPATH LANDMARK	MILES NORTH	FACILITIES
Byram boat ramp	0.8	Delaware access
Warford Rock	5.0	Overlook
Kingwood Station Road	5.5	Trail access
Fairview Road	6.6	Crossroad
Kingwood boat ramp	7.9	Delaware access
Frenchtown (Bridge Street)	8.9	Food/lodging

Destinations South of Bull's Island

TOWPATH LANDMARK	MILES SOUTH	FACILITIES
Prallsville Mill	2.8	Parking
Stockton (Bridge Street)	3.3	Food/lodging
Route 202 overpass	5.5	Landmark
Jimison Farmstead	5.6	Parking
Lambertville (Bridge Street)	6.7	Food/lodging
Firemen's Eddy	8.3	Delaware access
Belle Mountain	9.1	Landmark
Canal bridge	11.7	Landmark
Titusville (Church Street)	12.4	Canal bridge
Washington Crossing State Park	13.5	Restrooms/picnic area
I-95 overpass	16.3	Landmark

Fishing

Almost every New Jersey angler knows about the Delaware River's reputation for producing trophy fish. Huge carp linger around Bull's Island, where a state record weighing 42 pounds, 1 ounce was landed in 1987. Other state records caught in the Delaware River include a 29-pound tiger muskellunge, an 11-pound, 2-ounce American shad, and a 13-pound, 10-ounce walleye. Smallmouth bass, catfish, white perch, and American eel are abundant around Bull's Island.

The canal allows fishing as well and provides a good escape from the flotilla of boats that ply the Delaware during the summer. The section near Bull's Island is stocked seven times each year, totaling more than 14,000 trout. Gigantic carp can be found in the canal, where a state-record grass carp was landed in 1996 weighing in at a backbreaking 49 pounds, 3 ounces. Catfish, American eels, and largemouth bass are also abundant, along with lesser populations of smallmouth bass and pickerel.

Boating

The towpath can be crowded near the heavily touristed towns along the Delaware and may not mesh with the idea of a natural weekend spent birding or fishing. The solution is to ply the canal. Canoes, kayaks, and small boats with electric motors are allowed on 58 miles of water from Bull's Island to Trenton and from Trenton to the Raritan River. Bull's Island offers a canoe launch on the canal in addition to a boat ramp on the Delaware. Farther afield, a number of canoe access points line the canal from Trenton to Milford. If you're searching for seclusion, try the remote canoe access points at Jimison Farmstead or Firemen's Eddy. Bucks County River Country, across the Bull's Island bridge in Point Pleasant, rents canoes, kayaks, inner tubes, and rafts.

The Delaware River has no motor restrictions, and you can put in at any of the eight launch sites lining the shores. Bull's Island supplies a boat ramp, but you will also find ramps to the north at Byram and Kingwood Access in New Jersey and at Tinicum Park and Upper Black Eddy in Pennsylvania. South of Bull's Island, Jimison Farmstead, Lambertville, and Firemen's Eddy offer boat ramps in New Jersey. Only small boats can be launched from Tinicum Park or Firemen's Eddy, and the latter requires four-wheel drive if you're launching from a trailer. None of the boat ramps require a fee except Kingwood, which asks for a boat ramp permit or a hunting or fishing license.

Picnicking

If you don't mind dispensing with a picnic table, paddlers and bikers will find dozens of wooded clearings and serene coves lining the towpath and the Delaware River. Because trash is an ongoing problem on the river, many canoe liveries will not allow you to take along any containers. If you do, be sure to pack out everything you carry in. Several traditional picnic areas equipped with tables, restrooms, and water can be found at Bull's Island, Frenchtown, Stockton, Lambertville, and Washington Crossing in New Jersey, as well as Tinicum Park, Centre Bridge, and New Hope in Pennsylvania.

Mountain Biking

This is the perfect park to explore by bicycle. Although the towpath is not a challenging off-road experience, the number of small towns, quiet cafés, and historic sites along the trail could keep a traveler distracted for weeks. The 91.4-mile route along the Delaware River stretches over a variety of easy surfaces, including crushed rock, pavement, and packed dirt. A number of shops between Lambertville and Frenchtown rent bikes, including Lumberville General Store near Bull's Island, New Hope Cyclery on York Road, and Cycle Corner of Frenchtown on Bridge Street. Sections of the towpath on the Pennsylvania side are regularly affected by flooding, but the damaged areas are usually passable by mountain bike. See the Surrounding Points of Interest section for detailed accounts of the routes to the north and south of Bull's Island.

Horseback Riding

No horses are allowed on the canal towpath near Bull's Island, but a short drive will take you to the Raritan River section of the towpath, 33.9 miles long, where horses are welcome and trailer parking abounds. See the Main Canal Towpath section for directions and parking and trail details. Washington Crossing State Park, also covered below, offers a 2.5-mile horse trail and ample parking for trailers.

Birding

The canal, river, and adjacent strip of forested land provide diverse habitat for birds, where more than 150 species visit during migration and almost 90 species nest in spring. The canal attracts herons, egrets, and other waterbirds, and the woodland along the canal banks provides a good place to look for warblers. A variety of nesting warblers inhabit the islands of the Delaware River north of Bull's Island, most notably yellow-throated, prothonotary, and cerulean warblers. Ospreys, black vultures, and red-shouldered hawks can occasionally be seen circling over the water. Several of the rare and breeding species seen around Bull's Island include clay-colored sparrows, Mississippi kites, northern parulas, bald eagles, Louisiana waterthrushes, and yellow-throated vireos.

Winter Activities

Camping at Bull's Island ends in November, but cross-country skiing is welcome on the towpath, along with winter hiking and jogging. Boaters use the Delaware year-round, and the colder months produce good catches of walleye and smallmouth bass. Birding can be productive, as several species linger on the open water of the Delaware before heading south. Red-throated and common loons, lesser scaups, buffleheads, ring-necked and American black ducks, ring-billed gulls, and great blue herons can be seen through February. Bald eagles overwinter in the area but are usually seen farther north along the Kittatinny cliffs.

Flora and Fauna

About 24 acres southeast of the campground make up the Bull's Island Natural Area, a woodland dominated by river birch, slippery elm, red oak, silver maple, and sycamore. The island is one of many along the Delaware River, a natural corridor that encompasses a series of habitats as it travels south to the sea. The Delaware does not encounter one dam in its 330-mile journey past the borders of four states, making it the longest free-flowing river in the eastern United States. This unbroken flow is essential for fish species that depend on migration and spawning runs, such as American shad, striped bass, and river herring. The endangered shortnose sturgeon, a fish that migrates from salt water in order to breed, is known to spawn in the Lambertville area.

Dozens of rare and endangered species make use of the Delaware River corridor for migration, breeding, and foraging, including animals such as the bald eagle, bog turtle, and gray fox. Four endangered or threatened bat species inhabit the river areas around Upper Bucks and Hunterdon Counties. The Delaware River's upper and lower floodplains support a wide variety of trees such as white pine, Norway maple, black oak, sycamore, and willow. Rare vegetation such as sand cherry, prickly pear cactus, and hoary willow rely on the watershed for a foothold in New Jersey. Add to the list more than 20 species of fish, 180 species of birds, and countless reptiles, amphibians, shrubs, and herbs. The Delaware River Watershed receives various levels of protection along its course and has proven to be a fragile and perishable resource in a quickly developing area of New Jersey.

Surrounding Points of Interest

If you cycle down New Jersey's towpath and return on Pennsylvania's version, you will find towns facing each other in seeming competition. Historic stone mills, century-old farmsteads, bridgetender houses, and gift shops with suffixes like "on-the-Delaware" vie for superiority across each bridge, eddy, and bend in the river. Walk across the bridge from Bull's Island to Lumberville and you will come across the Black Bass Hotel, a 1740 country inn with tables overlooking the water. The Lumberville General Store began as a 1770 stone home and today offers bicycle rentals and a small deli. Similar shops are scattered along the river to the north and south, and the best way to discover many of the sights is to hop on a bicycle and explore.

Stockton and Centre Bridge

Three bridges span the Delaware along the stretch of river between Bull's Island and Washington Crossing State Park, 13.6 miles to the south. The tiny town of Stockton, only 3.3 miles to the south, is a village of eighteenth-century inns and mills along the Delaware River. Stockton Inn began as a stone cabin in 1710, later converted to include an inn, garden restaurant, and wishing well made famous by songwriter Richard Rodgers in the 1936 Broadway hit "There's a Small Hotel with a Wishing Well." The Woolverton Inn, built in 1792, is worth a visit for the grand style and surrounding countryside, but be prepared for the five-star prices if you want to spend the night. The remainder of Stockton retains the feel of a small river town with a lot of history, including an 1869 Presbyterian church and the oldest three-room schoolhouse in New Jersey, built in 1872.

You will find a number of sites within a short bike ride of Stockton. Prallsville Mill, a linseed oil mill that began operation in 1720, lies .5 mile to the north. A masonry mill replaced the original wooden structure in 1874, and the site is now home to an art gallery, gristmill, and parking for towpath hikers. Across the river from Stockton, the town of Centre Bridge was first settled in 1704 and holds several eighteenth-century homes and cottages, including the former studio of impressionist painter Edward Willis Redfield, who lived in Centre Bridge until his death in 1965. Traveling south from Centre Bridge brings you past a Pennsylvania historic district and Phillips Mill, a 1756 gristmill that serves today's artists as a center for forums and exhibits.

Lambertville and New Hope

Travel 3.3 miles south of Stockton and you will come to the tandem towns of Lambertville and New Hope, together representing the most visited area along the entire towpath. Both of the Colonial-era towns support all of the history, art, and architecture that makes seeking out small towns worthwhile. Museums, art centers, and historic inns abound on both sides of the river. You will also find endless gift shops, ice cream parlors, restaurants, theme shopping malls, and antique dealers. New Hope, across the bridge, harbors a visitor center and the offices of a conservation group called the Friends of the Delaware Canal.

Several interesting destinations lie to the north and south of the two cities. Head south of Lambertville for 1.7 miles to Firemen's Eddy, a boat ramp area providing one of the more serene access points on the Delaware River. Jimison Farmstead, 1 mile north of Lambertville, has occupied the land since 1711 and offers a large parking area on the canal with access for canoes. Head south of New Hope for 2.3 miles and you will arrive at the 134-acre Bowman's Hill Wildflower Preserve, which harbors more than 1,000 native plants and wildflowers.

Washington Crossing State Park

Travel 6.9 miles south of Lambertville and you will arrive at Washington Crossing State Park, marking the point where Washington's Continental Army crossed the Delaware before marching on the Hessian garrison at Trenton. On New Jersey's side of the Delaware, Nelson House marks the site where the Continental Army organized after the crossing, and Johnson Ferry House is where the officers gathered before the march on Trenton. On the Pennsylvania side is McConkey's Ferry Inn, where troops gathered on the night of December 25, 1776, before fording the river.

Seven main trails, four picnic areas, and four group campsites are scattered throughout the 3,126-acre New Jersey section. A good place to start is the visitor center, where you will find maps of the trails, restrooms, a playground, and a nearby open-air theater. Four marked hiking trails ranging from .9 to 2 miles begin near the theater, and several trails leave from the nature center about a mile to the north. One marked trail open to horseback riding extends 2.5 miles through a natural area north of the nature center, and one 5-mile trail allows mountain biking on the east side of the park. The four group campsites accommodate from fifteen to fifty campers and are equipped with fire rings, picnic tables, and chemical toilets. The campsites require a reservation and are open from April 1 through October 31.

Point Pleasant

Cross over the Bull's Island bridge into Pennsylvania and head north 1.8 miles to arrive at Point Pleasant. Bucks County River Country on Walters Lane rents canoes, inner tubes, rafts, and kayaks. Point Pleasant Village Store serves breakfast and lunch. Checking in at the Tattersall Inn will get you a private room in an eighteenth-century fieldstone mansion. About 1.8 miles to the north of Point Pleasant on Cafferty Road is Tohickon Valley Park, where you will find fishing in Tohickon Creek, twenty-two campsites, and four cabins. Drive about .9 mile north of Point Pleasant on Tohickon Hill Road and turn right on State Park Road to arrive at Ralph Stover State Park, home to a picnic area, whitewater kayaking, and a panoramic view of Tohickon Creek from High Rocks Overlook.

Erwinna

Travel 5.5 miles north of Point Pleasant and you will arrive at Erwinna, a town of scenic parks, plane rides, and historical inns. Overlooking the river are the eighteenth-century EverMay on the Delaware and the nineteenth-century Golden Pheasant Inn, two country escapes replete with amenities like twin fireplaces, private Jacuzzis, and predinner sherry served in the parlor. North of the two inns, the many picnic tables at Tinicum Park provide a good place to stop for a break. Here you will also find a boat ramp, restrooms, and a small campground. Van Sant Airport to the west offers biplane and glider rides, as well as an opportunity to see a collection of rare airplanes. Sand Castle Winery is just off River Road and usually schedules events on weekends. Antique dealers and gift shops are ever present along the Delaware, and Erwinna is no exception, adding its small share to the unbroken string of specialty shops stretching to New Hope.

Frenchtown

If you head north of Bull's Island on the New Jersey side to Frenchtown, you will pass two boat launch areas and Warford Rock, a scenic overlook of the Delaware River. Frenchtown itself was settled prior to the Revolutionary War but acquired its name when the French-speaking Paul Henri Mallet settled on 1,000 acres in 1795. The tiny borough retains the feel of a small river community, where café-lined streets, art studios, gift shops, and eighteenth-century inns occupy an area of one square mile. The Guesthouse at Frenchtown is a 1780 Colonial cottage, and the National Hotel has been renting rooms since 1851. Cycle Corner of Frenchtown sits on the corner of Bridge Street and Route 29, if you want to rent a bike or need repairs. Cross the Delaware River into Uhlerstown and head west on Uhlerstown Hill Road to see an 1832 covered bridge, the only one spanning Pennsylvania's Delaware Canal.

Milford and Upper Black Eddy

The towpath on the New Jersey side ends at Frenchtown, but you can continue on the Pennsylvania side to the towns of Milford and Upper Black Eddy, 3.2 miles north of Uhlerstown. Upper Black Eddy in Pennsylvania is surrounded by river scenery, state parks, and country stores. Ringing Rocks Park, about 1.5 miles west on Ringing Rocks Road, is a 7-acre field filled with boulders that ring like bells when struck properly. Several local musicians actually performed here for the Learning Channel using rocks of various sizes and tones. The park office for Pennsylvania's Delaware Canal State Park is nearby as well, 1.5 miles south of Upper Black Eddy on Lodi Hill Road.

Located across the Delaware River, the town of Milford was settled in 1750 and holds several affordable and unique restaurants mixed in with the usual specialty shops. Occupying an 1860 Victorian mansion and emulating a pub from the English countryside, the Ship Inn Restaurant was the first brewpub in New Jersey, offering a variety of microbrewed ales to accompany a pub-style menu. Milford Oyster House, set in a nineteenth-century stone mill, combines a restaurant and tavern with fresh seafood at reasonable rates. Milford Station is a casual restaurant on the Delaware that occupies an old train station, and the bakery down the road carries fresh-baked bread. If you feel like driving into the countryside, Volendam Windmill Museum is a 68-foot windmill on Adamic Hill Road once used for grinding grain, and Alba Vineyard is about 8 miles north in Finesville.

Main Canal Towpath

The towpath that extends 31.4 miles south from Frenchtown to Trenton already represents one of the longest trails in New Jersey, but the trail does not simply end in Trenton. An entirely new section heads northeast along the Raritan River part of the canal, known as the Main Canal, extending 33.9 miles from Trenton to New Brunswick. The path begins as crushed gravel, but the 30.4 miles of the trail above Bakers Basin Road consist of packed dirt. This is a popular route for runners and mountain bikers, and it is the only section of the towpath open to horses.

The towpath stretches past an array of parks, natural areas, and historical sites. The section between Princeton and Kingston offers a canal lock and locktender's house, access to Carnegie Lake, and parking for horse trailers. Griggstown, about 5 miles north of Kingston, supports a preserved bridgetender's house, a wooden canal bridge, canoe rentals, parking, and a picnic area. The park office for this section of the canal is at Blackwells Mills, 3.5 miles north of Griggstown, where you will find an 1835 canal house, a picnic area, and a wooden bridge spanning the canal. Adjacent to Blackwells Mills lies Six Mile Run Reservoir, a 3,000-acre area encompassing fields, horse trails, and conspicuously, no water. A reservoir planned for the site in 1970 never materialized, but the original name remained unchanged after the project was abandoned.

Where to Buy Supplies

If you are camped at Bull's Island, Lumberville General Store across the bridge carries staples such as bread, milk, and canned goods. Stockton, only 3.3 miles south of Bull's Island, has a small market and a few specialty restaurants. More substantive supplies can be found in the touristed towns along the canal. Lambertville and New Hope, about 7 miles south of the campground, contain pharmacies, gas stations, convenience stores, banks, and a variety of restaurants. Travel across the bridge to New Hope for two supermarkets. The capital city of Trenton is another 15 miles south of Lambertville, complete with sporting-goods stores, medical clinics, auto repair, hotels, and almost anything else a traveler needs.

Drive 8.9 miles north of Bull's Island to Frenchtown for a grocery store, cafés, pizza parlors, and delis. Frenchtown holds a bicycle shop offering rentals and repairs. In Milford, another 3.5 miles north, you'll find a pharmacy, food market, deli, and a variety of restaurants. If you are looking for historic hotels, bed-and-breakfast inns, specialty restaurants, antique stores, or ice cream parlors, travel to virtually any town along the Delaware. See the Surrounding Points of Interest section for specifics.

Cheesequake State Park

300 Gordon Rd.
Matawan, NJ 07747

Area. 1,361 acres.

Park office. The park entrance is in Middlesex County, 1.9 miles west of Matawan at the three-way intersection between Cliffwood Avenue, Morristown Road, and Gordon Road. From the intersection, drive north on Gordon Road for .8 mile to the park office on the right.

Highlights. Cheesequake Natural Area, Arrowsmith Point.

Activities. Camping, hiking, fishing, boating, picnicking, swimming, mountain biking, birding, cross-country skiing, snowshoeing.

Entrance fee. An entrance fee is charged from Memorial Day weekend through Labor Day.

Park hours. Year-round, from 8 A.M. to dusk.

For additional information: (732) 566-2161

Encompassing almost 1,400 acres of tidal salt marsh, upland hardwood forest, pineland, streams, and fields, Cheesequake State Park maintains a foothold in the midst of central New Jersey's fast-paced development. Only a few miles from Staten Island, the park still harbors more than 100 species of birds and a wide-ranging habitat that is difficult to find within the borders of any other single park. Fifty-three campsites and five marked trails give access to the quiet areas of Cheesequake, and a modern recreation area accommodates thousands of visitors every year. Picnicking, biking, birding, and fishing are popular pursuits in this small, green corner of Middlesex County.

Camping

Cheesequake's only family camping area and six group sites are situated in a wooded oasis bordered by the Garden State Parkway to the south and west and Route 689 to the east. No need to prepare for a stay in the wilderness—the modern campgrounds are located within 1.3 miles of a food concession, public beach, and six picnic areas. The

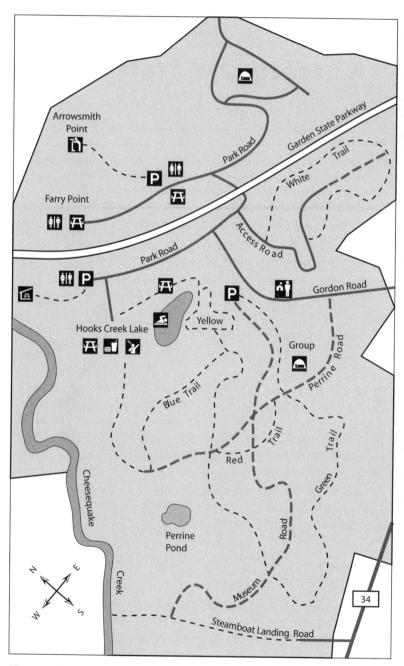

Cheesequake State Park

majority of the sites are large enough to accommodate almost any vehicle, although there is an 11-foot height restriction on trailers. The park is a popular weekend camping destination from the New York boroughs because it is situated within a few miles of several popular New Jersey restaurants, boardwalks, and beaches.

Family Campground

Ringed by a forest of chestnut oak and pitch pine, the family campground is separated from the main activity of the park. The office, recreation area, and Hooks Creek Lake lie on the other side of the parkway, while some of the more solitary attractions surround the campground. Arrowsmith Point and its nesting ospreys are less than a mile to the north. Farry Point, a good birding spot and the most secluded picnic area in the park, is a short drive beyond the osprey nesting grounds. A visit during the quiet days of early spring and late fall can be surprisingly serene, when the bustle of summer is reduced to a relaxing lull.

Directions. Turn right out of the park office, drive .3 mile, and turn right on the campground access road. Proceed .3 mile, turn right on Park Road, and continue .5 mile to the campground.

Sites and facilities. Cheesequake's fifty-three tent and trailer sites each contain a fire ring and picnic table, with water from ground pumps nearby. One restroom with flush toilets and hot showers lies next to the playground. A trailer sanitary station is located across from site 47. The campground is open from April 1 through October 31.

Recommended sites. Some of the campsites are perched on a hilltop, and others overlook small meadows. The north end of the campground benefits from less traffic noise, and here numbers 41, 43, 45, 46, and 47 sit on a slight rise away from the road. Site 46 is the most private of the group, and 47 holds a nice view of a meadow, although it is very close to site 48. Sites 16 and 20 are also set back from the road, with rows of trees screening both neighbors. Sites 25, 26, and 27 are fairly isolated but near highway traffic.

Gordon Field Group Campground

Gordon Field, divided into sites A through F, lies next to the Cheesequake Natural Area and many of the park's trails. The park office, interpretive center, and recreation area are all within walking distance. Each of the six sites accommodates up to twenty-five campers and is equipped with fire rings, grills, and picnic tables. Modern restrooms and ground pumps are close at hand, but the restrooms do not contain showers. Turn

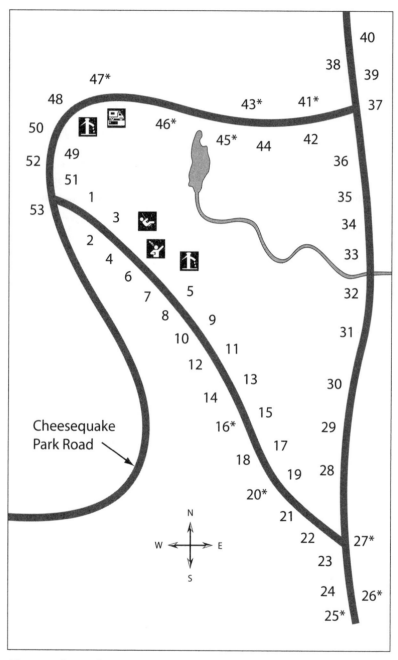

Cheesequake Family Campground

left out of the park office onto Gordon Road, drive .1 mile, and turn right onto the campground access road. Proceed .3 mile to Gordon Field. Group camping is available from May 1 through October 31.

Trails

Four hiking trails marked by color—yellow, green, blue, and red—run through the Cheesequake Natural Area and are intertwined in a series of loops totaling about 6 miles. The Yellow Trail begins at the recreation area and circles Hooks Creek Lake, joining the other three trails after winding .5 mile along the edge of a salt marsh and through patches of highbush blueberry. The Green Trail, the longest in the park at 3.5 miles, crosses through a variety of environments that define Cheesequake's landscape. The beginning is typical pine forest, but after you cross over two boardwalks, the trail enters a freshwater swamp of Atlantic white cedar, winterberry holly, and sweet bay magnolia. Circle around to the east, over another boardwalk, and you're in a dry forest again, surrounded by red oak, black birch, and a stand of 150-year-old white pine.

The Blue and Red Trails add another 1.7 miles to the circuit, but all of the trails through Cheesequake Natural Area are open exclusively to hiking, cross-country skiing, and snowshoeing. A fifth trail, the White Trail, is the only one in the park that allows mountain biking. At 1.4 miles, it stretches through what was once a second group campground known as Booth Field, first running alongside a closed access road, then

Trail Mileage and Difficulty

TRAIL	MILES	DIFFICULTY	BLAZE	USES
Blue Trail	1.0	E	blue	h,s,x
Green Trail	3.5	E	green	h,s,x
Museum Road	1.7	E	no blaze	h,s,x
Perrine Road	1.0	E	no blaze	h,s,x
Red Trail	0.7	E	red	h,s,x
Steamboat Landing Road	0.8	E	no blaze	h,m,s,x
White Trail	1.7	E	white	h,m,s,x
White Trail access road	1.0	E	no blaze	h,m,s,x
Yellow Trail	0.8	E	yellow	h,s,x

continuing on to parallel the Garden State Parkway. Check the Mountain Biking section for more on this trail and the surrounding dirt roads.

Activities

Cheesequake's recreation area sees the majority of action during warm weather. Hooks Creek Lake is surrounded by a swimming beach, three picnic areas, a food concession, two playgrounds, and modern restrooms. Fishing is allowed in Hooks Creek Lake, which is stocked with trout three times each year. The more remote areas of the park support hiking, mountain biking, birding, and cross-country skiing. One of the most rewarding endeavors at Cheesequake is a simple nature walk along the Green Trail, a hike that passes through a wide array of habitats ranging from freshwater marsh to pineland.

Cheesequake Natural Area

The different habitats found within Cheesequake can be seen all along the East Coast, but rarely will you find them concentrated in one small area. Located south of Hooks Creek Lake, the Cheesequake Natural Area makes up almost one-third of Cheesequake State Park. At 386 acres, it encompasses an amazing variety of terrain and wildlife that includes open fields, salt marsh, Atlantic white cedar swamp, six varieties of pines, and eleven different species of oaks. The swamp contains an array of uncommon plants and wildflowers, such as round-leaf sundew, yellow-fringed orchid, and marsh rose gentian. Four of Cheesequake's five trails access the area. The 3.5-mile Green Trail stretches through a good cross section of the many habitats, including a freshwater swamp, hardwood forest, and a rare stand of old-growth white pine. See the Flora and Fauna section for more information about the wildlife found in the Cheesequake Natural Area.

Arrowsmith Point

A short drive north from the family campground brings you to Arrowsmith Point, where ospreys have been nesting atop a set of poles in the salt marsh since 1997. Hike the short trail leading from the parking area until you come to a fork; then continue along to the right for the best view. Three poles usually support at least two pairs of ospreys, with adults on the nest by late March and chicks hatching as early as April. This can be a private walk before the warm weather brings a steady stream of birders in May. Take the left fork for an additional walk of about 200 yards, where a pavilion overlooking the salt marsh caters to hikers. Ospreys begin foraging in the area around mid-March, staying until the chicks are ready to fly south in late September.

Fishing and Boating

Hooks Creek Lake is stocked with more than 2,000 trout in early spring and another 500 in December. Up to 300 channel catfish and 100 bluegills are added certain years as well, and the lake sustains a small population of largemouth bass. Fishing is allowed by boat or from the shore, although boats are allowed on Hooks Creek Lake only from the day after Labor Day through the day before Memorial Day weekend. Canoes, kayaks, and small boats with electric motors are welcome. Anglers are also within 15 miles of several saltwater opportunities, including the Sandy Hook Gateway National Recreation Area, covered below.

Picnicking

Six picnic areas are scattered throughout the park, three next to the Garden State Parkway and three grouped around the recreation area. The most peaceful site rests next to Hooks Creek Lake, about 100 yards from the beginning of the Yellow Trail. Here you will find tables and grills on a small hill overlooking the lake. Water, grills, and parking are provided at all sites, and restrooms are within walking distance. Groups of twenty or more can reserve picnic areas at least five days in advance, but tables cannot be reserved on weekends between Memorial Day and Labor Day.

Swimming

Cheesequake's popular beach is open from Memorial Day through Labor Day. A developed recreation area surrounds the beach, complete with basketball courts, two playgrounds, a food concession, and modern restrooms with hot showers. Two picnic areas and parking for about 100 cars cater to visitors throughout the summer.

Mountain Biking

The White Trail begins east of the park office and runs 1.4 miles over a narrow dirt track. Although it parallels the parkway at some points, the trail is rarely used and usually quiet. An abandoned road leading to the White Trail adds another mile, making the total route a modest 2.4 miles of dirt track and paved road. Steamboat Landing Road (shown as

Dock Road on some maps) is another dirt track beginning on Route 34 about 2.6 miles west of the park office. Turn left out of the park office on Gordon Road, drive .8 mile, and continue straight onto Morristown Road. Proceed 1 mile, turn right on Route 34, and drive .8 mile to Steamboat Landing Road on the right. The road looks like a paved highway at first, but it soon turns into a dirt track leading through hardwood forest and cedar swamp. About .8 mile brings you to a spot known as Steamboat Landing on Cheesequake Creek, where early settlers shipped supplies 2 miles inland from the nearest port. Only .2 mile south of the landing, Museum Road splits off from Steamboat Landing Road and reaches into the Cheesequake Natural Area. Museum Road intersects with several of Cheesequake's marked trails, all off-limits to bikes, but you can ride about .4 mile up to the Green Trail and back.

Birding

Cheesequake is one of the few undisturbed tracts of land in Middlesex County along the Atlantic Flyway, and the park's wide-ranging habitat supports a number of species that are often elusive to casual observers. Warblers fly through in mid-May, including migrants such as Kentucky and worm-eating warblers. The salt marshes support black-crowned night herons, great egrets, and nesting green herons, as well as nesting ospreys at Arrowsmith Point. Flycatchers and thrushes inhabit the upland hardwood forest, and winter brings short-eared owls, common redpolls, and rough-legged hawks. Some notable species seen at the end of Steamboat Landing Road include black-necked stilts, black-billed cuckoos, king rails, solitary vireos, prairie warblers, and soras. Spring migration is the best time to visit this often overlooked birding area in central New Jersey.

Winter Activities

Although camping at Cheesequake ends in November, the park is open year-round for a handful of activities. The interpretive center remains staffed from Wednesday through Sunday during the winter, and cross-country skiing is allowed on the trails, open fields, and roadways. All of the trails allow snowshoeing, and you will sometimes see sledders on the hill next to the recreation area. A number of scheduled events occur throughout the winter, usually meeting at the interpretive center next to the office. Subjects range from basic backpacking techniques to guided walks with a naturalist. Check with the park's staff for a current schedule.

Flora and Fauna

The number of different habitats that are squeezed into this small plot of land creates a rare combination. Coastal salt marshes and freshwater cedar swamps dominate sections of the park, yet the Lenni-Lenape named this area Cheseh-oh-ke, meaning upland. Indeed, there are upland areas here as well, in the form of pine-oak forest and oak-hardwood forest supporting American beech, white pine, red maple, and a wide variety of oaks that includes eleven different species. A freshwater marsh, an area of pine forest, and a number of lakes, ponds, and streams add their contribution to the mix, creating a diversity found in very few places elsewhere in the state.

The unique ecosystem is responsible for an array of wildlife that seems almost ironic only 20 miles from New York City. The increasingly rare large marsh pink is found in the salt marsh, a dark pink flower with up to twelve lance-shaped petals. The cedar swamp holds yellow-fringed orchid, an extremely rare and very beautiful wildflower with light orange petals atop a two-foot stem. Trailing arbutus grows in the sandy soil along the trails. Round leaf sundew and wild geranium are found in the moist and shady climate of the cedar swamp. Pink lady's slipper can be found by the hundreds along the roads and trails of Cheesequake, gathered together in patches throughout the park. A comprehensive list of Cheesequake's plants and flowers is posted at the interpretive center, which is open seven days a week throughout the spring and summer.

Surrounding Points of Interest

Sandy Hook Gateway National Recreation Area

Since early in the last century, protecting New York Harbor has been the function of a thin piece of land jutting into Raritan Bay known as Sandy Hook. Remnants of the role this peninsula played in the nation's defense can be seen in historic Fort Hancock, which served its purpose until 1974 and still stands where it was built in 1898. The view from 85-foot Sandy Hook Lighthouse takes in a bird observatory, museum, some hiking trails, and several popular summer beaches. This is the oldest operating lighthouse in the United States, completed in 1764. The Sandy Hook peninsula is only a part of the larger Gateway National Recreation Area, America's fourth-busiest national park, receiving almost 9 million visitors every year.

Most of Sandy Hook's visitors head for one of the park's six beaches, but a number of quiet spots cater to bikers, birders, and anglers. A 5-mile bike path extends the length of the peninsula, weaving through a set of shore dunes and around two coves along the way. Spermaceti and Horseshoe Coves, great spots to find herons and other wading birds in the salt marshes near the boardwalk, begin about 1.9 miles north of the park entrance. Plum Island, about .5 mile from the entrance, is another good area for seabirds. The North Beach is a favorite place for anglers, with excellent fishing for bluefish, fluke, and striped bass. Take Route 36 east of Keyport for 13 miles and follow the signs for Sandy Hook Gateway National Recreation Area.

Where to Buy Supplies

Finding supplies is never a problem in the suburban areas around Cheesequake. Turn left out of the park onto Cliffwood Avenue and you will come to a strip mall on the corner of Matawan Road in less than a mile. The four corners of this intersection hold a deli with an ATM inside, bagel shop, Dunkin' Donuts, 7-Eleven, pizza parlor, pharmacy, and gas station. Turn right out of the park onto Morristown Road for almost anything else a traveler needs. You will come upon a Wawa convenience store on the corner of Steamboat Landing Road. Drive another 1.1 miles and bear right onto Route 9 north for delis, groceries, fast food, gas stations, pharmacies, and sporting goods. You will find two large shopping malls about 1 mile north of Route 34 on both sides of Route 9. The malls contain a Wal-Mart, Home Depot, fast food, and about fifty other retail stores.

Allaire State Park

P.O. Box 220
Farmingdale, NJ 07727

Area. 3,199 acres.

Park office. Monmouth County, 5.1 miles west of Manasquan Borough on the south side of Allaire Road.

Highlights. Allaire Village, Pine Creek Railroad.

Activities. Camping, hiking, fishing, canoeing, picnicking, mountain biking, horseback riding, birding, hunting, cross-country skiing, snowshoeing.

Entrance fee. A fee is charged to enter Allaire Village from Memorial Day weekend through Labor Day.

Park hours. The park grounds are open year-round, from dawn to dusk. Allaire Village is open Wednesday through Sunday from Memorial Day through Labor Day, and weekends only from Labor Day through November and the month of May.

For additional information: (732) 938-2371

Impeccably restored Allaire Village may look better today than it did when James P. Allaire began manufacturing pots and cauldrons on the site in 1822. Lack of fuel and the discovery of higher grades of ore in Pennsylvania forced the closing of Allaire's foundry only twenty-four years after it began. The land was eventually bought by Arthur Brisbane, a Hearst Newspaper executive, who donated 800 acres of his estate to New Jersey in 1941. Acquisition of land continued while the old village was restored, forming the core of Allaire State Park. A steam-engine train was added in the 1950s, and the Pine Creek Railroad still carries passengers along a 1-mile track near the village.

Beyond the wooden fences of Allaire Village, the park's 3,199 acres of lowland oak-pine forest supports more than 200 species of plants and animals. The well-maintained trail system includes several trails open to horseback riding and mountain biking, a few reserved solely for hikers, and one paved bike path that is envisioned to stretch from Trenton to the coast when complete. Flowing through the center of Allaire is the Manasquan River, where anglers will find four species of trout and

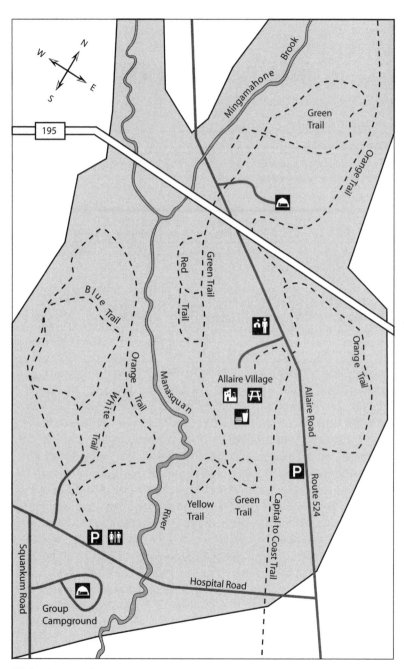

Allaire State Park

kayakers can paddle all the way to the Atlantic. To the west, a family campground is surrounded by modern restrooms, hot showers, and Allaire's wild and varied habitat.

Camping

Allaire's two campgrounds lie on opposite sides of the park. The family campground, where you will find tent and trailer sites along with four yurts and six shelters, is situated in a wooded area almost a mile west of the park office. A separate group campground holds six large sites on the south side of the park. Both campgrounds are easily accessible from paved access roads, perfectly suited for a family outing or casual camping experience. You will never feel lost in the wilderness at Allaire, but the sites are clean, well groomed, and close to modern facilities. Consider reserving ahead, as the campgrounds are usually busy on summer weekends.

Family Campground

A paved access road forms three separate loops through thin hardwood forest. Campsites line the road, some sitting close together on open grass lawns and others occupying a more wooded area as you head deeper into the campground. Four yurts to the west are like circular tents with a wooden floor, and six shelters on the east side of the campground sleep up to four people. About half of the sites are large enough to accommodate trailers. Near the campground entrance, the Green Trail gives access to the Mingamahone Brook and 500 acres of dense pineland on Allaire's northern border.

Directions. Turn left out of the park office on Allaire Road and drive .8 mile to the campground entrance on the right.

Sites and facilities. Allaire's forty-five tent and trailer sites, six shelters, and four yurts are each equipped with a fire ring and picnic table. The yurts each hold two double-deck bunks, and the shelters are one-room cabins, each with two double-deck bunks and a woodburning stove. The campground contains one modern restroom, hot showers, water pumps, a trailer sanitary station, and playground. Campsites, yurts, and shelters are open year-round.

Recommended sites. Drive past the first loop on the right, a series of sites on an open field, and turn into the second loop toward the east end of the campground. Number 26 is the most secluded site in this section, curled like a semicircle away from the road. Sites 23 through 25

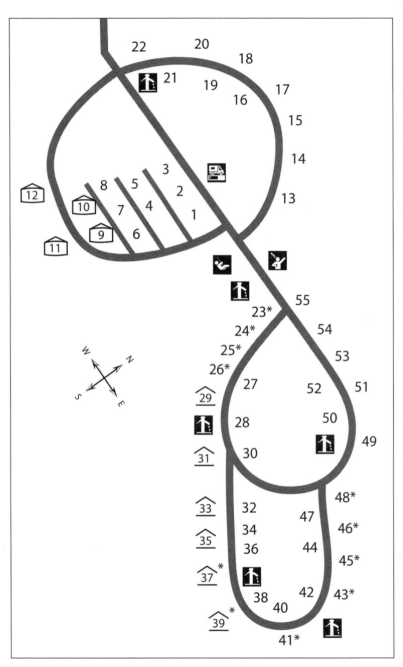

Allaire Family Campground

are good choices for privacy as well, ringed by trees and set back from the road. Continue east and you will find five quiet and wooded sites around the outside of the third loop, numbers 41, 43, 45, 46, and 48. The four yurts are all similar, situated on a grassy field near the campground entrance. Most of the shelters sit in a tight row, but numbers 37 and 39 gain a little distance from their neighbors and are backed by a forested rise.

Group Campground

Six group sites, designated by letters A through F, occupy a wide clearing in the forest near the southeast corner of the park. Sites E and F accommodate twenty-five campers each and are separated from the other four sites on the quiet east end of the campground. Sites A through D sit end to end on a long grass field and accommodate fifty campers each. You will find four chemical toilets and two water pumps scattered throughout the campground, but no showers. Each site holds picnic tables, fire rings, and grills. The campground is open year-round, and reservations are required. Turn right out of the park office on Allaire Road (Route 524). Drive 1.5 miles and turn right on Hospital Road. Proceed 1.6 miles to Squankum Road, turn left, and continue .6 mile to the group campground on the left.

Trails

Three trails near Allaire Village, although flat and open exclusively to hikers, make pleasant walks on a summer afternoon. The .5-mile Yellow Trail, beginning near the information center, is a groomed trail with log stairs and arched wooden bridges. A small waterfall on the Manasquan River flows beyond a wooden fence and a series of boardwalks. The 4.5-mile Green Trail leaves from the main parking area, and the 1.5-mile Red Trail splits off from the Green Trail to head through a forest of southern red oak, black walnut, and red maple. You can also begin the Green and Red Trails near the nature center, at the parking area on the park entrance road.

   Two other trails leave from near Allaire Village, one open to a variety of activities, and another used primarily by casual cyclists. The 16.5-mile Orange Trail, open to mountain biking and horseback riding, forms a circular route through mountain laurel, pitch pine, and chestnut oak. You can start from the parking area on the south side of Allaire Road, about .6 mile east of the park entrance. The trailhead is 200 yards west of the

Trail Mileage and Difficulty

TRAIL	MILES	DIFFICULTY	BLAZE	USES
Blue Trail	2.8	E	blue	e,h,m,s,x
Capital to Coast Trail	5.0	E	blue	h,m
Green Trail	4.5	E	green	h
Orange Trail (north)	16.5	E	orange	e,h,m,s,x
Orange Trail (south)	4.2	M	orange	e,h,m,s,x
Red Trail	1.5	E	red	h
White Trail	2.0	M	white	e,h,m,s,x
Yellow Trail	0.5	E	yellow	h

parking area, across the road, and through a wooden gate. The Capital to Coast Trail, a paved bike path beginning at the northeast corner of the main parking area, stretches 5 miles to the borough of Manasquan on the coast. The trail is envisioned to reach Trenton in future years, passing through a number of state and county parks in the process.

An area open to mountain biking and horseback riding lies at the southern end of Allaire, where sand roads and unmarked paths intersect three marked trails totaling about 10 miles. Another Orange Trail, a different trail from the northern Orange Trail, begins at a parking area on the west side of Hospital Road, about 1 mile south of Allaire Road. The area attracts deserving attention from mountain bikers, and a hitching post in the parking area caters to horseback riders. Two trails, the White and Blue, split off from the Orange Trail about .3 and .5 mile from the trailhead. The Orange and White Trails are the most difficult, encompassing steep hills and dirt roads totaling 6.2 miles. The Blue Trail is relatively flat, stretching 2.8 miles through a forest of mountain laurel and red oak. Hunting is permitted in this section of the park, so be aware of open seasons.

Activities

The Pine Creek Railroad and restored village will always attract the most attention at Allaire, but the park also offers diverse habitats and a natural environment suited to a variety of other outdoor pursuits. The Manasquan River is heavily stocked, one of the few rivers in New Jersey where anglers will find sea-run brown trout, and it is just long enough for an afternoon paddle to the coast. Mountain biking is popular in the southern, undeveloped section of the park, and many of Allaire's trails support horseback riding and cross-country skiing. The park also lies on the Atlantic Flyway, making it a good place to see migratory birds in the spring and fall.

Allaire Village

Much of Allaire's recorded history begins when a foundry named Williamsburg Forge came to the area in the 1790s. As with many industries relying on forest resources during that era, the property changed hands several times and eventually faced the prospect of a denuded forest and lack of fuel to run the furnaces. The site supported a bog iron furnace owned by Benjamin Howell at the beginning of the nineteenth century; then it was purchased in 1822 by the owner of a New York–based brass foundry, entrepreneur James P. Allaire. The ironworks produced pots, kettles, stoves, screws, and hand irons, as well as castings and pig iron for Allaire's foundry in New York. At its height, the village supported 400 people and dozens of shops and mills.

Today living history is on display at the restored village, which holds more than thirty buildings left standing from southern New Jersey's bog iron industry. An 1835 general store, an 1836 blacksmith shop, and many other restored structures line the walkways and millponds of the village. Local artisans in period garb demonstrate smithing, leatherworking, and carving throughout the spring and summer. A museum at the entrance doubles as an information center, where you will find maps and a pamphlet describing a self-guided tour of the village. Ironworking tools and the products of Allaire's foundry are on display, and a pictorial history of the area lines the museum walls.

Pine Creek Railroad

Allaire's steam-powered railroad is one of the oldest continually operating trains of its kind in the country and a popular attraction at the park. An open car with twenty-six benches, each capable of holding two people, sits between a diesel or steam-powered engine and one caboose. A variety of restored equipment is on hand, including an 1882 Irish steam engine, a 1942 diesel engine, and a number of passenger cars and cabooses. The narrow-gauge track forms a 1-mile oval circling a miniature depot. Picnic tables and wooden benches overlook the tracks, along with buildings salvaged from railroad yards of the past. Freneau Station of the Central Railroad of New Jersey and the watchmen's shanties from the old Pennsylvania Railroad remain preserved at trackside. Lines form during scheduled events, including nighttime Halloween rides and the annual play "The Great Train Robbery at Ole Pine Creek."

Fishing

Two rivers flow through the center of Allaire. The Manasquan is the territory of sea-run brown trout, a trophy fish that feeds in brackish and saltwater areas of the estuary, only to return upstream in an annual urge to spawn. The river receives more than 11,000 trout each year, but you can add the 4,000 rainbow trout stocked in the Manasquan Reservoir certain years and almost 300,000 sea-run brown trout that have been released in the tidal estuary since 1997. About 90 percent of all sea-run brown trout landed in New Jersey are caught from the Squankum Dam, where Route 547 crosses the Manasquan. Allaire's second river, the Mingamahone, is stocked with trout six times throughout the year. When combined with the trout that dwell at the confluence of the two rivers, the result is a productive and secluded fishing destination. You will also find a good population of pickerel and catfish in both rivers.

Boating

The Manasquan River supports canoes and kayaks, and the stretch from Allaire to the coast can be traveled within a few hours. Two easily accessible canoe launches are located where Southard Avenue and Preventorium Road each cross the Manasquan River. Above that point, the river is usually fraught with obstacles such as fallen trees. From either parking area, it's about a thirty-minute paddle to Allaire State Park and another hour to Spring Meadow Golf Course. An additional hour brings you to the Manasquan River Wildlife Management Area, where most canoeists take out. You can continue south through the Manasquan Inlet, but the stretch from the wildlife management area to the coast is mostly open water. Sea kayakers can put in at the canoe launch in the Manasquan River Wildlife Management Area, covered below.

Picnicking

Allaire's picnic area holds about 100 tables and grills south of the main parking area. The tables lie far enough from park activity to allow for quiet, situated in a wooded grove and around a small pond near the Green Trail. A covered pavilion, playground, restrooms, and water are nearby.

Mountain Biking

Roughly 1,000 acres south of the Manasquan River support a mixture of terrain that is popular with mountain bikers. Three marked trails form a matrix of dirt tracks, fire lanes, partially paved roads, and sand pits. Much of the area is unmarked, and some old blazes remain from former mapping efforts. The Orange, Blue, and White Trail markers are reliable, forming a total of about 10 miles through oak-pine forest and rolling terrain. A 16.5-mile trail on the north end of the park is open to mountain bikes as well—also marked in orange, but a different trail from the southern Orange Trail. Aside from the paved bicycle path next to the main parking area, trails near Allaire Village are off-limits to mountain bikes. See the Trails section for parking directions.

Horseback Riding

Horses are allowed on the trails to the north and south of Allaire Village outlined in the Mountain Biking section. The parking area servicing the trails south of the Manasquan River offers ample space for trailers and a hitching post near the trailhead. See the Trails section for directions. Another parking area with enough space to accommodate trailers gives access to the northern Orange Trail. The parking area lies .6 mile east of the park entrance on the south side of Allaire Road, but you have to ride back along the busy paved road for about 200 yards to reach the trailhead. Circle A Riding Academy on Herbertsville Road in Howell offers guided rides through the park.

Birding

Allaire receives less attention among birders than the nearby shore areas, but the park is still an inevitable stop for migratory birds on their journey along the Atlantic Flyway. Great-crested and Acadian flycatchers, barred owls, indigo buntings, blue-headed vireos, and palm, black-throated green, prothonotary, and blue-winged warblers are only a few of the rarities seen in the forests of the Manasquan River Basin. The Orange Trail on the north end of Allaire is productive for warblers, vireos, and flycatchers. A number of breeding birds can be seen throughout the park, including barred owls, Northern Waterthrushes, orchard orioles, Cooper's hawks, and wild turkeys. A pair of bald eagles has been nesting at nearby Manasquan Reservoir since 2002, with perhaps the most visible eagle's nest in New Jersey. See the Surrounding Points of Interest section for details.

Hunting

Two small areas totaling 1,276 acres are open to limited deer hunting. The section of Allaire south of the Manasquan River provides most of the open land. The Orange, Blue, and White Trails run through the area, so hikers should take note. A small section of the park north of Hurley Pond Road allows hunting as well. Allaire is in deer management zone 51.

Winter Activities

Campsites remain open year-round, and the shelters provide wood-burning stoves for heat. Cross-country skiing and snowshoeing are allowed on all of the trails save the walking trails near Allaire Village, and sea-run brown trout spawn from October through February on the Manasquan River. Allaire also hosts a variety of scheduled activities throughout the colder months. Among the more popular events are Halloween train rides, holiday tours by lantern, and a George Washington birthday celebration. Visit during the Christmas season and you will see children lined up for Santa's yearly visit to the Pine Creek Railroad. Dates and times for certain activities change every year, so check with the park office for a list of scheduled winter events.

Flora and Fauna

Allaire State Park is part of the Manasquan River Watershed, an area that has been depositing sediment in successional floods for millions of years. The floodplain supports deciduous forest and lowland marshes. The upland oak-pine forest holds American sycamore, shortleaf pine, and white, scarlet, and chestnut oaks. A total of 62 tree species make up the varied forests of the watershed, along with 34 different shrubs and 206 varieties of wildflowers. Hundreds of animals inhabit the land as well, including 93 fish, 23 reptile, and 21 mammal species. More than 240 types of birds are at least migratory residents, and hikers may even come across New Jersey's only spiny lizard, the northern fence lizard.

Several endangered animals maintain a tenuous foothold in and around Allaire, including the timber rattlesnake, bog turtle, and Pine Barrens tree frog. Half of the world's extremely rare swamp pinks are found in New Jersey, and a few small populations cling to the banks of the Manasquan River. The plant blooms for one week in early spring, sending up a single spherical cluster of pink flowers from a straight green stem. Another endangered plant, Knieskern's beaked-rush, requires continuously wet and sandy soil, a unique set of conditions found only in forested wetlands like those surrounding Allaire State Park.

Surrounding Points of Interest

The Manasquan River stretches through Allaire and on to the Atlantic coast, passing a number of wildlife areas, canoe access points, and inland fishing destinations along the way. Travelers will find a developed recreation area and a pair of nesting bald eagles at the Manasquan Reservoir a few miles to the west. To the east, the Manasquan River Wildlife Management Area encompasses more than 700 acres of deciduous forest and floodplain near the Atlantic Ocean. Monmouth Battlefield State Park entails a bit of a drive, but it is a worthwhile detour for anyone interested the Revolutionary War and New Jersey's historic landmarks.

Manasquan River Wildlife Management Area

The Manasquan River widens as it weaves through this 744-acre wildlife management area, a popular fly-fishing destination and one of the best sections of the river for anglers. A record-setting sea-run brown trout measuring 32 inches was caught here in 2002, although new records are sure to be set as the fledgling stocking program continues. A single access road leads to the river through a forest supporting pitch pine, red maple, red cedar, and white oak. The launch point at the end of the road suits canoes and small boats. Hunting is allowed for deer, small game, and waterfowl, and a dog-training area lies south of the river. Drive 2.2 miles east of the park office on Allaire Road (Route 524). Proceed straight across the intersection onto Ramshorn Road, and continue .2 mile to the wildlife management area entrance on the right.

Manasquan Reservoir

A highly developed park surrounds this 4-billion-gallon reservoir, where you will find a visitor center, environmental center, boat ramp, restrooms, and vending machines. A paved 5-mile trail circles the lake through eastern white pine, box elder, and a variety of oak trees. The visitor center rents canoes and electric-powered boats during the summer, and fishing is excellent for largemouth, smallmouth, and hybrid striped bass. Among New Jersey's fifty or so nesting pairs of bald eagles, the pair at Manasquan Reservoir is one of the earliest to arrive at its nest each year. The eagles are easy to view, as a telescope at the environmental center is trained on the nest and hooked to a television monitor from late January through April. Turn left out of the park office on Allaire Road, drive 1.2 miles, and turn left on Route 547. Proceed .6 mile and turn right on Old Tavern Road. Continue 2.8 miles, turn right on Windeler Road, and proceed .3 mile to the Manasquan Reservoir entrance on the right.

Monmouth Battlefield State Park

This park is a 15-mile drive from Allaire, but it's worth the effort if you are interested in Revolutionary War history. About 5 miles of all-purpose trails, two picnic areas, and an information center overlook the scene of the Battle of Monmouth at this 2,928-acre park just west of Freehold. On June 28, 1778, George Washington's outnumbered force of 13,500 men met 20,000 British and Hessian troops in open-field combat. Washington's victory put an end to the last major Revolutionary War battle in the north. Several historic buildings surround the battlefield, among them the 1745 Rhea-Applegate House, the 1746 Craig House, and the Old Tennent Church, built in 1751. The park entrance is 2.5 miles west of Freehold on the north side of Business Route 33.

Where to Buy Supplies

Turn right out of the park office and drive 5.1 miles southeast on Route 524 to Manasquan. The large borough contains banks, pharmacies, grocery stores, gas stations, marinas, and most items common to modern and growing towns. You will find dozens of bait-and-tackle shops north of Manasquan, and Brielle to the south has a bicycle shop and at least three marinas. Farmingdale is slightly closer to Allaire but offers only a hardware store, convenience store, pizzeria, and bagel shop. Turn left out of the park office, drive 1.2 miles, and turn right on Route 547. Proceed 2.2 miles to Farmingdale.

The Southern Region: Burlington, Ocean, Camden, Atlantic, Salem, Cumberland, Cape May

More than half of New Jersey's parkland lies in the southern third of the state. Perhaps the most defining feature of the region is the Pinelands National Reserve, a 1.1-million-acre expanse stretching from the Atlantic Ocean in the east to Parvin State Park in the west. This is where travelers have a chance to truly become lost in the wilderness, an area of small towns, cranberry bogs, and remote rivers that meander through vast stretches of pristine pineland. Wharton State Forest alone encompasses more than 115,000 acres, and campers looking for an escape are assured a haven from the crowds at one of Wharton's nine isolated campgrounds.

Heading south means spending time in the pinelands, but the area is also defined by the sea. Barnegat Bay provides some of New Jersey's best saltwater fishing, and anyone bound for Cape May can witness an annual migration that attracts birders from around the world. Fortescue, Heislerville, Egg Island, and a number of other hidden wildlife areas cling to the Delaware Bay shoreline, where travelers will find a peaceful and rarely explored corner of the Garden State.

Brendan T. Byrne
State Forest

P.O. Box 215
New Lisbon, NJ 08064

Area. 36,647 acres.

Park office. Burlington County, 1 mile east of Route 70 on the north side of Route 72.

Highlights. Whitesbog Village, Pinelands National Reserve, Batona Trail.

Activities. Camping, hiking, fishing, picnicking, mountain biking, horseback riding, birding, hunting, cross-country skiing, snowshoeing, snowmobiling.

Entrance fee. None.

Park hours. Year-round, from dawn to dusk.

For additional information: (609) 726-1191

The Lebanon Glass Works set up industrial furnaces in the Pine Barrens in 1851 and denuded the forest of trees before shutting its doors in 1867. Almost a century later, the southern New Jersey pinelands was zoned for an international airport and a city of 250,000 residents, complete with highways, high-rise buildings, and concrete parking lots. Then Brendan T. Byrne was elected governor of New Jersey in 1974. The legislature, business leaders, and developers protested at every step, but in 1977 the governor enacted Executive Order 56, creating the Pinelands Review Committee. The Pinelands Protection Act was signed into law three years later, creating America's first national reserve. The original 1 million acres of pinelands protected under the legislation has since grown to 1.1 million acres, and this is now recognized by the United Nations as one of the most unique ecosystems on the planet.

The section of the pinelands within Brendan T. Byrne State Forest has lived up to its namesake's vision. Developed recreation areas do not exist within the park, nor will you find swimming beaches, concession stands, or an abundance of pavement. This is a place to explore the forest from a simple and basic campsite. Hundreds of miles of trails and fire roads, countless rivers and streams, dozens of ponds and lakes min-

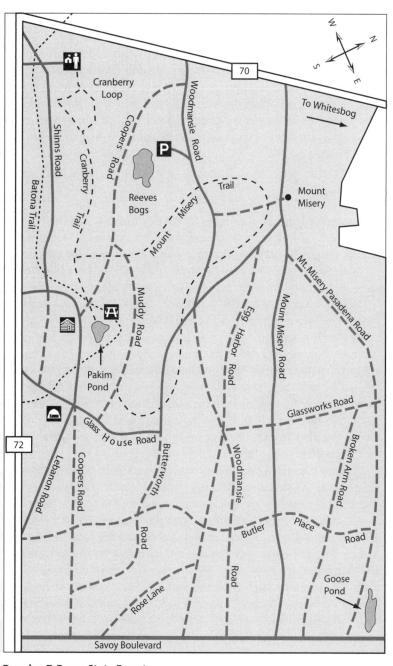

Brendan T. Byrne State Forest

gle with the pines in a 36,647-acre area on the edge of an even larger national reserve. The beginning of the Batona Trail marks the outskirts of the Pinelands National Reserve, which stretches south to Wharton State Forest, Belleplain State Forest, and beyond. The area is home to more than 850 species of plants and 350 species of birds, mammals, reptiles, and amphibians. Brendan T. Byne State Forest, on the northern edge of the reserve, is the gateway to this vast wilderness—an area of small towns, miles of unbroken solitude, and slow-moving rivers the color of sepia tea.

Camping

There's something about camping in the Pine Barrens that can't quite be defined. Just as the salt air and ocean spray give the seashore a unique feel, so the dappled light and muffled sounds of the pines create a sense of place. Bounded by forest and blanketed by a fine white sand that defines the pinelands, campsites at Brendan Byrne are wide and isolated. Camping is basic, but you are never far from hot showers, water from ground pumps, and even rudimentary laundry facilities. Most sites can accommodate small trailers, and large groups will find three sites on the east end of the family campground capable of holding up to 100 campers. Three yurts are located in the family campground as well, and three isolated cabins rest on the shore of Pakim Pond. You will find no food concession or swimming beaches nearby, but rather than a place to linger, the campground serves as a way to access Brendan Byrne's most powerful asset—the surrounding trails and roads through the Pinelands National Reserve.

Directions. Turn left out of the park office onto Shinns Road and drive 2.1 miles to the stop sign. Turn left, proceed .6 mile past Pakim Pond picnic area on the left, and continue another .5 mile to the campground.

Sites and facilities. Brendan Byrne's seventy-nine tent and trailer sites, three yurts, and three group campsites all contain fire rings and picnic tables. The necessities are close at hand, including hot showers, modern restrooms, drinking water, and a telephone. Yurts are round tents with a wood frame, each equipped with two double-deck bunks. The group camping area, divided into sites A, B, and C, contains its own restroom with modern toilets but no showers. A trailer sanitary station lies at the campground entrance. The campground is open year-round.

Recommended sites. Three separate access roads loop through the forest, and the only one lacking a wilderness feel is the first, contain-

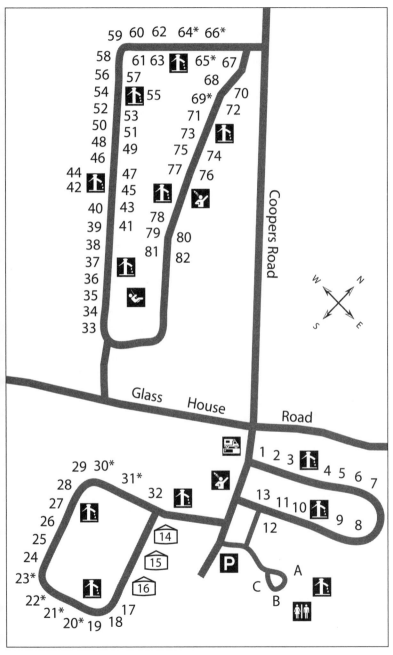

Brendan T. Byrne Family Campground

ing sites 1 through 13. The second loop contains the best site in the park, number 20, situated some distance from the road and isolated from its neighbors. Other notable sites for privacy include numbers 21, 22, 23, 30, and 31. Showers and a laundry room are located in the third loop, so it's a bit more traveled, but number 66 is private, ringed by trees, and large enough for trailers. Site 65 is insulated from the road, although it sits in the median surrounded by other sites, and numbers 64 and 69 are recessed about 20 yards into the forest.

Cabins

The lake view and solitude make Brendan Byrne's cabins perfect for anyone seeking contemplation and quiet sunsets. The back door of each cabin leads to a private wooden dock on Pakim Pond reminiscent of a Tom Sawyer fishing scene. A wooded clearing between the dock and the cabin holds a picnic table and grill, and showers are a short walk away at the campground restrooms. The cabins each consist of a main room, kitchen, and bathroom equipped with a modern toilet. Two double-deck bunks, a wooden table, two benches, two chairs, and a fireplace occupy the main room. The kitchen contains an electric stove and oven. Follow the directions for the family campground, and you will come to the cabins on the left side of the road next to the Pakim Pond picnic area. The cabins are available from April 1 through October 31.

Trails

Brendan Byrne supports a network of trails, fire roads, and dirt paths that stretch past working cranberry bogs, remote tributaries, and isolated cedar swamps. The 50-mile Batona Trails cuts through Brendan Byrne on its way to Bass River State Forest near the coast. About 10 miles of the trail lies within the borders of Brendan Byrne, beginning at Pakim Pond. Follow the trail west along Shinns Branch Road, then veer into the forest west of the park office. Continue across Route 70 and along Bisphams Mill Creek until you arrive at the park border at Route 72. Parking areas at the Brendan Byrne office and Pakim Pond picnic area provide good access to this hiking-only trail.

Four other marked trails originate at the office, and most of them follow one of the many rivers that flow through the forest. Mount Misery Trail, marked in white, extends 8.5 miles past a cranberry bog to the northern end of the park, skirting the South Branch and McDonalds

Trail Mileage and Difficulty

TRAIL	MILES	DIFFICULTY	BLAZE	USES
Batona Trail	9.4	E	pink	h,s,x
Broken Arm Road	3.0	E	no blaze	b,e,h,m,s,x
Butler Place Road	5.5	E	no blaze	b,e,h,m,s,x
Butterworth Road	5.1	E	no blaze	h,m,s,x
Coopers Road	5.3	E	no blaze	e,h,m,s,x
Cranberry Loop Trail	1.1	E	red	h,m,s,x
Cranberry Trail	2.7	E	red	h,m,s,x
Egg Harbor Road	4.2	E	no blaze	b,e,h,m,s,x
Glass House Road	2.1	E	no blaze	h,m,s,x
Glassworks Road	2.2	E	no blaze	b,e,h,m,s,x
Lebanon Road	1.2	E	no blaze	h,m,s,x
Mount Misery Pasadena Road	5.3	E	no blaze	b,e,h,m,s,x
Mount Misery Road	5.7	E	no blaze	h,m,s,x
Mount Misery Trail	8.5	E	white	h,m,s,x
Muddy Road	2.1	E	no blaze	e,h,m,s,x
Rose Lane	1.6	E	no blaze	b,e,h,m,s,x
Shinns Road	4.2	E	no blaze	h,m,s,x
Woodmansie Road	4.5	E	no blaze	b,e,h,m,s,x

Branch of the Rancocas Creek Watershed along the way. The 2.7-mile Cranberry Trail, marked in red, follows Shinns Branch to the cabins and picnic area at Pakim Pond. The Cranberry Trail is paved and designated for wheelchair access between the office and Pakim Pond. Cranberry Loop Trail veers off from the Cranberry Trail to form a 1.1-mile loop through a small patch of forest near the office. A fourth trail, a bike trail marked in orange, stretches 10.8 miles through the park, using a variety of existing dirt roads. All four trails allow mountain bikes, cross-country skiing, and snowshoeing.

Horses, motorcycles, and snowmobiles are restricted to the 50 miles of dirt roads that crisscross the forest, not such a bad fate considering the many thin fire trails that extend into the heart of the Pine Barrens. Glassworks Road travels past the three main tributaries of Rancocas

Creek to end at North Branch Road on the northern end of the park. Butler Place Road is a little more remote, extending 5.5 miles from Route 72 in the south, past a cedar swamp, and across three tributaries to Goose Pond in the north. If you're still not satisfied after exploring Brendan Byrne, neighboring Greenwood Forest to the east adds another expansive network of roads and trails open to cross-country skiing, horseback riding, hiking, biking, and snowshoeing. Keep in mind that many of the roads require four-wheel drive, and travelers should carry a topographic map, water, and basic emergency supplies.

Activities

Brendan T. Byrne is New Jersey's second-largest state forest. Miles of marked trails, fire roads, and dirt paths lead past more than 36,000 acres of protected land, home to plants and animals that flourish in the unique habitat of the pinelands. Brendan Byrne's roads are perfectly suited to horseback riding, and anyone willing to explore will find working cranberry bogs, remote cedar swamps, and nineteenth-century villages. A short walk from the campground leads to a quiet picnic spot on Pakim Pond, and farther afield, mountain biking, cross-country skiing, or snowshoeing can access one of the largest tracts of protected wilderness on the East Coast.

Whitesbog Village

The area became known as Whitesbog when Joseph J. White began farming cranberries on the land in the 1860s. Joseph White's operation became one of the largest cranberry farms in New Jersey, and the nearby bogs are still farmed today, producing more than 150,000 pounds of cranberries each year for distribution throughout the United States. Daughter Elizabeth White also cultivated New Jersey's first highbush blueberry plants here in 1916.

The Whitesbog Preservation Trust is in charge of restoring the village and sponsors an annual blueberry festival and other seasonal events. The village bears examples of the changes in agriculture throughout the nineteenth and twentieth centuries, including a general store and cranberry-packing building. A 3-mile dirt road extends from the village, around 3,000 acres of cranberry bogs, and through an area of pitch pine forest and a cedar swamp. The bogs along this stretch harbor hundreds of wintering tundra swans through March. You can visit the cranberry bogs and historic village on Whitesbog Road from dawn to dusk daily.

From the intersection of Routes 70 and 72, drive 5.5 miles east on Route 70 and turn left on Whitesbog Road, a well-maintained dirt road. Proceed 1.3 miles to the village of Whitesbog.

Fishing and Boating

The shallow rivers of Brendan Byrne reflect runoff from soil rich in iron ore and organic matter. As a result, the game fish most sought after by fishers cannot survive in the Pine Barrens. Pakim Pond supports modest numbers of pickerel, catfish, and sunfish, but the best course of action for anglers and boaters is to head for Barnegat Bay, where the inlets and ocean produce some of the best saltwater fishing on New Jersey's coast. A few nearby parks offer fishing as well, including Island Beach State Park and Colliers Mills Wildlife Management Area. See the Surrounding Points of Interest section for more information.

Picnicking

Brendan Byrne's picnic areas lie on the shore of Pakim Pond and are fairly serene if you arrive on a weekday or during the off-season. Two covered pavilions and thirty tables overlook the pond near the parking area, with grills, restrooms, and water from ground pumps on the site. Groups of twenty or more can reserve the picnic areas up to five days in advance. Turn left out of the park office onto Shinns Road and drive 2.2 miles to the stop sign. Turn left and proceed .6 mile to the Pakim Pond picnic area on the left.

Mountain Biking

The Pine Barrens are flat, and those seeking mountainous terrain have few options. Pines extend beyond the horizon in all directions. A 10.8-mile bike route, marked in orange, follows dirt roads past Pakim Pond, Shinns Branch, and Reeves Cranberry Bogs. Mount Misery Trail is a bit more interesting because it uses more trails than roads to create an 8.5-mile ride leading to a 115-foot hill at the northern end of the park. You will find a United Methodist summer camp at the top of the hill. Biking is allowed on the remaining trails throughout the forest with the one exception of Batona Trail. Fine white sand is abundant along all of Brendan Byrne's trails and roads.

Horseback Riding

None of Brendan Byrne's marked trails allow horses, but that shouldn't bother anyone willing to explore the miles of dirt roads that weave through the forest. Parking for trailers can be found throughout the area, including the campground, park office, and Pakim Pond.

Birding

Birders should not visit Brendan Byrne without making a trip to the cranberry bogs and cedar swamps of Whitesbog, known for large numbers of tundra swans in late winter and early spring. The bogs attract sandpipers by the dozen during spring droughts, including Baird's, buff-breasted, least, pectoral, semipalmated, solitary, spotted, and stilt sandpipers. Lesser and greater yellowlegs can be found in the bogs as well, along with American golden and semipalmated plovers. American black ducks, green-winged teals, and mallards arrive when the bogs are swollen, along with occasional bald eagles, northern shrikes, and loggerhead shrikes. Drive the dirt roads circling the cranberry bogs for the best results. Nearby Reeves Cranberry Bogs, about 4.5 miles to the west, are almost as productive and can harbor more tundra swans than Whitesbog depending on the day.

The birding opportunities drop considerably once you travel away from the cranberry bogs, but the pines of Brendan Byrne support species such as red-headed woodpeckers, summer tanagers, and Acadian flycatchers. A variety of warblers fly through in spring and some nest, including black-throated green warblers. Other species occasionally seen in the pines include Canada warblers, black-billed cuckoos, long-eared owls, and common nighthawks. You can cover a variety of habitat by looking near Pakim Pond, at Reeves Bogs on Woodmansie Road, among the pines bordering Shinns Road, and along Cranberry Trail.

Hunting

Almost 90 percent of the forest is open to the hunting of deer, small game, wild turkeys, and waterfowl. The typical pinelands habitat is not a favorite among hunters, although Wharton State Forest to the south is gaining in popularity. Brendan Byrne falls within deer management zone 21.

Winter Activities

Brendan Byrne's campground is open year-round, and winter activities surround the extensive road and trail system weaving through the Pine Barrens. Hiking and mountain biking become a bit easier during the colder months, when the sand roads firm up to produce better traction. The roads and trails are open to cross-country skiing, and most of the roads allow snowmobiles. Heavy snowfalls occur only occasionally in the Pine Barrens, so opportunities for activities like snowmobiling are rare. Winter travelers should carry the essentials for wilderness survival when venturing out.

Flora and Fauna

The Pinelands National Reserve contains 83 percent of New Jersey's state forest land and the majority of the state's endangered species. More than 850 species of plants have been identified in the Pinelands National Reserve, including 84 listed as threatened or endangered by state, federal, or worldwide organizations. The rare curly grass fern was first discovered near Quaker Bridge in 1808, and carnivorous plants thrive here because they are capable of supplementing the poor nutrients in the soil with nitrogen from insects. Pitcher plant, round-leaf sundew, and Venus flytrap can be found in the low-lying, shaded areas of the forest. Add these to a long list of endangered orchids, ferns, shrubs, and grasses, and the list will still be incomplete.

Many of the numerous animal species that inhabit the forest also are endangered and have been the subject of state, federal, and international protection. A total of 39 mammal, 299 bird, 91 fish, and 59 amphibian and reptile species occur in the pinelands, including 44 endangered or threatened species. The Pine Barrens tree frog is one of the better-known endangered inhabitants, marking its presence every spring with a chorus that has come to be a symbol of the Pine Barrens. At least 15 of the 91 species of fish found throughout the reserve are common in the acidic waters of Brendan Byrne, including some species found nowhere else in the state, such as the black-banded sunfish. Another oddity is the eastern mudminnow, a fish that has developed a gas bladder for breathing air during times of stagnant water or drought.

The Pinelands National Reserve, once thought to be a barren, inhospitable place because of the high acidity and poor nitrogen levels in the soil, is now home to more than 1,200 species of plants and animals. Brendan Byrne's 36,647 acres make up but a fraction of the total reserve, which flows south from the borders of Brendan Byrne to Wharton, Bass River, and Belleplain State Forests and beyond.

Surrounding Points of Interest

Most of the destinations surrounding Brendan Byrne are a continuation of the Pine Barrens, but some of the parks have a special appeal. Points of interest range from well-traveled state parks with developed recreation areas to rugged wildlife management areas containing no facilities at all. A few are within 5 miles of Brendan Byrne, such as the adjacent Greenwood Forest. Barnegat Bay and several seashore destinations lie 30 miles away, adding a dimension so different from the pinelands experience that driving to the coast requires a small mental adjustment.

Greenwood and Pasadena Wildlife Management Area

Brendan Byrne's extensive system of dirt roads and trails continues into the adjacent Greenwood and Pasadena Wildlife Management Area. Once known simply as Greenwood Forest, this is New Jersey's largest wildlife management area, encompassing 29,712 acres of upland pine-oak forest, Atlantic white cedar swamps, streams, and small lakes. The land is wild and undeveloped, and although many unmarked trails crisscross the forest, hiking usually requires some creative bushwhacking. A few unmarked trails and roads begin on the west side of Route 539 between Routes 70 and 72. A boardwalk trail through Webb's Mill Bog, an area known for its variety of orchids and sundew plants, begins about 6.5 miles north of Route 72 on the east side of Route 539. Greenwood Forest is stocked with almost 3,000 quail each year, so it is popular with hunters of small game, deer, wild turkeys, and waterfowl. Three small lakes support a small population of pickerel, perch, and catfish, and the dirt roads are open to hiking, mountain biking, cross-country skiing, and snowshoeing. Horseback riding is allowed but requires a permit from the Division of Fish and Wildlife.

Double Trouble State Park

Continue east from Greenwood Forest on Route 618 and you will come to Double Trouble State Park, situated next to the Garden State Parkway. The 7,881-acre park represents a continuation of the Pine Barrens, but it is vastly more developed than Greenwood Forest to the west. Restrooms, picnic tables, and a 1.5-mile nature trail occupy a landscape of cedar swamps and upland pine forest. A restored historic village is the main attraction, where a former cranberry farm and sawmill are surrounded by a nineteenth-century general store, restored schoolhouse, and workers' cottages. Cedar Creek offers the best canoeing near Brendan Byrne outside of Wharton State Forest, running from Bamber Lake in Greenwood Forest through Double Trouble State Park and on to the coast.

Manchester and Whiting Wildlife Management Areas

Manchester and Whiting Wildlife Management Areas sit next to each other along Route 70 and are almost a continuation of Brendan Byrne, located about 3 miles northeast of the state forest border. Combined, they make up 4,276 acres of pine-oak forest, cedar swamp, and small rivers bordered by marshland. The area is a popular hunting destination known for deer, small game, and wild turkeys, although the roads and unmarked trails are open to hiking and mountain biking year-round and cross-country skiing in the winter. A parking area in the Whiting Wildlife Management Area gives access to Bauer Pond and the Michaels Branch of Wrangel Brook, where anglers will find fair numbers of largemouth bass. Boats with electric motors are allowed in the small, 10-acre pond.

Colliers Mills Wildlife Management Area

Drive north of Manchester and Whiting Wildlife Management Areas and you will come to the 12,662 acres of Colliers Mills Wildlife Management Area, near the corner of Routes 528 and 539. This is one of New Jersey's more developed wildlife management areas, complete with an office, dog-training area, and shooting range. The headwaters of Toms River form an area supporting two lakes, several ponds, a cedar swamp, and six cranberry bogs. You can access Turn Mill Lake, Colliers Mill Pond, and Success Lake from the entrance on Route 640. Of the three, Turn Mill Lake offers the best fishing. Small boats with electric motors are welcome here, and fishing is good for largemouth bass, pickerel, yellow perch, catfish, and sunfish. The roads and unmarked trails are open to mountain biking and hiking, and hunting is allowed for deer, small game, wild turkeys, and waterfowl.

Barnegat Bay

The coast along Barnegat Bay encompasses quiet seaside towns, state-run marinas, oceanside parks, and river inlets stocked with trout. A few picturesque county parks jut into the sea on peninsulas, including Cattus Island County Park, north of Toms River, and Berkeley Island County Park, at the mouth of Cedar Creek. Sedge Island Wildlife Management Area, a group of small islands 1 mile off the southern tip of Long Island Beach State Park, supports a research center focusing on the surrounding system of estuaries. It is also a great sea kayaking destination. Eno's Pond County Park and Forked River State Marina are together at the outlet of Forked River, an area offering trails, boardwalks, picnic tables, and an observation deck. The former whaling town of Toms River traces its origins to 1767 and is home to the Toms River Seaport Society Maritime Museum, the Ocean County Historical Society Museum, and a number of historical buildings.

Rivers, inlets, and coves offer fishing and boating along the coast from Brick to Barnegat Lighthouse State Park. Fishing hot spots along this stretch include Silver Bay, Toms River, and Cedar Creek. Barnegat Inlet, between Island Beach and Barnegat Lighthouse State Parks, is known for trophy bluefish, weakfish, fluke, and striped bass. Forked River and nearby Oyster Creek Channel have long been known for their populations of winter flounder and striped bass. The bay is also a popular sea kayaking location because of the maze of marked channels, creek mouths, and islands to explore along the coast. The protected waters and minimal tidal currents make the bay an easy paddle. Numerous marinas throughout the area offer sea kayak rentals and fishing charters.

Island Beach State Park

This 10-mile-long barrier island separates the Atlantic Ocean from Barnegat Bay. More than 3,000 acres of white sand beaches, pristine dunes, tidal salt marshes, and freshwater wetlands occupy a coastline devoid of the usual development, especially if you're willing to walk a mile beyond the well-traveled parking areas and access points. Part of the island is set aside as a botanical preserve, protecting more than 400 species of rare coastal plants. The island is known for migratory seabirds, peregrine falcons, and the state's largest osprey colony. A 1-mile developed section of the beach offers restrooms, swimming, a nature center, and access to a few miles of hiking trails. Fishing is allowed from the shore, where bluefish, striped bass, summer flounder, and weakfish are the main catch. From the intersection of Routes 70 and 72 near the Brendan Byrne office, drive east on Route 70 for 18.1 miles and exit to the right on Route 37 south. Proceed 13.1 miles and exit to the right on Route 35 south. Continue 2.5 miles to Island Beach State Park.

Where to Buy Supplies

Come to Brendan Byrne prepared, because supplies are not close at hand. The nearest stores line the traffic circle where Routes 70 and 72 come together, known locally as the Four Mile Circle, where you will find a Wawa convenience store, gas station, auto repair garage, pizza parlor, and tavern. The next-closest city is Browns Mills. From the Four Mile Circle, drive 5.2 miles north on Four Mile Road and turn right on Pemberton-Browns Mills Road. Proceed 2.3 miles to Browns Mills. Stores are widely scattered throughout the town, but you will find pharmacies, banks, one grocery store on the east end of town, and a variety of restaurants.

If you require a major city, follow the directions to Long Island Beach State Park, and you will arrive at Toms River near the Garden State Parkway. The city carries most of the conveniences common to large and prospering areas. Along the way to Toms River, you will pass the small towns of Whiting and Lakehurst, about 12 and 17 miles from the Four Mile Circle. Both towns contain pharmacies, grocery stores, gas stations, convenience stores, and fast food.

Wharton State Forest

4110 Nesco Rd.
Hammonton, NJ 08037

Area. 115,111 acres.

Park office. The Atsion office is in Burlington County, 7.5 miles north of Hammonton on the east side of Route 206. The Batsto office is 7.1 miles east of Hammonton on the north side of Route 542.

Highlights. Batsto Village, Apple Pie Hill, Batona Trail, wilderness camping, river canoeing.

Activities. Camping, hiking, fishing, boating, picnicking, swimming, mountain biking, horseback riding, birding, hunting, cross-country skiing, snowshoeing, snowmobiling.

Entrance fee. A fee is charged to enter the Atsion recreation area and Batsto Village from Memorial Day weekend through Labor Day.

Park hours. Year-round, from dawn to dusk.

For additional information:
Atsion office: (609) 268-0444
Batsto office: (609) 561-0024

Wharton State Forest makes up the largest undeveloped tract of land in New Jersey, part of a 1.1-million acre expanse known alternately as the Pinelands National Reserve, the southern New Jersey pinelands, and the Outer Coastal Plain. Locals know the region simply as the Pine Barrens. It is an area defined by small towns and corner general stores, slow-moving rivers, and sand roads made of almost pure white quartz. The high acidity of Pine Barrens soil supports few agricultural crops, a phenomenon that prompted early settlers to deem the area barren. Yet the pinelands as a whole contain more unbroken forest than the remainder of New Jersey, occupying almost 25 percent of the state's total land area. This is the largest unbroken forest on the Eastern Seaboard between Boston and the Chesapeake Bay, capable of holding the combined acreage of the next five largest New Jersey state forests within its borders.

Travelers looking for a wilderness experience within New Jersey should end their search here. Wharton State Forest contains nine camp-

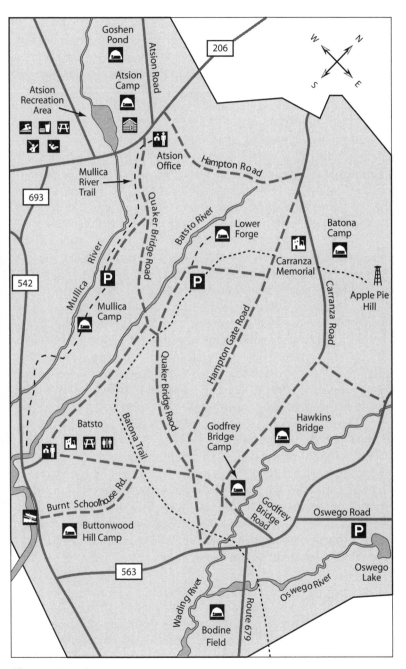

Wharton State Forest

grounds, 500 miles of remote fire roads, and four rivers that create a canoeing paradise for anyone who has ever picked up a paddle and pined for solitude. Some of the campgrounds are so remote that they can be accessed only by canoe or by trail. Some of the rivers cut through the center of the Pine Barrens, with nothing along the route but a wilderness campsite. Most of the roads do not appear on normal street maps.

For those interested in staying closer to civilization, the recreation area at Atsion offers a peaceful beach that is surrounded by picnic tables, grills, lakeside trails, and a bathhouse with hot showers. Nine quiet cabins line Atsion Lake, where boating, fishing, and swimming are worthwhile pursuits during the summer. Farther south, the restored village of Batsto is a popular tourist attraction, harboring more than forty structures left standing from the town's nineteenth-century iron industry.

Visitors to Batsto Village will find a recorded history of the area dating back to the early seventeenth century, when Swede Eric Mullica sailed up an uncharted river to the present location of Atsion. Exploitation of the pinelands by the iron-ore and glassmaking industries is well documented, but early uses of the forest ranged from cotton mills to paper mills, and it even served as a haven for privateers who transported supplies along remote Pine Barrens trails during the late eighteenth century. Moments in the history of Wharton include Pine Barrens outlaw Joe Mulliner, who robbed stagecoaches near Lower Forge; the construction of a bridge after several Quakers drowned fording the Batsto River (the present site of Quaker Bridge); and a battle of scientists in 1808 over which botanist would be credited with the discovery of the curly grass fern.

Land and industry traded hands and functions many times, ending with entrepreneur Joseph Wharton, who bought 96,000 acres of pineland with the intention of building canals throughout the region and exporting water to Philadelphia. The New Jersey legislature put an end to the idea when it passed a law prohibiting exportation of water. New Jersey finally bought the land from Wharton's heirs in 1955, forming the core of Wharton State Forest.

Camping

Wharton contains nine campgrounds, more than any other state park or forest in New Jersey. One of them, Atsion Family Campground, is a traditional camping area offering picnic tables, water pumps, fire rings, and modern restrooms with showers. The other eight are considered wilderness sites, which describes a wide spectrum of accessibility, iso-lation, and wilderness appeal. They range from pineland groves set on the banks of a remote river to sandy clearings next to a forest pond. You can drive into and park at some of the sites, but others can be reached only by river or by trail. The eight wilderness sites contain pit toilets, and two of the campgrounds, Lower Forge and Buttonwood Hill, have no water. The most isolated sites, Mullica River and Lower Forge, are inaccessible by motor vehicle. If you're looking for modern conven-iences, Wharton's nine log cabins sit on the shore of Atsion Lake—secluded enough to allow for privacy, yet all within a short drive of the park office and recreation area. With the exception of Atsion, all of Wharton's campgrounds are open year-round.

Atsion Family Campground

Atsion is the most developed of Wharton's nine campgrounds, and the only one that offers modern restrooms, hot showers, and a trailer san-itary station. All of the sites are well spaced from one another, set in wooded clearings and encircled by trees. They are also large, many of them wide enough to accommodate trailers, and a few sites rest on the shore of Atsion Lake. On the opposite side of the lake sits a recreation area, where you will find a swimming beach, playgrounds, and picnic tables. This is not one of Wharton's more remote campgrounds, less than a mile from Route 206, but it is still far from the nearest town or retail center. During the summer, you will find firewood for sale and a self-service vegetable stand at a local farm across the road. Heed the sign: "Please put money in box—thanks for your honesty."

Directions. Turn left out of the Atsion office onto Route 206, drive .1 mile, and turn right on Atsion Road. Proceed 1 mile to the Atsion Fam-ily Campground on the left.

Sites and facilities. Atsion's fifty tent and trailer sites are each equipped with a fire ring and picnic table. One modern restroom with hot showers and a trailer sanitary station sit near the entrance. Water from ground pumps is within walking distance of all sites. The camp-ground is open from April 1 through mid-December.

Recommended sites. Most of the sites at Atsion are well spaced and wooded. Of the seven sites near Atsion Lake, numbers 8, 10, and 22 offer the best view of the water and are fairly private. The other four, 4, 6, 12, and 20, have a barrier of trees blocking the view. Away from the lake, number 15 is separated from its neighbors, 48 is set back from the road, and 42 is encircled by trees. About ten of the sites are large

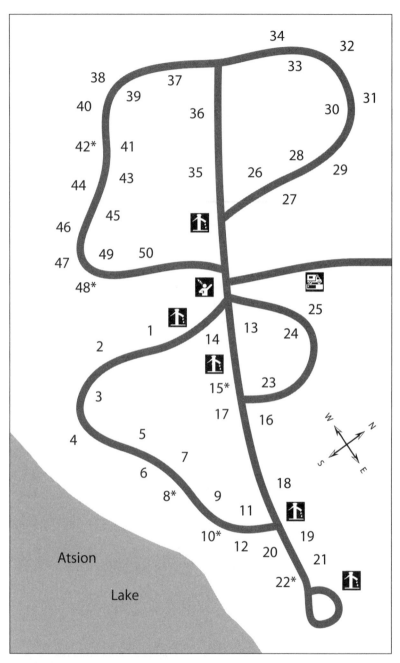

Atsion Family Campground

enough to accommodate trailers, including recommended sites 10 and 48. Other trailer sites include 2, 4, 6, 13, 16, and 38. Numbers 19 and 20 are perfect for small campers, but trees near the entrance exclude large trailers.

Atsion Lake Cabins

If New Jersey's cabins were to be rated for country appeal, privacy, and amount of rocking chair space on the back porch, Wharton's would hold a place at the top of the list. Nine log cabins rest on the shore of Atsion Lake. The wide back porches—most of them screened, all within a few feet of the shore—overlook the lake with a view of the surrounding pinelands. The seventy-five-year-old cabins are situated well off the road in quiet clearings, looking like homesteads from America's old West. Some offer upstairs bedrooms, a few are single story, and all supply a fireplace in the main room.

Directions. Turn left out of the Atsion office onto Route 206, drive .1 mile, and turn right on Atsion Road. Cabins line the south side of Atsion Road from Route 206 to the Atsion Campground.

Cabins and facilities. One-story cabins include numbers 1 and 5, each with two bedrooms, and cabin 6 with one bedroom. Cabins 2 and 3 have an upper floor, with a bedroom on each level. Cabins 4, 7, 8, and 9 are made up of two stories, with one bedroom below and two above. Each bedroom sleeps two people (cabin 8 is the one exception, accommodating a total of eight people). The kitchen is equipped with an electric stove and refrigerator, and modern bathrooms contain hot showers. An outdoor table and grill face Atsion Lake. Cabins are available from April 1 through October 31.

Recommended cabins. Aside from the interior layout, you will find only minor differences between the nine cabins. Numbers 6 and 7 are separated from each other slightly more than the others. Cabins 8 and 9 are next to each other but still private, with back porches resting about five feet from the lake. Numbers 4 and 5 are close neighbors, and 5 has a wooden back porch within feet of the water, though it's the only porch without a screen. Cabin 4 offers a wooden back deck in addition to a screened-in porch. Although right on the lake, numbers 1 through 3 also lie directly on Atsion Road.

Goshen Pond Campground

Goshen Pond represents a compromise between the development of Atsion Campground and the complete wilderness of Mullica River and

Lower Forge Campgrounds. The Goshen Pond entrance lies close to Route 206, yet you must drive along the rough access road for .8 mile to reach the campground. A forested clearing meets the shore of Goshen Pond, where you will not find designated campsites. Rather, campers can pitch a tent anywhere within the campground limits, and makeshift fire pits serve as fire rings. The serenity at Goshen Pond depends on how many tents are pitched during the day, but it is usually peaceful, with very few visitors. The pond turns pink at sunset, and spring peeper frogs always come out to lull you to sleep at night. One water pump is centrally located, and pit toilets are scattered throughout the site. Drive .5 mile west of the Atsion Family Campground and turn left at the wooden Goshen Pond sign.

Mullica River Campground

Mullica River is one of two campgrounds at Wharton that are inaccessible by motor vehicle. The campground can be reached by canoe or by walking .8 mile from the parking area on Mullica River Road. The parking area lies 4 miles south of the nearest paved road, along a rough and rugged dirt track that is not recommended for the average family car. You will come to a forested clearing on the slow-moving Mullica River, where the typical white sand of the Pine Barrens is dotted with pitch pines, shrubs, and patches of green grass. Campers can pitch a tent anywhere within the campground limits, and ground fires are allowed in makeshift fire pits. Although the site is relatively small, you stand a good chance of being the only person in the campground. One water pump and two pit toilets are centrally located.

From Atsion, drive south on Quaker Bridge Road for 2.2 miles to the wooden Mullica River Camp sign and turn right on the thin dirt track (Mullica River Road). Proceed 2 miles to the parking area marked by three orange rings on a tree; then walk south along the yellow-blazed Mullica River Trail for .8 mile to the campground. From Batsto, drive north on the dirt road at the western edge of Batsto Village (the road parallels a wooden fence surrounding the village). Follow the dirt road (Batsto River Road, but it's not marked) for .7 mile to a sand parking area and a fork in the road. Bear right at the fork, hugging the shore of Batsto Lake. Proceed 3.8 miles, always following the main dirt track, and turn left on an unmarked dirt road. Drive .3 mile to the parking area on the left. Quaker Bridge and Mullica River Roads are potholed dirt tracks under the best of conditions, and some vehicles may not be able to make the journey.

Lower Forge Campground

Lower Forge, located near the geographic center of Wharton State Forest, is also inaccessible by motor vehicle. You must either canoe in along the Batsto River or hike .3 mile from the parking area on Lower Forge Road. The parking area at Lower Forge technically is accessible by car, but it lies 5 miles from Route 206 along weatherbeaten dirt roads. You will come to a clearing bounded by forest and the Batsto River, where you can pitch a tent among the pitch pines, patches of grass, and white sand covered with pine needles. A few access points to the Batsto River lie 30 feet down an embankment, but much of the river is bordered by shrubs and out of view of the campground. As with most of Wharton's wilderness campgrounds, there are no designated sites at Lower Forge, and fire pits are makeshift. The campground has one pit toilet but no water.

From Atsion, drive 3.9 miles south on Quaker Bridge Road, cross the Batsto River, and turn left on Lower Forge Road. Drive .8 mile to the parking area on the right, then walk west from the parking area for .3 mile to the campground. From Batsto, drive north on Goodwater Road for 4.8 miles, bear slightly right onto Lower Forge Road, and proceed .8 mile to the Lower Forge parking area on the right. See the driving advisory at the end of the Mullica River Campground section before setting out.

Batona Campground

Pitch pines and white sand make up Wharton's northernmost campground, set on the Skit Branch of the Batsto River. A series of wetlands follows the river south, bordering the northern edge of the campground. Batona is easily accessible along mostly paved roads. Near the entrance, a memorial commemorates the 1928 plane crash of Capt. Emilio Carranza on his return flight from New York to Mexico City. The pink-blazed Batona Trail runs along the campground access road, leading 3.6 miles north to Apple Pie Hill and a panoramic overlook of the pinelands. This is Wharton's fourth-largest camping area, and privacy is easy to find, as you can pitch a tent anywhere within the campground limits. One hand pump supplies water, and pit toilets are situated throughout the grounds.

From the Atsion park office, drive north on Route 206 for 3.3 miles and turn right on Forked Neck Road. Proceed 3.1 miles, through a residential area, and turn right on Carranza Road. Drive 4.4 miles and turn left on the dirt access road opposite the Carranza Memorial. Continue .3 mile to the Batona Campground. Driving from Batsto, you will encounter a number of dirt roads. Drive 4.2 miles east on Route 542 (Pleasant Mills

Road) and turn left on Route 563. Proceed 11.4 miles to Friendship-Speedwell Road, where the dirt roads begin, and turn left. Continue 2.5 miles to Carranza Road, turn right, and drive 3.2 miles to the campground access road on the right. Proceed .3 mile to Batona Campground.

Buttonwood Hill Campground

Buttonwood Hill is the smallest campground at Wharton, with a capacity of twenty-five campers. It is also one of the easiest to access, situated about 50 yards from Route 542. Four picnic tables with fire rings occupy a tiny clearing about 100 feet wide. The tables sit on a grass lawn, backed by trees and fronted by the dirt road. One outhouse lies about 35 yards north of the campground on Burnt Schoolhouse Road. Across Route 542, the Crowley Landing boat ramp area offers water, picnic tables, and modern restrooms. Drive 1.9 miles east of the Batsto office on Route 542 and turn left on Burnt Schoolhouse Road, an unmarked dirt road. The campground is about 50 yards north of the corner on the right.

Godfrey Bridge Family Campground

Aside from Atsion, Godfrey Bridge is the only campground at Wharton with numbered and designated campsites. Although each site contains a picnic table and fire ring, Godfrey Bridge is still basic, equipped with one water pump and five pit toilets. This is about as close to the water as you will get at Wharton, as seven of the sites rest within feet of the Wading River. The remaining sites occupy a forest of pitch pines and hardwoods amid Wharton's familiar white sand. About half of the sites are large enough to accommodate trailers, and the best of the seven river sites are 17, 18, 20, and 21.

The campground consists of two sections separated by .2 mile. The first section, near the Wading River, contains one water pump but no pit toilets. The second section contains five pit toilets but no water pump. Drive 4.2 miles east of Batsto on Route 542 and turn left on Route 563. Proceed 6 miles to Godfrey Bridge Road and turn left (a Wading Pines Camping Resort sign on the corner points the way). Proceed 1 mile to the first Godfrey Bridge loop and 1.2 miles to the second loop. Wading Pines Camping Resort across the river offers a general store and canoe rentals.

Hawkins Bridge Campground

Mullica River and Lower Forge are Wharton's most remote campgrounds, but Hawkins Bridge is not far behind. It lies 2 miles from the nearest paved road on the west bank of the Wading River. A dirt track

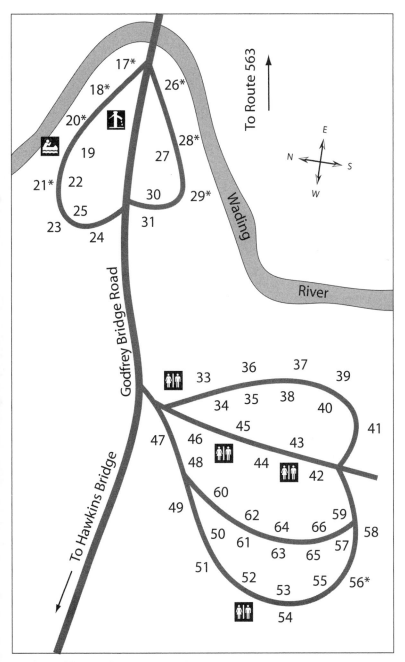

Godfrey Bridge Family Campground

circles the large campground, where privacy is easy to find amid the mixture of open sandy areas, oak-pine forest, and scattered underbrush. Unlike some of the other remote campgrounds at Wharton, you will find more hardwood trees here than sand and pines. The campground is also accessible by motor vehicle. Pit toilets and one water pump service Hawkins Bridge, but the pump was out of service at last check. Drive west from Godfrey Bridge Campground for about .3 mile and turn right at the first intersection, an unmarked dirt road. Proceed 1.4 miles north along the dirt road and turn right into the Hawkins Bridge Campground.

Bodine Field Campground

A wide, sandy clearing is dotted with pines, brush, and grass. The Wading River flows through the campground, but most of the river is bordered by bushes and out of view. You can pitch a tent anywhere within the campground limits at this large and open area. Bodine Field is home to two canoe landings, one on the west side of the campground and one on the Beaver Branch of the Wading River, about .1 mile to the south. Pit toilets are scattered throughout the campground, and one water pump is centrally located. Drive 4.2 miles east of Batsto on Route 542 and turn left on Route 563. Proceed 5.3 miles to Route 679 (Chatsworth Road) and turn right. Continue 1.7 miles, turn right at the Bodine Field sign, and drive .5 mile to the campground on the right.

Trails

A number of marked trails run through Wharton, most notably the 50-mile Batona Trail and the 9-mile Mullica River Trail. Four other trails circle Batsto Village, ranging from 1 to 3.8 miles in length, and two short trails access the Atsion recreation area. A few of the marked trails make use of Wharton's many fire roads crisscrossing the forest. The roads range from those with graded surfaces to potholed jeep tracks barely represented on the best topographic map. They stretch from historic villages to Pine Barrens overlooks; from huge cedar swamps to river headwaters. Most of Wharton's trails are open exclusively to hikers, but the dirt roads allow a wide range of activities, including mountain biking, horseback riding, and some motorized vehicle uses.

The Batona Trail is the best-known and most trafficked trail in the forest. About 25 of its 50 miles cross through Wharton before it continues on to Bass River State Forest to the east and Brendan T. Byrne State Forest to the north. Batona's pink blazes begin near Harrisville Lake on the

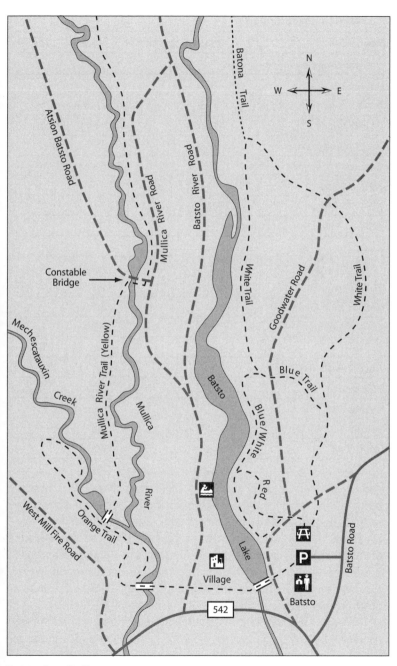

Batsto Area Trails

Trail Mileage and Difficulty

TRAIL	MILES	DIFFICULTY	BLAZE	USES
Batona Trail Destinations				
Route 679	0.0			
Batsto	9.9	E	pink	h
Quaker Bridge	16.0	E	pink	h
Lower Forge parking	17.0	E	pink	h
Carranza Memorial	22.3	E	pink	h
Batona Camp	22.8	E	pink	h
Apple Pie Hill	26.4	E	pink	h
Mullica River Trail Destinations				
Atsion	0.0			
Mullica River Road	2.2	E	yellow	h
Mullica parking	4.2	E	yellow	h
Mullica River Camp	5.0	E	yellow	h
Constable Bridge	7.5	E	yellow	h
Batsto	9.0	E	yellow	h
Batsto Area Trails				
Blue Trail	1.7	E	blue	h
Orange Trail	1.8	E	orange	h
Red Trail	1.0	E	red	h
White Trail	3.8	E	white	h

eastern edge of the park, stretch 9.9 miles west to Batsto, then turn north and extend 12.9 miles past Lower Forge Campground, the Carranza Memorial, and Batona Campground. A popular 4.1-mile section runs from the Carranza Memorial to Apple Pie Hill, a scenic overlook of the pinelands. You can park at the Carranza Memorial and walk north through the Batona Campground to Apple Pie Hill, producing an 8.2-mile round-trip. Batona was named by a local hiking club using an acronym for "back to nature" and allows hiking only.

The yellow-blazed Mullica River Trail extends from Atsion to Batsto, paralleling Wharton's longest river most of the way. The trail begins near Atsion by following Quaker Bridge Road southeast for 2.2 miles; then it turns right on Mullica River Road and heads south to Batsto. Sections of the trail veer off from the road into the forest, producing a serene and secluded 9-mile hike. Along the way, the trail passes a number of quiet fishing spots and the Mullica River Campground about 5 miles south of Atsion. Portions of the Mullica River Trail share Quaker Bridge Road, and those sections are open to horseback riding and mountain biking.

Four other marked trails, open solely to hikers, run through the Batsto Natural Area north of Batsto Village. The Blue and Red Trails combine to form a 2.7-mile loop beginning along the east shore of Batsto Lake before circling through a dense pitch pine forest. The 3.8-mile White Trail veers off from the Blue Trail to continue north along the Batsto River. The Orange Trail, a secluded 1.8-mile walk along the Mullica River and Mechescatauxin Creek, meets the Mullica River Trail west of Batsto. The trailhead for the Blue, Red, White, and Batona Trails lies at the north end of the Batsto office parking area. The Orange Trail begins at the dirt parking area near the western edge of Batsto Village.

Activities

Wharton's 115,111 acres attract wilderness travelers of all passions. Almost any pursuit that will put you in the center of the pinelands is worth the effort. Canoeing is one of the most rewarding ways to see the forest, and the sand roads are popular with horseback riders. Historic sites such as the Carranza Memorial and scenic overlooks like Apple Pie Hill are popular hiking destinations. Atsion's recreation area in the north and Batsto Village in the south receive the bulk of Wharton's summer travelers. You will find swimming at the Atsion recreation area, along with modern restrooms, a food concession, and picnic tables. The nineteenth-century village at Batsto is a busy historical attraction, where a visitor center and museum host travelers throughout the year.

Batsto Village

The Batsto area has been used by humans since the Lenni-Lenape named the area Batstu, or "bathing place," prior to the arrival of Europeans. Settlers began developing Batsto in 1766, when ironmaster Charles Read built a foundry near the mouth of the Batsto River. What remains on the site today are forty-three original buildings dating to the nineteenth century, including Joseph Wharton's 1876 mansion, an 1828 gristmill, and an 1830 stone horse barn. A trail leads around the village and crosses a wooden footbridge over the Batsto Lake dam, where an 1882 sawmill overlooks the scene. Several books and pamphlets detailing a complete history of the area are available at the Batsto park office. A museum, nature center, and visitor center are open from 9 A.M. to 4 P.M. daily.

Carranza Memorial

In the early hours of July 13, 1928, rescue workers recovered the body of Mexican aviator Emilio Carranza in the remote pinelands of what is now Wharton State Forest. Captain Carranza had flown a goodwill mission from Mexico City, landing in New York to complete the second-longest flight in aviation history at the time—surpassed only by Lindbergh's flight one year earlier. Despite severe weather, a telegram from Mexican officials ordered Carranza to hasten his return journey. Captain Carranza departed on the night of July 12 with only a compass, map, and flashlight for navigation. His plane was never seen in Mexico City. On the morning of July 13, his body was discovered at the present location of the Carranza Memorial. Every year, on the closest Saturday to July 12, the American Legion Post 11 holds a memorial ceremony to coincide with a similar service in Mexico. The 12-foot stone monument marking Emilio Carranza's crash site is located across the road from the Batona Campground.

Apple Pie Hill

Apple Pie Hill is like a ship's mast placed in the middle of a serene and waveless ocean. At 205 feet, it may be small, but you can see the curvature of the earth from the top. A panoramic view from Apple Pie Hill takes in the Pinelands National Reserve, a level plain covered with pines stretching to the north and east. A 60-foot fire tower topping the hill is maintained by the New Jersey Forest Fire Service, but the surrounding land lies in the Franklin Parker Preserve, a 9,400-acre tract of land that represents the largest privately owned conservation area in New Jersey. The preserve, under the stewardship of the New Jersey Conservation Foundation, connects Wharton State Forest in the west with Brendan T. Byrne State Forest to the north and Bass River State Forest to the east.

You can hike to Apple Pie Hill along the Batona Trail, beginning at the Carranza Memorial, an 8.2-mile round-trip that climbs two small hills, skirts a cedar swamp, and crosses the Skit Branch of the Batsto River. You can also drive by taking Route 532 about 1.5 miles west of Main Street in Chatsworth to Ringler Avenue, a small paved road on the left marked by two broken-down brick pillars. Turn left on Ringler Avenue, drive .3 mile, and continue straight ahead where the road turns into dirt. (Do not follow the paved road, which veers left.) The dirt road bends around for 1.7 miles to a parking area next to the Apple Pie Hill fire tower.

Fishing

Many lakes and rivers throughout the forest allow fishing, but Wharton's acidic water means the catch is exactly the same in each one of them. Fishing is good for pickerel and catfish in Atsion, Batsto, and Oswego Lakes, as well as the Batsto, Oswego, Mullica, and Wading Rivers. You will also find a lesser population of sunfish in all of the above water bodies and a few American eels in the rivers. None of the lakes offer boat ramps, but they all allow small boats with electric motors. One rather secluded parking spot for anglers lies along the Mullica River off Quaker Bridge Road, although four-wheel drive is recommended. Drive 2.2 miles south on Quaker Bridge Road from the Atsion park office and turn right at a thin dirt side road. Proceed .2 mile to the river.

Boating

Four rivers—the Batsto, Mullica, Oswego, and Wading—all make their way through a portion of Wharton's 115,111 protected acres. They combine to host more paddlers every year than the Delaware itself. The Wading and Oswego rivers on the park's eastern border are the most traveled of Wharton's four rivers, as they cut through a more developed area of the forest. The Mullica and Batsto Rivers run parallel to each other through Wharton's isolated interior, so they typically see fewer paddlers. Campgrounds lie on the Mullica, Batsto, and Wading Rivers, allowing for a two-day paddle if you camp for the night. Four nearby canoe liveries offer rentals, pickup and drop-off service, and one- or two-day packages.

The best rivers for a wilderness escape are the Mullica and the Batsto, which both meander through the heart of Wharton State Forest. The section of the Mullica River from Atsion to Pleasant Mills is protected under the federal Wild and Scenic Rivers Act. As a result, the seven-hour journey beginning at Atsion and ending at Pleasant Mills, with an overnight stay at Mullica River Campground, is one of the most satisfying wilderness paddles in the Pine Barrens. The Batsto River also offers an overnight campground at remote Lower Forge, one of the few campgrounds that restrict motor vehicles. The eight-hour journey down the Batsto from Hampton Furnace to Batsto Lake will put you near the remote center of Wharton State Forest.

If you prefer company, the Wading and Oswego Rivers can support a flotilla on sunny summer days. Three campgrounds lie along the Wading River—Hawkins Bridge, Godfrey Bridge, and Bodine Field—all of them available for overnight stays. The two rivers are popular because their launch sites are readily accessible by car, and both provide easy paddling for beginners. The journey down the Wading River from

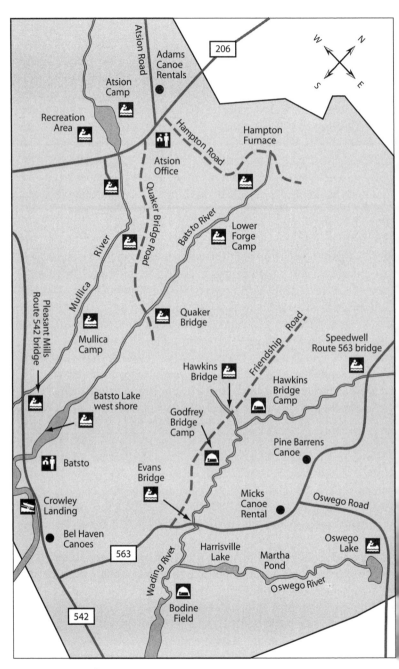

Canoe Access Points

Canoe Trip Times

RIVER	BEGIN	END	HOURS
Batsto River	Hampton Furnace	Lower Forge	2.5–3.5
	Lower Forge	Quaker Bridge	1.0–1.5
	Quaker Bridge	Batsto Lake	3.0–4.0
Mullica River	Atsion Lake	Mullica Camp	2.5–3.5
	Mullica Camp	Pleasant Mills	4.0–5.0
Oswego River	Oswego Lake	Martha Pond	2.0–3.0
	Martha Pond	Harrisville Lake	1.0–2.0
Wading River	Speedwell	Hawkins Bridge	2.5–3.5
	Hawkins Bridge	Godfrey Bridge	1.0–1.5
	Godfrey Bridge	Evans Bridge	1.5–2.5
	Evans Bridge	Bodine Field	1.0–2.0
	Bodine Field	Beaver Branch	0.25–0.75

Speedwell to Beaver Branch is a seven- to nine-hour trip, but you can reduce the time by about three hours if you put in at Hawkins Bridge where it spans Tulpehocken Creek. The Oswego River from Oswego Lake to Harrisville Lake is only about four hours, although many paddlers prolong the trip by portaging around the Harrisville Lake dam and continuing south on the Wading River.

For those who prefer powered boats, electric motors are allowed in Atsion, Batsto, Harrisville, and Oswego Lakes, as well as the Mullica River. Crowley Landing on the Mullica River, across the road from Buttonwood Hill Campground, holds a concrete boat ramp large enough for two boats side by side. You will find a floating dock, but no boat ramp, at the Atsion recreation area on the west side of the beach.

Picnicking

Wharton's two main picnic areas are located at the Atsion recreation area and next to the Batsto office. Both lie at the center of park activity, with restrooms, grills, and water close at hand. The fifty or so tables at Atsion line the east and west sides of the recreation area access road, far enough from the beach and parking area to offer privacy. The Batsto picnic tables occupy a grass clearing on the north side of the office parking area, where about twenty tables sit next to modern restrooms.

A more serene option is the little-known picnic area at Crowley Landing, where you will find a dozen tables nestled in wooded groves directly on the Mullica River. A wooden bridge over an inlet leads from Crowley Landing to twenty more tables, with grills, modern restrooms, and drinking water nearby. Crowley Landing is located on Route 542 across the road from Buttonwood Hill Campground.

Swimming

Clean and clear Atsion Lake is surrounded by the pitch pines and white sand of Wharton State Forest. A wide beach overlooks nine log cabins across the lake, and the cordoned-off swimming area is larger than at most parks. The recreation area contains modern restrooms with showers, a food concession, first-aid station, water fountains, and a telephone. Two playgrounds and about forty picnic tables border the parking area, along with a second set of modern restrooms, an activity field, and two short trails. The 1.3-mile Blue Trail follows the shore of Atsion Lake to the west, and the .7-mile Red Trail leads from Atsion Lake to the parking area. The beach is open to swimmers from Memorial Day weekend through Labor Day.

Mountain Biking

The white sand that constitutes Wharton's dirt roads, almost 90 percent silica, is sometimes referred to as sugar sand by local mountain bikers. It is a substance that simulates riding on two deflated tires. Plans are in the works to mark two mountain bike trails through the forest using a combination of negotiable sand roads and hard dirt tracks. A 16-mile loop for advanced riders and a 5-mile beginners' loop will leave from the Batsto Village Parking Area. Future plans also call for side trails to veer off into the forest. Until then, all of Wharton's sand roads are open to mountain bikers, and road conditions depend on weather, four-wheel-drive activity, and recent maintenance.

Horseback Riding

Horse trailers seem to be a permanent fixture at the huge parking area behind the Atsion office. Quaker Bridge Road leaves directly from the parking area, a secluded sand road that is suited to horses more than it is to mountain bikes, motorized vehicles, or hiking shoes. The ride to Mullica River Road and back is 2.2 miles. Some riders continue south on Mullica River Road, which is less traveled and pressed thin by pines. The round-trip to Mullica River Campground and back to Quaker Bridge

Road adds 5.6 miles to the ride. You will find dozens of access points to the Mullica River along the route.

Birding

Wharton's rivers, cedar swamps, and open fields support a number of species that are not easily seen elsewhere in the Pine Barrens. The cedar swamps near Batona Campground and along the Oswego River support saw-whet owls, northern waterthrushes, and a variety of warblers. Camping at Wharton in the spring or summer will always reward you with the call of whippoorwills at night, and chuck-will's-widows can be heard but are less common. Eastern towhees seem to inhabit every bush at Goshen Pond Campground, and red crossbills, hermit thrushes, hooded warblers, and common nighthawks can sometimes be seen near Harrisville Lake and along Carranza Road. Red-headed woodpeckers are known to linger around Batsto Village. Birders should consider the destinations covered in the Belleplain State Forest chapter, as well as Edwin B. Forsythe National Wildlife Refuge, covered in the Bass River State Forest chapter.

Hunting

About 95 percent of Wharton's 115,111 acres is open to the hunting of deer, small game, waterfowl, and wild turkeys. The popularity of deer hunting has increased at Wharton in recent years, mainly because of the return of large deer as a result of conservation efforts. The forest is particularly busy with hunters during the muzzleloader and six-day firearms seasons, which occur in Wharton from the end of November through December. Check the current regulations for specific days and annual changes. The bulk of Wharton falls within deer management zone 23, and the remainder of the forest lies in zones 19, 24, 25, and 26.

Winter Activities

Camping is available year-round at Wharton's eight wilderness campgrounds. Hiking and mountain biking are worthwhile pursuits during the winter, when the roads are less likely to be pulverized by four-wheel-drive vehicles and the sand firms up for better traction. Cross-country skiing and snowshoeing are allowed on the 500 miles of sand roads throughout the forest, and snowmobiling is permitted on most of the roads. The main obstacle for winter trail activities—other than hiking and biking—in the Pine Barrens is the amount of annual snowfall, which rarely exceeds 1 foot. Winter travelers should carry the essentials for wilderness survival when venturing out.

Flora and Fauna

More than 1,200 species of plants and animals inhabit Wharton State Forest and the surrounding pinelands. The trees alone number almost 50 species, including at least 5 types of pine and 8 species of oak. White poplar, sassafras, black walnut, sweetbay magnolia, American persimmon, and southern catalpa are present, along with many more. Another 800 species of plants occupy the forest, almost 10 percent of them threatened or endangered. Bog asphodel is a quickly disappearing plant that produces an exotic bloom of yellow flowers. Its beauty and rarity combine to hasten its demise, as bog asphodel is a favorite of indiscriminate plant collectors. Swamp pink, Knieskern's beaked rush, and American chaffseed are just a few extremely rare plants that rely on Pine Barrens habitat.

Almost 350 animal species occur in the park as well, but perhaps the most unusual residents are the amphibians. Wharton's rivers maintain an acidity level that is too stressful for the eggs of most aquatic animals, yet a handful of amphibians have adapted to the unique conditions. The blue-spotted salamander makes use of milder vernal pools in the spring to lay its eggs, whereas Pine Barrens tree frogs seek out water with a high acidity level. The eastern tiger salamander is New Jersey's largest salamander, measuring up to 8 inches long, with distinctive dark green spots resembling army camouflage. The endangered southern gray tree frog and threatened eastern mud salamander add to the list of rare amphibians that have adapted to conditions in the pinelands. Refer to the other Southern Region chapters for more information about the flora and fauna of the Pine Barrens.

Surrounding Points of Interest

Wharton's size makes it a destination unto itself, and it would be wise to reserve side trips for a separate journey. That said, Wharton is the largest state forest within the Pinelands National Reserve, so the surrounding points of interest are many. Belleplain State Forest lies to the south and is surrounded by dozens of wildlife areas known for their unmatched birding, fishing, and boating. Bass River State Forest and the salt marshes of Great Bay Boulevard meet the Atlantic Ocean to the east, near Edwin B. Forsythe National Wildlife Refuge. All of these areas and many more are covered elsewhere in this guidebook. See the Brendan T. Byrne, Bass River, and Belleplain State Forest chapters for more information.

Penn State Forest

Penn State Forest is a continuation of the vast pinelands represented in Wharton State Forest, but this 3,366-acre wildlife area is undeveloped and contains no marked trails. It is also a prime location to see a section of the pinelands composed of stunted pines less than 6 feet tall. The phenomenon is globally rare, and New Jersey contains the most acreage of pygmy pines in the world. One parking area gives access to Oswego Lake, where fishing, canoeing, and boats with electric motors are welcome. Drive .7 mile north of Godfrey Bridge Campground on Route 563 and turn right on the unmarked paved road (Oswego Lake Road). Proceed 3 miles to the parking area on the right. One large tract of pygmy pines is located near the corner of Stave Road and Lost Lane. Turn right out of the parking area, drive about 100 yards, and turn left on the unmarked dirt road (Sooey Road). Proceed straight ahead for 2.7 miles, turn right on Lost Lane, and continue 1 mile to Stave Road. The dirt roads are not marked, and four-wheel drive is recommended.

Where to Buy Supplies

Hammonton is the nearest major retail center to both Batsto and Atsion. The small city lies 7.5 miles south of Atsion on Route 206 and 7.1 miles west of Batsto on Route 542. From Batsto, drive 7.1 miles west on Route 542 and turn right on Route 30. The city contains a Wal-Mart, banks, gas stations, pharmacies, grocery stores, fast food, diners, and a variety of restaurants. A few widely scattered gas stations, restaurants, and convenience stores line Route 206 to the north of Atsion. Pic-A-Lily Bar and Restaurant is 1.2 miles north on the right. Within the next 7 miles, you will pass a bar and grill, barbecue restaurant, and diner. Two gas stations sit on the outskirts of Tabernacle, 7.8 miles north of the Atsion office.

Campers at Godfrey Bridge or Hawkins Bridge Campground can find supplies at Wading Pines Camping Resort, located across the river from Godfrey Bridge Campground. The resort's general store offers basic camping supplies and food, from lighter fluid and insect repellent to hot dogs and bagels. Bel Haven Canoe and Kayak, located about 3.4 miles east of Batsto on the north side of Route 542, carries items such as wet suits, paddles, and flotation cushions. Mullica River Marina is on the south side of Route 542, about 2.3 miles east of Batsto, where you will find fuel and other boating supplies.

Bass River State Forest

762 Stage Rd.
Tuckerton, NJ 08087

Area. 27,635 acres.

Park office. Burlington County, 4.8 miles west of Tuckerton on the north side of Stage Road.

Highlights. Absegami Natural Area, Batona Trail.

Activities. Camping, hiking, fishing, boating, picnicking, swimming, mountain biking, horseback riding, birding, hunting, cross-country skiing, snowshoeing, snowmobiling.

Entrance fee. A fee is charged to enter the recreation area from Memorial Day weekend through Labor Day.

Park hours. Year-round, from 8 A.M. to 8:00 P.M.

For additional information: (609) 296-1114

The state began acquiring land in 1905, when Gov. Edward C. Stokes established the Forest Park Reservation Commission to protect depleted forests. Bass River became New Jersey's first state forest later that year and recently marked its centennial birthday with a series of events celebrating the park's history. Absegami, or "little stream," was the name the Lenni-Lenape Indians gave to the small river flowing through the forest, but the little stream became a lake when Bass River's tributaries were dammed in 1930 to form the clear waters of Lake Absegami. The Civilian Conservation Corps (CCC), Roosevelt's answer to unemployment during the Great Depression, went about building cabins, fire roads, and bridges around the lake, and a recreation area was born. Remnants of the old CCC camp can still be seen on the Pink Trail in the southern section of the park.

Bass River's recreation area is highly developed, with three camping areas, cabins, shelters, and lean-tos surrounding Lake Absegami. A sandy beach on the east side of the lake is surrounded by two picnic areas, a food concession, and enough parking to accommodate the busiest weekend. Dozens of trails and sand roads crisscrossing the 27,635-acre pine and oak forest are enough to provide a sense of escape,

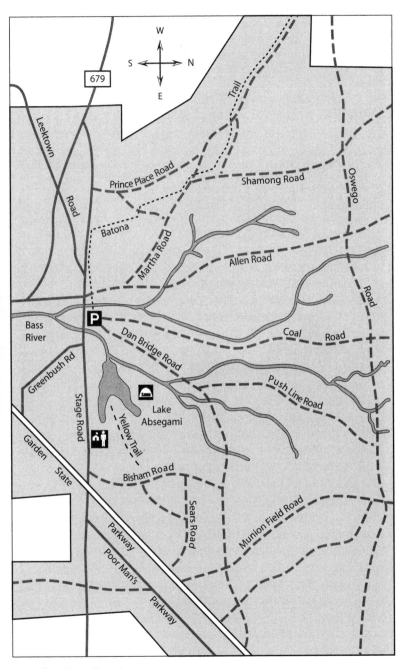

Bass River State Forest

many of them open to mountain bikers, horseback riders, and cross-country skiers. The 50-mile Batona Trail heads west from the park to Wharton State Forest and Apple Pie Hill, the highest point in the southern New Jersey pinelands.

Camping

Bass River's 176 campsites offer enough variety to satisfy anyone planning to spend the night. Much of the activity revolves around Lake Absegami, where visitors will find two family campgrounds, one campground catering to large groups, six cabins, nine lean-tos, and half a dozen shelters. Hot showers, modern restrooms, and drinking water are a short walk from any of the camping options. Cabins and shelters provide prime shorefront views, but alas, none of the tent sites lie directly on the water. The two family campgrounds occupy a forest of pitch pine and chestnut oak, and the solitude of Bass River's undeveloped pineland is never more than a trail away.

North Shore Family Campground

North Shore provides easy access to the recreation area and boat launch, with Lake Absegami situated less than a mile to the south beyond a small stream. The individual sites never quite make you feel lost in the wilderness, but only a handful of spots next to the road will discourage an overnight stay. Many of the sites are large enough to accommodate trailers, and a thin row of trees and brush serves as a border between neighbors. The Blue Trail heads south from the campground to the recreation area, and the Yellow Trail leads east through a quiet forest of white pine and red maple.

Directions. Turn right out of the park office and follow the access road for 1.1 miles to the campground.

Sites and facilities. North Shore's ninety-three tent and trailer sites are each equipped with fire rings and picnic tables. Three modern restrooms are within walking distance of all sites; the one in the middle of the campground contains hot showers and a washer and dryer. A playground sits next to the showers, four water pumps are scattered throughout the campground, and a trailer sanitary station lies next to the entrance. The campground is open from April 1 through October 31.

Recommended sites. Many of the campsites at North Shore sit end to end directly on the paved access road, making careful selection crucial if you are in pursuit of solitude. Number 144 curves into the woods

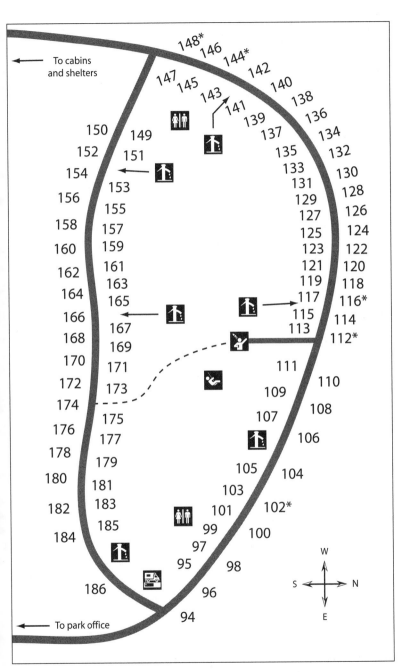

North Shore Family Campground

around a curtain of trees, and 148 is encircled by forest at the northwest corner of the campground. The next best options for privacy in descending order are 102, recessed from the main road; 116, where you will find a water pump across the way rather than a campsite; and 112, which sits by itself opposite the shower and playground. The remainder of the sites at North Shore are nearly identical to one another, although numbers 100, 106, 118, 140, and 142 sit slightly off the road.

South Shore Family Campground

You can see Lake Absegami from the east side of the campground, but none of South Shore's campsites lie at the water's edge. This is no great detriment, as the most serene places to pitch a tent are the farthest from Lake Absegami. The sounds of afternoon swimmers at the beach become distant, and then absent, as you travel away from the lake toward the far end of the campground. A few of the sites are secluded enough to produce a sense of privacy, and many can accommodate trailers.

Directions. Turn left out of the park office and follow the park access road for .3 mile to the campground.

Sites and facilities. South Shore's eighty-three ground sites and nine lean-tos are each equipped with a fire ring and picnic table. Lean-tos are one-room cabins, each furnished with a woodburning stove. Four modern restrooms, water from ground pumps, and two playgrounds are scattered throughout South Shore. The restroom next to campsite 63 contains hot showers and a washer and dryer. Campsites and lean-tos are open year-round.

Recommended sites. Drive past the sites in the median as you enter the campground, most of them open to the sky and bunched together, until you pass the lean-tos and see site 21 on the right. This is not a bad option for a trailer, ringed by trees and overlooking a slight rise, but the sites become more serene as you drive on. Numbers 24 and 25, fairly private in their own right, lead to four quiet spots on the edge of the campground. Sites 27 and 31 are recessed into the forest, and 29 forms a semicircle that curls away from the road into the woods. The next site you come to, number 33, is supremely secluded, hemmed in by the forest and large enough to accommodate a trailer. The lean-tos are all fairly peaceful, but number 6 lies at the end of the row in a wooded clearing.

Group Campground

Six group sites, A through F, stretch along the campground access road midway between the park office and North Shore Campground. The

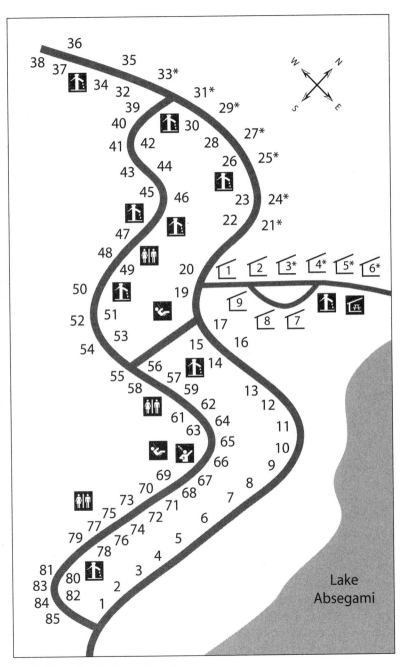

South Shore Family Campground

sites are almost identical, with the exception of site C, a sandy area with no trees. The others are forested enough to at least obscure the view of neighboring campers. Water, picnic tables, one fire ring, and a pit toilet are close at hand, but the campground does not contain showers. Each site accommodates twenty-five campers, and the campground is open year-round.

Cabins and Shelters

Six cabins and six shelters on the north shore of Lake Absegami are the closest you can get to sleeping on the water at Bass River. A thin finger of Lake Absegami separates the beach from the cabins, and the south-facing view includes a sweeping vista of the lake bounded by pitch pine and red maple. Cabins and shelters each contain a living room and two bunk rooms, but the cabins are slightly larger, with an additional kitchen, modern bathroom, and fireplace.

Directions. Follow the directions for North Shore Campground and continue about .6 mile through the campground to the cabins and shelters.

Cabins and facilities. Each cabin sleeps six, with double-deck bunks in the main room and each of two bedrooms. All cabins contain a fireplace, modern bathroom with hot showers, and kitchen with an electric stove and refrigerator. A screened-in porch faces the lake, and you will find a charcoal grill and picnic table a few steps outside the back door. The cabins are available from April 1 through October 31. Contact the park office for reservations.

Shelters and facilities. The six shelters share three water pumps and one modern restroom with hot showers. Each shelter accommodates up to four people, with a double-deck bunk in each of two bedrooms. A central living room is equipped with a woodburning stove, and you will find a grill, picnic table, and benches outside. The shelters are available from April 1 through October 31.

Recommended cabins and shelters. The sound of beachgoers at the recreation area diminishes as the cabin numbers rise. Cabin 3 holds the clearest view of the lake, followed closely by the scene from numbers 4 and 5. Cabin 6, on the end, is the quietest option, but a barrier of trees separates the cabin from the shore. Lined up next to the cabins, six shelters are well spaced and secluded, each with a picnic table no more than 20 yards from Lake Absegami. All of the shelters occupy private groves in a serene setting, but shelter 1 offers the best view of the water, followed by shelters 3 and 2.

Trails

The defining pink blazes of Batona Trail stretch 50 miles through the Pinelands National Reserve, a 1.1-million-acre area containing Wharton, Brendan T. Byrne, and Bass River State Forests. Batona marks its southern end at the corner of Stage Road and Coal Road, about 1.1 miles west of the park office. From there, the trail heads west along Stage Road, then north into Bass River's interior, before bending westward toward Wharton State Forest. Batona is one of the flattest 50-mile hikes you'll ever encounter, and hiking is the only activity allowed on the trail. If you develop a passion to walk Batona's entire length, see the Wharton State Forest chapter for more details.

Bass River also encompasses seven short hiking and biking trails, most of them surrounding Lake Absegami. The Red, Orange, and Blue Trails are the three shortest, together forming a 1.5-mile hike between the recreation area and the two campgrounds. The Yellow Trail leaves the recreation area behind, stretching wide and flat through serene pine-oak forest for the first mile before joining a deeply rutted fire road on the outskirts of the park. The Yellow Trail ends at the eastern end of the 2-mile Plum Trail, a walk through cedar and pines leading back to the park office.

The 2.5-mile Pink Trail and 1.3-mile Green Trail begin south of Stage Road across from the park entrance. The Pink Trail passes an old CCC camp about 100 yards south of the corner of Stage and East Greenbush Roads. A parking area and a plaque near Greenbush Road describes the corps' contribution to Bass River State Forest. An eighth trail, the Absegami Trail, circles the Absegami Natural Area and is covered below.

Miles of sand and dirt roads intersect the trails as well, all of them open to mountain biking, horseback riding, cross-country skiing, and most motorized vehicles. Two roads begin near the Batona trailhead on Stage Road, about 1.1 miles west of the park office. Coal Road cuts through secluded pineland along the West Branch of the Bass River, passes a small bog, and continues on to remote Oswego Road about 3.5 miles north of Stage Road. Dan Bridge Road, leaving from the same trailhead, crosses three Bass River tributaries and stretches about 4.5 miles through dense pines to the Garden State Parkway. The total altitude variation along either road is about 60 feet. Carry water and emergency supplies if you venture out along any of Bass River's dirt roads, as you will be hemmed in by forest along the entire route.

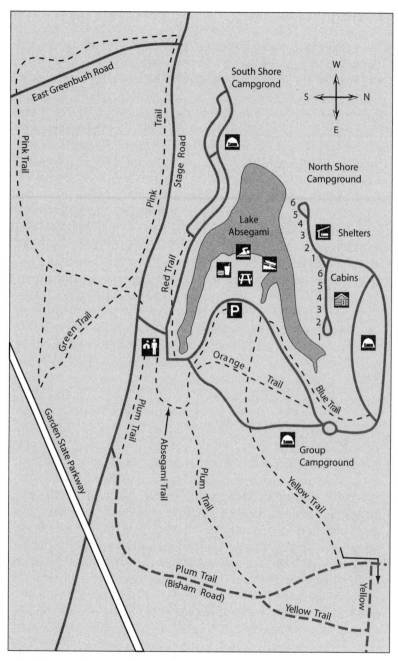

Lake Absegami Area Trails

Trail Mileage and Difficulty

TRAIL	MILES	DIFFICULTY	BLAZE	USES
Absegami Trail	0.5	E	white	h,s,x
Blue Trail	0.6	E	blue	h,m,s,x
Green Trail	1.3	E	green	h,m,s,x
Orange Trail	0.5	E	orange	h,m,s,x
Pink Trail	2.5	E	pink	h,m,s,x
Plum Trail	2.0	E	blue	h,m,s,x
Red Trail	0.4	E	red	h,m,s,x
Yellow Trail	2.2	E–M	yellow	h,m,s,x
Batona Trail Destinations				
Coal Road	0.0			
Stage Road	0.8	E	pink	h
Martha Road	6.7	E	pink	h
Route 679	8.0	E	pink	h
Evans Bridge	8.7	E	pink	h

Activities

Bass River State Forest mixes wilderness with a developed recreation area. Miles of sand roads leading through the Pinelands National Reserve are open to all sorts of activities, from hiking to snowmobiling. This is Bass River's most rewarding asset, its isolated roads accessing the surrounding pine forest and a habitat supporting hundreds of rare plants and animals. Closer to the park office, the recreation area at Lake Absegami is surrounded by a swimming beach, picnic tables, and modern restrooms with showers. It's usually busy during the summer months, but Lake Absegami provides the opportunity to cast a line or row a boat to a quieter shore. Absegami Natural Area offers an alternative to the developed recreation area, with an easy, self-guided hike through pine and oak woods.

Absegami Natural Area

Absegami Trail begins at the park office and forms a .5-mile loop through 128 acres of pine forest and cedar swamp. The trail is designed to provide an introduction to a variety of Pine Barrens habitats. A boardwalk and a few wooden bridges pass Atlantic white cedar, sweet bay magnolia, and a mixture of pines. Fewer than 30,000 acres of Atlantic white cedar forest remain in New Jersey, much of it lost to wildfires, deer browsing, and development of coastal wetlands. The presence of red maple trees along the trail shows a natural transition from Atlantic white cedar swamp to hardwood forest. Absegami Trail allows hiking and cross-country skiing, but no bikes.

Fishing and Boating

Fishing is good for pickerel, catfish, and sunfish in 63-acre Lake Absegami. Small boats with electric motors are allowed on the lake, and you will find a boat ramp 100 yards north of the recreation area on the campground access road. The surrounding Bass, Wading, and Mullica Rivers are not great fishing destinations, but the area around the park provides a few boating opportunities. Great Bay Boulevard Wildlife Management Area offers interesting kayaking through tidal salt marsh, and you can rent boats at First Bridge Marina on Great Bay Boulevard. See the Surrounding Points of Interest section for more information. Also see the Wharton State Forest chapter for information about canoeing the Mullica, Wading, and Oswego Rivers.

Swimming and Picnicking

About eighty picnic tables surround Bass River's classic sandy beach. Half of the tables sit in forested groves on the edge of Lake Absegami, and one covered pavilion on the south side of the beach holds two grills and two long picnic tables. A bathhouse with modern restrooms and hot showers is nearby, and a food concession sells everything from hot dogs to suntan lotion. The wide, white beach is reminiscent of an ocean shore, but beware, the recreation area is very popular during the summer. Swimming is allowed from Memorial Day weekend through Labor Day.

Mountain Biking

All of the roads and marked trails within Bass River allow mountain bikes, with the one exception of Absegami Trail. Expect flat terrain and a lot of fine, white sand. If you want to stay near the campground and still avoid well-traveled areas of the park, the Yellow and Plum Trails combine to form an easy 3.2-mile loop through serene pine and oak forest. The Yellow Trail begins beyond a steel guardrail at the southeast end of the group campground. From the guardrail, follow the Yellow Trail for .6 mile to a dirt crossroad (Bisham Road, but it's not marked). Turn left and cycle .2 mile until you come to Sears Road, an unmarked dirt road on the right. Turn right on Sears Road and cycle .6 mile to another unmarked dirt road, Falkinsburg Branch Road, and turn right. The road forks almost immediately. Bear right at the fork and continue south for .5 mile until you return to Bisham Road. Turn left, cycle .7 mile along Bisham Road, and then turn right on the Plum Trail, which parallels Stage Road for .6 mile to end at the park office.

Horseback Riding

Horses are not allowed on the marked trails within the recreation area, but all of the sand roads and outlying trails are perfectly suited to horseback riding. Bass River's dirt roads encompass enough terrain to satisfy a ride of almost any length. See the Trails section for destinations and distances.

Birding

Bass River supports a number of species typical of the Pine Barrens, including pine warblers, red-eyed vireos, red-headed woodpeckers, eastern towhees, and common yellowthroats. Check the cedar swamps along Absegami Trail for rarities such as sedge wrens, saw-whet owls, and prothonotary warblers. Bald eagles have been seen in the park as well, but they are not common, and an occasional heron will forage near the marshy areas of Lake Absegami. If you're camping, listen for the night sounds of the eastern screech owl, whippoorwill, and common nighthawk.

The number of birding destinations surrounding Bass River makes it easy for this 27,635-acre forest to get overshadowed. Cape May, covered in the Belleplain State Forest chapter, and Edwin B. Forsythe National Wildlife Refuge, in the Surrounding Points of Interest section, are two nearby sanctuaries that draw birders from around the world. Great Bay Boulevard Wildlife Management Area, also covered below, lies only 5 miles east of the park office and is a great place to look for egrets, herons, and shorebirds.

Hunting

Almost 99 percent of the forest is open to the hunting of deer, small game, waterfowl, and wild turkeys. The typical pinelands habitat is not a favorite with hunters. The bulk of Bass River lies within deer management zone 24, although a small piece of the forest south of the Garden State Parkway falls in zone 22. Stafford Forge Wildlife Management Area is a popular hunting destination, as it is stocked with 2,000 pheasant each year. See the Surrounding Points of Interest section for directions.

Winter Activities

Winter camping is a small but growing pastime in New Jersey. Small, because it's somewhat of an art, and growing, because it's a great way to beat the crowds. Bass River's campsites and lean-tos are open year-round, and the average overnight visitation is a modest five to ten campers per week after November. Miles of sand roads allow snowmobiles, and all of the trails are open to snowshoeing and cross-country skiing. Hiking is the most common winter pastime, as heavy snowfalls are infrequent this far south. Lean-tos are equipped with woodburning stoves throughout the winter.

Flora and Fauna

New Jersey's southern pinelands gained international attention when John McPhee released his best-selling book *The Pine Barrens* in 1968. Ten years later, the United States designated 1.1 million acres of the pinelands as the country's first national reserve, and in 1983, the United Nations followed suit by declaring the region an international biosphere reserve. Bass River State Forest makes up a small part of the reserve, an area known as the New Jersey Pine Barrens. The 1.1 million acres encompass three state forests, miles of slow-moving rivers, and small country towns that blend into the landscape with ease.

It is difficult to believe that early settlers deemed the area barren, mainly because the acidic soil supports few agricultural crops. Today environmentalists see the Pine Barrens as one of the richest and most diverse ecosystems on earth. More than 850 plant species have been identified in the Pinelands National Reserve, in addition to dozens of endangered birds, mammals, amphibians, and reptiles. Bass River State Forest itself lies near a phenomenon known locally as the Pygmy Pine Forest, a great expanse of pitch pines that reach an average height of only 6 feet. Visitors can see the stunted forest at nearby Stafford Forge Wildlife Management Area, covered below. For more information about the wildlife of the pinelands, refer to the Wharton State Forest and Brendan T. Byrne State Forest chapters.

Surrounding Points of Interest

North of Bass River, the pinelands continue into Stafford Forge Wildlife Management Area, a large tract of land popular with hunters. To the east, Bass River's forest meets the coast, joining an area of salt marshes and tidal wetlands. Several sanctuaries along the shore provide nesting and feeding grounds for migratory birds, as well as a last haven for a number of rare plants. Three such sanctuaries lie within a ten-minute drive of Bass River State Forest.

Stafford Forge Wildlife Management Area

This 15,837-acre area is known mainly for its pheasant hunting, but the road beyond Stafford Forge claims one other rare distinction. The northern border of this wildlife management area is a prime location to see what is known locally as the Pygmy Pine Forest, a section of the Pine Barrens containing vast tracts of dwarf pitch pines that reach an average height of 6 feet at maturity. The phenomenon is globally rare, and New Jersey contains the most acreage of pygmy pines in the world. Wind, salt air, and poor soil conditions combine to create an effect that allows you to see over the top of an entire forest canopy from your car window. Pitch pines normally grow to a height of 40 to 70 feet. Turn left out of the park office onto Stage Road, drive 4.1 miles, and turn left on Route 9. Proceed .8 mile into Tuckerton and turn left on Route 539 (North Green Street). The stunted pines line both sides of Route 539, beginning at 7 miles and ending at 9 miles to the north of Tuckerton.

Great Bay Boulevard Wildlife Management Area

Many of New Jersey's wildlife management areas are mainly destinations for birders, anglers, and hunters, but Great Bay Boulevard is an interesting drive even if you're not passionate about fishing. One thin road stretches 7 miles between Great Bay and Little Egg Harbor, where salt marshes blanket the sea in every direction. Several parking areas along the way offer views of salt marshes and distant marinas on the horizon. One parking area at the end is a common destination for sea kayakers, with a thin trail leading to the beach and a great view of the bay.

Fishing, crabbing, and clamming are popular, and the marinas all supply boat ramps, rentals, and supplies. Birding is excellent in the marshes along the road, where egrets look like common fixtures and a row of osprey nests adorns the power poles 4 miles south of the first parking area. Swallows, gulls, terns, and herons are common in the salt marshes, and plovers, sandpipers, and a variety of shorebirds frequent the bay at the end of the road. From the Bass River office, follow Stage Road east for 4.1 miles and turn left on Route 9. Proceed .5 mile into Tuckerton, turn right on Great Bay Boulevard, and follow the road 6.7 miles to the end.

Edwin B. Forsythe National Wildlife Refuge

You don't have to be a bird-watcher to be impressed by the number of waterbirds diving into the impounds at the Brigantine section of Edwin B. Forsythe National Wildlife Refuge. Keep your life list ready, because an 8-mile drive through this 46,000-acre refuge of tidal wetland provides a chance to see the hundreds of species that migrate through every year. The variety of birds recorded at Forsythe is impressive, almost 300 species, including rarities such as piping, American golden, and black-bellied plovers; upland, curlew, and solitary sandpipers; as well as roseate and least terns, American white pelicans, and sooty shearwaters. This coastal region has long provided the primary nesting habitat for Atlantic brants and American black ducks, as well as tricolored and yellow-crowned night herons, glossy ibises, blue-winged teals, American kestrels, and many more.

The refuge supports a number of trails through undeveloped sections, but the fresh and brackish water impounds at Brigantine are a good place to start. Take the Garden State Parkway south to Exit 48 (Route 9 south). Drive 5.6 miles south on Route 9 into Oceanville and turn left on Great Creek Road. Proceed .6 mile to the refuge office on the right, where you will find maps and information. There is an entrance fee throughout the week.

Where to Buy Supplies

The borough of Tuckerton lies 4.8 miles east of the park office, and you will find a number of stores along the way. Turn left out of the park office onto Stage Road and drive 3.8 miles to a flashing traffic light (Giffordtown Lane). Turn right and drive .2 mile to Route 9. At the four-way intersection, you will find a pizza parlor, drug store, McDonald's restaurant, and Acme supermarket with a pharmacy and ATM inside. If you turn left on Route 9, the Tuckerton border is .4 mile to the west. The large borough contains convenience stores, restaurants, delis, gas stations, banks, and pharmacies. If you turn right at the Acme Market intersection onto Route 9, you come upon a Cumberland Farms convenience store on the left after .1 mile and a bicycle shop across the street. The nearest major city is Atlantic City, 14 miles south on the Garden State Parkway to Exit 38.

Parvin State Park

701 Almond Rd.
Pittsgrove, NJ 08318

Area. 1,952 acres.

Park office. Salem County, 5 miles west of Vineland on the south side of Route 540.

Highlights. Parvin Lake, Parvin Natural Area.

Activities. Camping, hiking, fishing, boating, picnicking, swimming, mountain biking, horseback riding, birding, cross-country skiing, snowshoeing.

Entrance fee. A fee is charged to enter the recreation area from Memorial Day weekend through Labor Day.

Park hours. Year-round, from dawn to dusk.

For additional information: (856) 358-8616

The remains of five Lenni-Lenape encampments around Parvin add some irony to the fact that the first recorded landowner in the area was settler John Estaugh, who was granted a title to almost 3,000 acres in 1742. Lemuel Parvin settled on the land in 1796 and dammed Muddy Run stream to power a sawmill, creating Parvin Lake in the process. The state bought 918 acres in 1933 and, with the help of the Civilian Conservation Corps, established Parvin State Park. Ten years later, in 1944, the area was used to house prisoners of war from Rommel's Afrika Corps, who were sent from Fort Dix to work in local food-processing plants. Japanese-American interns were already there, shipped in to work the fields while their children occupied a camp at Parvin.

Today this 1,952-acre park stands as a bit of an anomaly, as it holds the only public campground amid the vast farmland and open space of Cumberland and Salem Counties. Parvin and Thundergust Lakes are small but active, surrounded by a modern campground, eighteen cabins, picnic tables, a swimming beach, and food concession. A boat ramp gives access to Parvin Lake, where anglers will find good fishing for largemouth bass. Almost 15 miles of trails weave through a diverse forest composed of fifty types of trees, an area open to mountain biking, horseback riding, and cross-country skiing.

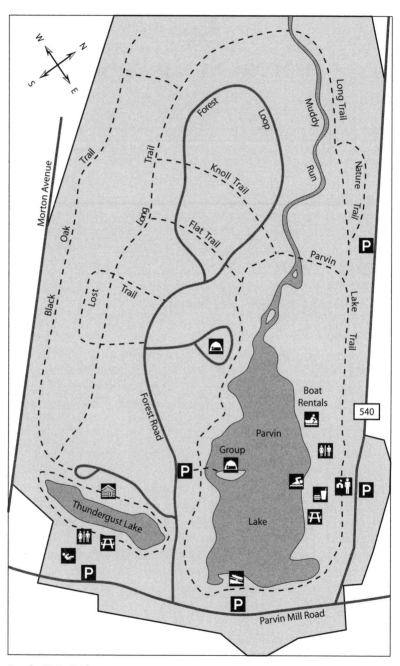

Parvin State Park

Camping

Parvin's one family campground, four group sites, and eighteen cabins surround the park's two lakes. A modern family campground borders the south shore of Parvin Lake, where tent and trailer sites sprawl out beneath a canopy of mixed oak and pine trees. A wooden footbridge leads to the four group sites, which are situated on a forested island about 30 yards offshore. The eighteen secluded cabins ring Thundergust Lake less than a mile to the south, many of them directly on the water and all in private clearings far from the main road.

Jaggers Point Family Campground

A small point of land juts into Parvin Lake, where fifty-six tent and trailer sites occupy a developed campground complete with modern restrooms, hot showers, and laundry facilities. Jaggers Point is a trailer-friendly campground, and several of the sites can accommodate vehicles of almost any size. A wide access road leads to the lake, forming a series of loops through pitch pine, chestnut oak, and red maple. Most of the sites are easily accessible, bordering the paved access road and open to the sky. A few of the sites lie near the water but not directly onshore. Parvin Trail intersects the north end of the campground, heading west into Parvin Natural Area and east along the shore of Parvin Lake.

Directions. Drive east from the park office for .3 mile and turn right on Parvin Mill Road. Continue .3 mile, turn right on Forest Road, and proceed .6 mile to the campground on the right.

Sites and facilities. Parvin's fifty-six tent and trailer sites are equipped with fire rings and picnic tables. A playground sits next to site number 7, and ten water pumps are scattered throughout the campground. One modern restroom contains flush toilets, hot showers, and laundry facilities. A trailer sanitary station is located at the campground entrance, and a canoe launch reserved exclusively for campers lies between sites 13 and 15. Jaggers Point is open year-round.

Recommended sites. The three waterside sites—10, 11, and 13—are the most sought-after spots in the park, although a barrier of brush blocks any view of Parvin Lake. Number 13 is the best of the three, where an adjacent canoe launch adds some open space and access to the water. Several of the sites away from the lake provide slightly more privacy. Site 49 is recessed into the forest and encircled by bushes, 16 is hemmed in by trees, and 22 sits well away from the road. Sites 33, 34, and 41 enjoy mild isolation, sharing no immediate neighbors. Numbers 8 and 52 can accommodate the largest trailers, and smaller trailers will easily fit in about one-third of the remaining sites, including recommended sites 11, 13, 16, and 41.

Island Point Group Campground

About .3 mile east of the family camping area, a wooden footbridge arches 30 yards from the shore of Parvin Lake to the group campground. Island Point is a small forested island holding four group campsites designated by letters A through D. Sites A, B, and C each contain two fire rings, picnic tables, and a water pump, with a modern restroom located beyond the bridge. Site D is more isolated than the others, situated at the end of a short path where Parvin Lake is within view (none of the other sites offer a view of the water). Site D contains two picnic tables and one fire ring, but no water pump. Parking is available on Forest Road, so all supplies have to be carried at least 30 yards over the bridge. The group sites are open from March 1 through November 30.

Thundergust Lake Cabins

Parvin's eighteen cabins rest near the shore of Thundergust Lake. Each accommodates four people, with two double-deck bunks, a woodburning stove or fireplace, electric stove, refrigerator, and modern bathroom complete with hot water and a shower. Cabins 6 and 16 are wheelchair accessible, and each of them accommodates six people. Each cabin is equipped with an outdoor picnic table and grill. Cabin 10 holds the clearest view of the lake, and 1 through 3 are situated near the lake but not directly onshore. The cabins equipped with a fireplace rather than a woodburning stove include 1 through 4, 8, 15, 17, and 18. Drive east from the park office for .3 mile and turn right on Parvin Mill Road. Continue .3 mile, turn right on Forest Road, and proceed 40 yards to the cabin entrance on the left. The cabins are open from April 1 through October 31.

Trails

Parvin borders the western edge of New Jersey's Pine Barrens. As a result, the ten trails weaving through the park's 1,952 acres are relatively flat. Three of the longest trails—Long, Forest Loop, and Black Oak—stretch through Parvin Natural Area, a 465-acre protected area encompassing the western half of the park. The red-blazed Long Trail is the most scenic, squeezed thin by brush in its 2.7-mile route along Muddy Run, past an Atlantic white cedar swamp, and through an

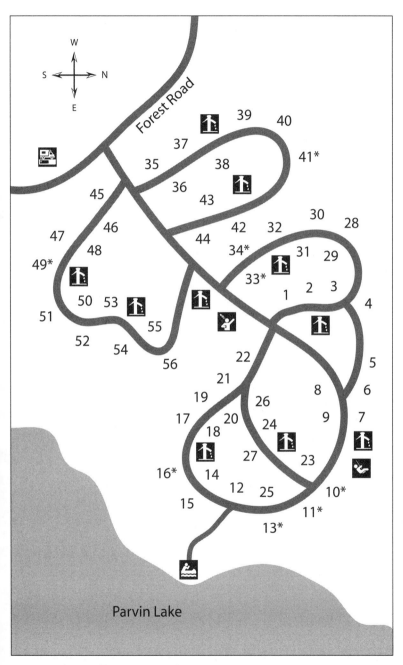

Jaggers Point Family Campground

Trail Mileage and Difficulty

TRAIL	MILES	DIFFICULTY	BLAZE	USES
Black Oak Trail	2.4	E	brown	e,h,m,s,x
Flat Trail	0.3	E	pink	h,m,s,x
Forest Loop	2.1	E	blue	h,m,s,x
Forest Road	1.0	E	blue	h,m,s,x
Knoll Trail	0.6	E	orange	h,m,s,x
Long Trail	2.7	E	red	e,h,m,s,x
Lost Trail	0.8	E	orange	e,h,m,s,x
Nature Trail	0.6	E	white	h
Parvin Lake Trail	3.1	E	green	h,m,s,x
Thundergust Lake Trail	1.0	E	yellow	h,m,s,x

upland pine-oak forest. The blue-blazed Forest Loop is suited for a leisurely bicycle ride, as it makes use of an unused paved road that cuts through a forest of shortleaf pine, southern red oak, and shagbark hickory. Black Oak Trail, marked with brown blazes and the best option for horseback riders, begins at the Thundergust Lake cabin complex and extends 2.4 miles through scarlet oak and white pine.

Parvin Lake Trail allows mountain biking and cross-country skiing along its 3.1 mile course through pitch pine, sassafras, and at least five types of oak. Marked in green, the trail connects several well-traveled areas of the park, including the park office, Long Trail, both campgrounds, and the boat launch on Parvin Lake. Its northern section ends at the white-blazed Nature Trail, a hiking-only trail that runs .6 mile through an Atlantic white cedar swamp. Parvin Trail's southern end reaches the cabin complex and Thundergust Lake Trail, a thin path along the lakeshore offering limited views of the water. Beware, though: Many of the trails become swampy during wet weather, and the Long, Nature, and Thundergust Trails can disappear entirely when overgrown in midsummer.

Activities

Two picnic areas flank the recreation area at Parvin Lake, where swimming is popular throughout the summer. A boat ramp caters to anglers, and a food concession accompanies a first-aid station, hot showers, canoe livery, and two playgrounds. Parvin's ten trails are open to a wide range of pursuits, from mountain biking to horseback riding, and birders will not regret a hike through Parvin Natural Area beginning at the white-blazed Nature Trail.

Fishing

Fishing is allowed in Parvin and Thundergust Lakes and Muddy Run. Largemouth bass are abundant in both lakes, and Parvin Lake also supports a good population of perch, pickerel, carp, and catfish. Parvin Lake is a lunker bass lake, which simply means it is managed to encourage the production of large bass. This is accomplished through a number of special restrictions, such as a 15-inch minimum size limit, among others. If you are looking for crappie, head for Thundergust Lake, where yellow perch and catfish are common as well. Muddy Run is a great destination for privacy, where you will find an abundance of catfish and bluegill sunfish, a few pickerel, and an occasional largemouth bass.

Boating

Both lakes allow boats with electric motors. A boat ramp on Parvin Lake caters to all visitors, and campers can use the canoe launch next to campsite 13 at Jaggers Point Campground. Thundergust Lake does not offer a boat ramp, but you can launch small boats from the parking area on the west side of Parvin Mill Road. When water levels are high, the canoe ride across Parvin Lake and down Muddy Run is a worthwhile paddle leading through the 465-acre Parvin Natural Area, although the river may not be passable during dry periods. Canoe rentals are available at the beach concession.

Picnicking

The main picnic area borders Parvin Lake, where about seventy-five tables and grills circle the beach near restrooms, water, and a playground. The twenty-five or so tables closest to the food concession are very busy on sunny days. The Thundergust Lake picnic area offers two covered pavilions, a restroom, activity field, and playground, but the lake is not within view. Groups of twenty or more can reserve the pavilions at Thundergust Lake at least five days in advance. Both areas are open from April 1 through October 31.

Swimming

Parvin's beach is surrounded by a developed recreation area complete with hot showers, restrooms, picnic tables, playgrounds, and parking for about fifty cars. The food concession sells everything from suntan lotion to barbecue tongs. A small, cordoned-off section of Parvin Lake is open to swimming from Memorial Day weekend through Labor Day.

Mountain Biking

All of the trails at Parvin allow mountain bikes save the .6-mile Nature Trail on the north end of the park. Parvin's trails are flat, but long enough to produce a pleasant ride through distracting scenery. Forest Loop, Black Oak, and Long Trails weave through Parvin Natural Area, a section of the park supporting 50 types of trees, 60 species of shrubs, and 200 varieties of flowering plants. Forest Loop is paved for bikers seeking a casual ride, but the other two trails can get a bit swampy during wet weather. Long Trail becomes overgrown in places during the summer, and wooden planks are used to cross several low-lying sections. See the Trails section for blazes and mileage.

Horseback Riding

Long, Black Oak, and Lost Trails combine to form almost 6 miles of trails open to horseback riding. Forest Road is closed to motorized vehicles beyond Jaggers Point Family Campground, so traffic noise is never a factor. See the Trails and Mountain Biking sections for more information.

Birding

Long Trail and Forest Loop stretch through Parvin Natural Area, a section of the park known for nesting wild turkeys, barred owls, yellow-billed cuckoos, and a long list of warblers. A few rarities that occur here include bald eagles, Cooper's hawks, long-eared owls, peregrine falcons, and northern harriers. Many of the common ducks can be seen on both lakes, along with occasional sightings of black-crowned night herons, pied-billed grebes, and ospreys. Prothonotary warblers nest along Muddy Run, and great blue and green herons, great egrets, and more than a dozen species of ducks feed along the banks. The Nature Trail is another popular birding destination, known for Kentucky warblers, Acadian flycatchers, Louisiana waterthrushes, and blue-gray gnatcatchers. Naturalists at Parvin host guided bird walks periodically throughout the year; check with the park office for a current schedule.

Hunting

Hunting is not permitted within Parvin State Park. Edward G. Bevan Wildlife Management Area, about 15 miles south on Route 55, is known for its excellent pheasant hunting. Peaslee Wildlife Management Area, 10 miles east of Bevan, is stocked with almost 6,000 quail each year. New Jersey's wildlife management areas are purchased and maintained with revenues from hunting and fishing licenses, so hunters are always welcome. Both areas allow hunting for deer, small game, waterfowl, and wild turkeys.

Winter Activities

Jaggers Point Family Campground is open year-round, but the cabins are closed during the colder months. All of the trails allow hiking, cross-country skiing, and snowshoeing, and winter is a good time to escape the summer crowds. Guided walks occur throughout the winter, usually meeting at the Parvin Lake parking area.

Flora and Fauna

Parvin represents a transition between New Jersey's Pine Barrens and upland hardwood forest. The result is an unusual combination of plant life covering a variety of terrain, from river floodplains to rolling hills. Pitch pine, black cherry, red maple, and white, red, scarlet, and chestnut oaks are just a few of the many types of trees found at Parvin. About 400 acres in the western section of the park is designated as the Parvin Natural Area, home to 60 types of shrubs, a variety of ferns and mosses, and more than 170 species of birds that nest or migrate through in spring. Wild azalea, winterberry holly, mountain laurel, greenbrier, and sweet pepperbush are all common. One rare resident is the endangered swamp pink, a plant that blooms in early spring by sending up a single cluster of pink flowers from a straight green stem.

Surrounding Points of Interest

Head south of Parvin and anglers will come to Union Lake Wildlife Management Area. Union Lake is the largest lake in southern New Jersey, known for its excellent fishing. Drive west along the Cohansey River for a quiet driving tour that encompasses several of New Jersey's little-known wildlife areas. Continue north along the Delaware River, and you can combine several destinations in a one-day trip. Fort Mott State Park, Supawna Meadows National Wildlife Refuge, and one of the largest heronries on the Atlantic coast, at Pea Patch Island, are all within a few miles of one another on the Delaware River.

Union Lake Wildlife Management Area

The Maurice River feeds 898-acre Union Lake, the largest lake in southern New Jersey and a premier destination for anglers seeking largemouth bass. A fish ladder below the Union Lake dam allows river herring to enter the lake, creating an abundant food supply for many game fish. The conditions have resulted in huge populations of not only largemouth bass, but pickerel, yellow perch, carp, and crappie as well. A large parking area and wide concrete ramp cater to boaters, and outboard motors up to 9.9 horsepower are allowed on the lake. The wildlife management area entrance is located on the north side of Route 608 (Carmel Road), about .7 mile north of Route 49 in Millville. You can access the Maurice River from the boat ramp at the end of Fowser Road, off Route 47 (Second Street) in Millville.

Cohansey River Watershed

An interesting day trip includes a drive along the Cohansey River, taking in several relatively unknown wildlife areas that support nesting ospreys, foraging bald eagles, and miles of salt marsh along the Delaware Bay. The Cohansey River Watershed stretches through 5,000 acres of tidal salt marsh and forested wetlands, encompassing Dix, New Sweden, and Mad Horse Creek Wildlife Management Areas. Head 3.3 miles south of Bridgeton on Route 609 and turn right on Route 553 (Fairton Road). Drive .3 mile and turn right on Route 601 (Back Neck Road), which parallels the Cohansey River to the north. This area can produce a bald eagle sighting. At least six pairs nest along the Cohansey River, and many forage throughout the watershed in winter. Great blue herons, northern harriers, snowy egrets, and other birds of the tidal marshes can be seen along the drive.

Several parking areas line Back Neck Road before the road dead-ends at the Cohansey River. A PSE&G restoration site along the way offers a boat ramp, nature trails, and two pairs of nesting ospreys. Black cherry, eastern red cedar, sweet gum, and black gum border the parking area. Take a detour south on Schoolhouse Road, and you will arrive at the tiny town of Sea Breeze near the mouth of the Delaware River. This is a quiet spot to watch shorebirds and other wildlife. Gulls and terns are common along the coast, cattle egrets perch in the trees along Schoolhouse Road, and sanderlings flock to the area by the hundreds during the summer. The town of Sea Breeze, today composed of a few seasonal houses, was once a summer resort complete with hotels, bathhouses, billiard rooms, and a steamboat landing that attracted vacationers from Philadelphia.

Fort Mott State Park

A series of forts began construction in 1872 to protect shipping along the Delaware River from foreign threats, but building accelerated when Spain heightened the fear in 1898 during the Spanish-American War. Fort Mott was completed around the turn of the century, then fitted with three 10-inch and three 12-inch guns to guard the Delaware Inlet. A walking tour circles the park's welcome center, gift shop, picnic tables, playground, and restrooms. Finn's Point Trail, at the end of Cemetery Road, allows hiking, mountain biking, and cross-country skiing.

Fort Delaware, on Pea Patch Island, is connected to Fort Mott by a round-trip ferry service that runs from April through July. Fort Delaware served as a prison camp for Confederate soldiers during the Civil War, and many of the soldiers who died there are buried at Finn's Point National Cemetery, located adjacent to Fort Mott. The mortality rate at the prison camp was high, resulting in almost 3,000 dead in 1863 as a result of disease, starvation, and neglect. Finn's Point Cemetery marks the burial place of 2,436 Confederate war dead, and a group of marble headstones near the northwest corner of the cemetery commemorates 13 German prisoners of war who died while imprisoned at Fort Dix during World War II.

In addition to Fort Delaware, Pea Patch Island holds the largest Atlantic coast heronry north of Florida. Up to 12,000 pairs of nine different species arrive each spring, including great blue, little blue, and tricolored herons; black-crowned and yellow-crowned night herons; great, snowy, and cattle egrets; and glossy ibises. Pea Patch Island provides one of the few breeding grounds remaining along the Atlantic Flyway, since much of the habitat along the Eastern Seaboard has been destroyed by coastal development. Thousands of nesting herons and egrets make daily journeys from Pea Patch Island to the rich feeding grounds of nearby Supawna Meadows National Wildlife Refuge. Fort Mott, Pea Patch Island, and Finn's Point National Cemetery are located on the Delaware River, five miles northwest of the town of Salem.

Supawna Meadows National Wildlife Refuge

Almost 3,000 acres of tidal salt marsh along the Delaware River serve as a sanctuary for nesting, migrating, and wintering birds. Shorebirds, ducks, and gulls make use of the tidal areas throughout the year, including purple sandpipers, greater yellowlegs, green-winged teals, hooded mergansers, and herring gulls. Waterbirds are not the only inhabitants here, as 20 percent of the park consists of upland fields and woodland, which support American woodcocks, eastern meadowlarks, northern bobwhites, savannah sparrows, and wood thrushes. A great number of raptors migrate through or nest as well, including ospreys, red-tailed hawks, northern harriers, great horned and short-eared owls, and American kestrels.

Two trails access the salt marsh and upland fields near Fort Mott. The Wetlands Pond Loop and Grassland Trails are essentially one, leaving from a parking area on the south side of Lighthouse Road about .1 mile east of Fort Mott Road. The Grassland Trail leads .2 mile to an observation deck overlooking one vast stretch of salt marsh, where mallard, black, and pin-tail ducks are common. Wetlands Pond Loop Trail veers off from the Grasslands Trail and extends 1.2 miles south to the park headquarters, which is usually deserted. You will come across two tidal ponds in the first half mile, home to New Jersey's only brackish water turtle, the diamond-backed terrapin. Tree swallows arrive by the thousands in spring and remain throughout the summer, feeding on bayberries along the trail.

Finn's Point Rear Range Lighthouse

Finn's Point Rear Range Lighthouse is a convenient destination, as it lies only 1.3 miles north of Fort Mott. A wooden kiosk in the parking area serves as a gateway to Supawna Meadows and provides maps and information about the wildlife refuge. The lighthouse was built in 1876 and helped guide ships between Delaware Bay and the Delaware River for the following seventy-five years. The light became obsolete when the channel entering Delaware Bay was widened in 1950 to support larger vessels. A front range light once stood on the banks of the Delaware River, and mariners navigated the channel by lining up the two lights, one behind the other. The rear range light fell into disrepair, until it was refurbished in 1983 and came under the stewardship of Supawna Meadows National Wildlife Refuge.

Where to Buy Supplies

Drive about 5 miles east from the park office on Route 540, and you will come to downtown Vineland. The city offers everything a traveler needs, including banks, pharmacies, grocery stores, sporting goods, car repair, delis, and restaurants. Vineland's retail stores begin only a few miles east of the Parvin office. Downtown Millville is about 6 miles south of Vineland on Route 47, where you will find almost as many services. A third option is to travel 8 miles south of Parvin to Bridgeton, a town that contains banks, fast food, grocery stores, and a number of restaurants.

Belleplain State Forest

P.O. Box 450
Woodbine, NJ, 08270

Area. 21,320 acres.

Park office. Cape May County, 1.4 miles west of Woodbine on the south side of Route 550.

Highlights. Lake Nummy, 187 campsites, surrounding points of interest.

Activities. Camping, hiking, fishing, boating, picnicking, swimming, mountain biking, horseback riding, birding, hunting, ice fishing, cross-country skiing, snowshoeing, snowmobiling.

Entrance fee. A fee is charged to enter the recreation area from Memorial Day weekend through Labor Day.

Park hours. Year-round, from dawn to dusk.

For additional information: (609) 861-2404

This 21,320-acre forest on the edge of the Pine Barrens represents the southernmost public park to offer camping in New Jersey. With 187 sites scattered among three campgrounds, it's difficult to be dissatisfied at Belleplain. The campgrounds and much of the activity surround Lake Nummy, a 26-acre lake created in the late 1930s from a former cranberry bog. A modern recreation area is surrounded by a wide swimming beach, picnic tables, a food concession, playgrounds, and a bathhouse with hot showers. Boaters and fishers can use the floating dock at Lake Nummy or the boat ramp at East Creek Pond a few miles to the south. Farther afield, more than twenty marked and unmarked trails allow all sorts of activities, including mountain biking, horseback riding, cross-country skiing, and snowshoeing.

If you are willing to travel, Belleplain lies near a number of worthy destinations along the coast and is a good alternative to the expensive summer hotels in Cape May. Any angler unhappy with Belleplain's options can head for the saltwater fishing grounds of Delaware Bay or the many inlets along the Atlantic coast. History buffs are within a short drive of two lighthouses and the historic districts of the cape. One of the best birding spots in the country lies at the southern tip of New Jersey,

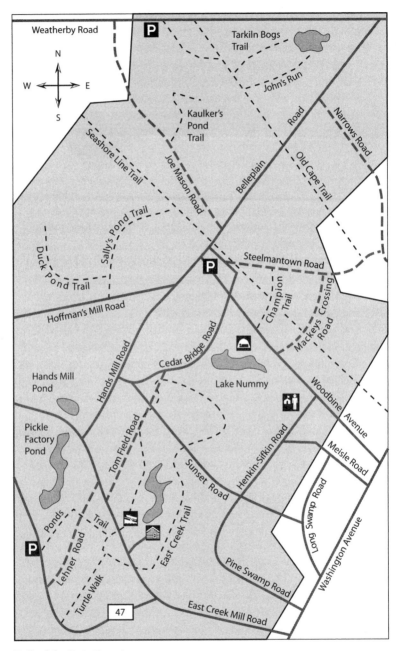

Belleplain State Forest

where migrating shorebirds stop to feed on Delaware Bay horseshoe crab eggs in spring. The many inlets, bays, and natural areas surrounding Belleplain add to the attraction of this easily accessible park.

Camping

Three campgrounds fan out through the forest to the north and south of Lake Nummy. North Shore, Meisle Field, and CCC Campgrounds combine to offer 187 sites, more than any other public camping area in New Jersey. About half of the campsites are large enough to accommodate trailers, and Meisle Field holds five yurts and fourteen lean-tos. Eight sites rest near the water, all of them at the more popular North Shore Campground. Two group sites west of the lake each accommodate seventy-five campers, and one group cabin lies 5 miles south of the park office on East Creek Pond. No need to pack a bevy of supplies at Belleplain, where modern restrooms, drinking water, and even laundry facilities are common to all family campgrounds.

North Shore Family Campground

North Shore is adjacent to the recreation area and holds the only sites at Belleplain that lie directly on the shore of Lake Nummy. As a result, the campground tends to see more activity than its counterpart to the south. Campsites range from wooded clearings large enough to accommodate trailers to quiet spots on the water encircled by trees. They see a steady flow of campers during warm weather, and pitching your tent on a weekday or during the off-season will go a long way to increasing privacy. Reserve ahead if you're interested in one of the waterside sites, as they are usually full on summer weekends.

Directions. Turn right out of the park office onto Henkin-Sifkin Road, drive .5 mile, and turn right on Meisle Road. Proceed 100 yards and stop at the booth to pay admission or show your camping permit. Continue 1 mile beyond the gate, always bearing right along the shore of Lake Nummy, and turn right into North Shore Campground.

Sites and facilities. North Shore's eighty-three ground sites each hold a picnic table and fire ring. You will find three modern restrooms evenly distributed among the sites, but only the one in the middle of the campground offers hot showers and laundry facilities. A playground sits next to the showers, and twenty water pumps are scattered throughout the campground. North Shore is open year-round.

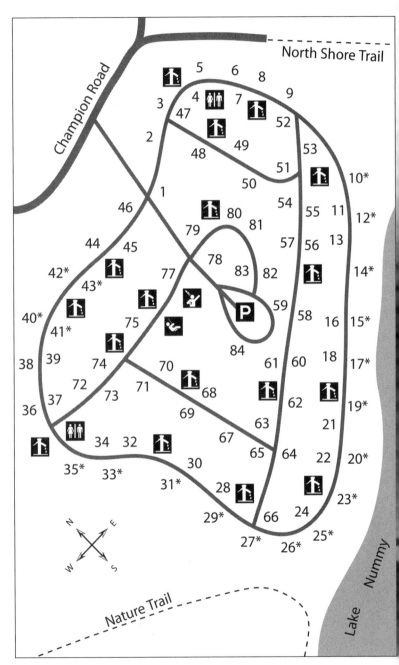

North Shore Family Campground

Recommended sites. The eight sites facing the shore of Lake Nummy (10, 12, 14, 15, 17, 19, 20, and 23) are the most sought after in the park, although some of them sit behind a barrier of trees blocking any scene of the lake. Sites 15 and 17 hold a clear view of the water—both worthy options, but number 17 is a bit open to the road. Number 14 offers a slightly obscured view of Lake Nummy through trees, as does number 23, a wooded site set back from the road. Sites 10, 12, 19, and 20 are separated from the lake by a thin row of trees, but they have no opposite neighbors and are fairly private. The best offshore sites, odd numbers 25 through 35, line the outside of the campground, with no neighbors behind them and a view of woodland across the way.

Meisle Field and CCC Family Campgrounds

These two campgrounds are essentially one, separated by a small paved road on the southwest side of Meisle Field. The campgrounds are encircled by forest, and a pleasant walk along the Nature Trail ends at the beach and recreation area to the north. This is the quieter side of Lake Nummy, but open space between sites is a bit sparse. Meisle Field holds five yurts, which are circular canvas tents containing two double-deck bunks and a wood floor. You will also find fourteen lean-tos, unfurnished one-room cabins that accommodate up to six campers. Yurts and lean-tos are each equipped with a picnic table, outdoor grill, and fire ring.

Directions. Follow the directions for North Shore Campground. The entrance to Meisle Field is immediately on the left after the admissions booth.

Sites and facilities. The eighty-five ground sites, fourteen lean-tos, and five yurts each supply a picnic table and fire ring. Three restrooms are scattered throughout the grounds, two of them equipped with hot showers and laundry facilities. One playground sits in the center of the campground, and water from ground pumps is within walking distance of all sites. The campsites, yurts, and lean-tos are available year-round. The trailer sanitary station on the south side of the campground is open from March 1 through November 30.

Recommended sites. Sites 102 and 105 are large and private. A wide band of trees separates the nearby restroom from both campsites. Numbers 210 through 219 sit in a forested section of Meisle Field and share no immediate neighbors. Even numbers 124 through 134 offer some privacy as well, as they line the outside of the campground and are backed by forest. The best of the lean-tos, numbers 11 through 14, each occupy secluded clearings surrounded by pitch pine and chestnut oak.

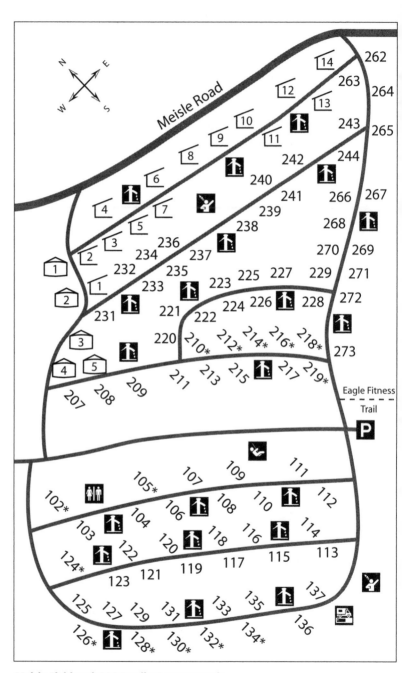

Meisle Field and CCC Family Campgrounds

Group Campground

Belleplain's two group sites rest in a wooded grove about 100 feet away from the road. Each site contains two pit toilets, two large grills, about eight picnic tables, a water pump, and fire ring. Drive .5 mile beyond the entrance gate, past the turn for North Shore Campground, to the group campsites on the left. Each site accommodates seventy-five campers and is open year-round. Groups must reserve at least five days in advance.

East Creek Group Cabin

Belleplain offers only one cabin, located on the south shore of East Creek Pond, and it is always booked eleven months in advance. A wide backyard holding several picnic tables is surrounded by a forest of pine, oak, and wildflowers. The view of East Creek Pond from the back porch is relaxing, where wooden chairs face an outdoor grill, fire pit, and boat dock on the water. The cabin accommodates thirty campers, with seven double-deck bunks and one single bunk in each of two bedrooms. The living room is furnished with a fireplace, sofas, and chairs. Two modern bathrooms contain hot showers, and the full kitchen holds a refrigerator, electric stove, and oven. The cabin is open year-round and is equipped with a propane heating system. Drive east from the park office on Route 550 (Belleplain-Woodbine Road), proceed 1.4 miles, and turn right on Route 557 (Washington Avenue). Continue 3.1 miles and turn right on Route 47 (Delsea Drive). Drive .7 mile and bear right on Route 347 (East Creek Mill Road). Proceed on East Creek Mill Road for another 1.5 miles to the cabin on the right.

Trails

Totaling more than 40 miles, Belleplain's flat trails accommodate a wide array of pursuits. Only a few of them are more than 2 miles long, and many are smooth and broad enough to serve as country roads. With the exception of Eagle Fitness Trail and the Nature Trail circling Lake Nummy, all of the trails at Belleplain allow hiking, mountain biking, horseback riding, cross-country skiing, and snowshoeing. Even motorcycles and snowmobiles are permitted on many of the dirt roads and marked trails.

East Creek Trail is the longest in the park, forming a 7.2-mile loop from Lake Nummy to East Creek Pond and back. The trail is well marked, yet thin enough to produce a sense of escape, stretching through a mixture

Trail Mileage and Difficulty

TRAIL	MILES	DIFFICULTY	BLAZE	USES
Champion Trail	0.8	E	no blaze	b,e,h,m,s,x
Duck Pond Trail	2.0	E	no blaze	b,e,h,m,s,x
Eagle Fitness Trail	0.5	E	no blaze	h
East Creek Trail	7.2	E	white	e,h,m,s,x
Goosekill Trail	0.3	E	green	e,h,m,s,x
John's Run Trail	1.0	E	no blaze	b,e,h,m,s,x
Kalker's Pond Trail	1.7	E	no blaze	b,e,h,m,s,x
Lehner Road	1.3	E	no blaze	e,h,m,s,x
Mackeys Crossing Road	1.3	E	no blaze	b,e,h,m,s,x
Meisle Trail	0.6	E	orange	e,h,m,s,x
Narrows Road	2.4	E	no blaze	b,e,h,m,s,x
Nature Trail	0.9	E	white/yellow	h
North Shore Trail	0.7	E	red	e,h,m,s,x
Old Cape Trail	4.5	E	no blaze	b,e,h,m,s,x
Ponds Trail	2.2	E	blue	e,h,m,s,x
Sally's Pond Trail	1.4	E	no blaze	b,e,h,m,s,x
Seashore Line Trail	7.2	E	yellow	b,e,h,m,s,x
Steelmantown Road	2.9	E	no blaze	b,e,h,m,s,x
Tarkiln Bogs Trail	0.9	E	no blaze	e,h,m,s,x
Turtle Walk Trail	1.4	E	no blaze	b,e,h,m,s,x

of habitat ranging from pitch pine and red maple to open fields and Atlantic white cedar swamps. Seashore Line Trail is the second longest, tempting for mountain bikers and horseback riders. Beware, though: It is a popular four-wheeling route, and the driving can get a bit fast. Old Cape Trail, the third longest in the park, runs from Steelmantown Road to Belleplain's northern border and is less frequented by motorized vehicles.

Four short trails surround Lake Nummy, all of them extremely easy. A pleasant walk from Meisle Field Campground to the recreation area combines Meisle Trail with the wide and sandy Goosekill Trail and the Nature Trail. North Shore Trail extends .7 mile through dense woodland, where a tree canopy arches overhead to create the feeling you're achieving some distance from civilization. Eagle Fitness Trail leaves from Meisle Field Campground, providing a short and flat afternoon walk through pineland and hardwood forest while you're in camp.

Miles of sand roads weave through Belleplain's 21,320 acres of mixed pine and oak forest, many of them serving as connectors to several of the marked trails. Steelmantown Road intersects a number of dirt roads and trails leading to the northern border of the forest. Combining Steelmantown and Mackeys Crossing Roads with Old Cape and John's Run Trails produces a 5.2-mile one-way journey through dense pineland and low-lying marsh. Joe Mason Road heads north to the border of Peaslee Wildlife Management Area at Weatherby Road, where you will find an entirely new set of unmarked trails and fire roads.

Activities

Belleplain's recreation area sees much of the park's activity during warm weather. Lake Nummy's thin and sandy beach seems as if it were designed to mesh with the surrounding forest. Pine trees shade about fifty picnic tables near the shore, where a white strip of sand circles Lake Nummy. You can rent a canoe at the food concession or take a hot shower in the bathhouse. Farther afield, Belleplain's well-maintained trails and roads support a wide array of pursuits, from mountain biking to snowmobiling, and a boat ramp caters to anglers at East Creek Pond.

Fishing and Boating

Lake Nummy and East Creek Pond both offer good fishing for largemouth bass, pickerel, and catfish. East Creek Pond is a slightly better spot for largemouth bass and holds a good population of yellow perch as well. You will find a boat ramp on the south shore of East Creek Pond and a floating dock to launch small boats on Lake Nummy. The lakes allow electric motors, and canoe rentals are available at the beach concession. See the East Creek Group Cabin section for directions to East Creek Pond. Also see the Surrounding Points of Interest section for nearby boating and fishing destinations.

Picnicking

Pineland surrounds the shore of Lake Nummy, where about fifty tables intermix with the forest in no particular arrangement. The area is busy during the summer, but it's a beautiful spot if you can find a quiet day.

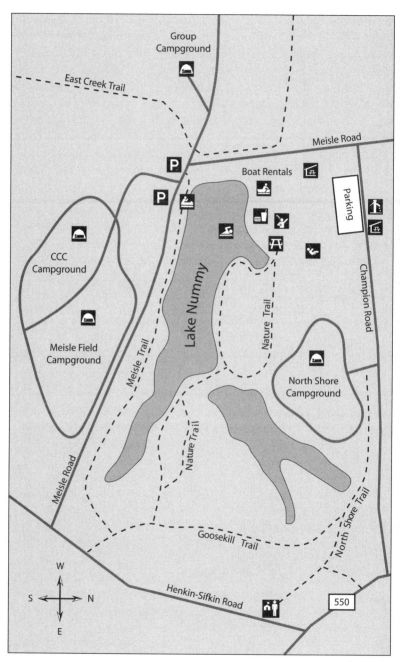

Belleplain Recreation Area

The picnic area on the west side of the parking lot is a bit more private and rarely crowded, surrounded by trees in a wooded clearing. A covered pavilion also sits directly on Champion Road next to a huge activity field. Restrooms and water are nearby, and each site is equipped with charcoal grills and tables. Groups of twenty or more must reserve at least five days in advance.

Swimming

Rather than a wide and sandy strip of land, the picturesque beach at Lake Nummy is a mixture of water and woods. Pine and oak trees lead almost to the water's edge, where a thin ribbon of white sand outlines Lake Nummy. Picnic tables and grills border the shoreline near a bathhouse and showers. The food concession offers almost anything you need for a day at the beach, from hot dogs and ice cream to playing cards, Frisbees, and sunscreen. The beach is open to swimmers from Memorial Day weekend through Labor Day.

Mountain Biking

Mountain bikes are allowed on all of the trails throughout Belleplain except the Nature and Eagle Fitness Trails. The dirt roads and trails throughout the forest vary from the white quartz sand prevalent throughout the Pine Barrens to surfaces more suitable for riding, such as packed dirt. Many of the roads are coated with a layer of pine needles, making cycling a bit easier than on naked sand. East Creek Trail is composed of pine needles over packed dirt and will give you a serene ride through a cross section of Belleplain's habitat. If you prefer to head north, Steelmantown Road, Champion Trail, Mackeys Crossing Road, Old Cape Trail, and Seashore Line Trail will partially avoid the fine sand that tends to irritate mountain bikers.

Horseback Riding

Riding is allowed on all of Belleplain's trails except the Nature and Eagle Fitness Trails, but beware of the trails that allow motorized vehicles. The three trails near Lake Nummy are quiet and popular with horseback riders. From the parking area at the southwest corner of Lake Nummy, Meisle Trail heads .6 mile east to Goosekill Trail. Turn left on Goosekill Trail, ride .3 mile, and turn right on North Shore Trail. Proceed .2 mile and turn left on Mackeys Crossing Trail, leading .2 mile to Route 550. You can turn around at Route 550 or cross over the highway to Mackeys Crossing Road and continue into the northern reaches of Belleplain State Forest.

Birding

For birders, a journey to Belleplain requires a side trip to nearby Cape May, the preeminent birding destination in New Jersey and one of the top locations in the country. It is not unusual to find birders from around the world during a visit to this southernmost point in the state. The funnel shape of the cape creates a bottleneck of migratory birds in fall, particularly from late September through early October. Almost 400 species fly through each year, including a great number of rarities. The horseshoe crab spawning in May attracts more than 1 million migrating birds, many on their way from South America to breeding grounds in the Arctic. See the Surrounding Points of Interest section for details.

Butterflies

Many butterfly species use the sun's reflection off white sand roads to help them warm up after cool spring nights, and more than sixty species have been recorded near the sand roads of Belleplain. Early spring brings mourning cloaks, cabbage whites, question marks, and spring azures. Elfins and orange sulphurs arrive in late spring, followed by falcate orangetips, Juvenal's duskywings, pearl crescents, and painted ladies. Around May 1, you will start to see juniper hairstreaks, viceroys, common buckeyes, and silver spotted skippers.

Butterfly-watchers will not regret a side trip to Cape May, especially in the fall, when thousands of monarchs stop to rest at the cape on their way south. Peak migration occurs from late September through early October. The Cape May Bird Observatory in Goshen, just north of the junction between Routes 47 and 646, keeps a butterfly and humming-bird garden. The preserve attracts butterflies by the hundreds, including black, tiger, and spicebush swallowtails; rare skippers; Hayhurst's scallopwings; pearl crescents; and many more. The observatory also maintains a dragonfly pond and attracts nessus sphinx and other moths with plates of overripe fruit.

Hunting

Most of Belleplain State Forest, about 20,000 acres, is open to the hunting of deer, small game, waterfowl, and wild turkeys. The area is popular during wild turkey season, which occurs from mid-April through May. Belleplain falls within deer management zone 34 and turkey-hunting area 22. Peaslee Wildlife Management Area begins at Belleplain's northern border (north of Route 548) and is stocked with almost 6,000 quail each year. Peaslee covers more than 25,000 acres, but a good place to begin is at the parking areas lining Hesstown Road north of Route 49.

Winter Activities

Camping is available year-round at Belleplain. East Creek Group Cabin is equipped with central heat, and the fourteen lean-tos at Meisle Field Campground contain propane heaters. Belleplain's low annual snowfall means that hiking is the most common winter pursuit, but half of the trails are open to snowmobiles, and virtually all of the trails allow cross-country skiing and snowshoeing. Belleplain's lakes do not freeze through every year, but ice fishing is allowed on Lake Nummy and East Creek Pond, given safe conditions. Pickerel and yellow perch are the main winter catch.

Flora and Fauna

Belleplain lies on the southern border of the New Jersey Pine Barrens, sharing many of the traits common to Wharton and Bass River State Forests to the north. Because Belleplain was pieced together in a series of land acquisitions spanning seventy years, the park also encompasses a mixture of pine-oak forest, lowland swamps, and acquired farmland in various stages of succession. Stands of Norway spruce, Atlantic white cedar, a variety of pines, and white, scarlet, and chestnut oaks are surrounded by an understory of grasses, lichens, mosses, and ferns.

Belleplain's varied composition results in a melding of the common and the uncommon. The globally endangered sensitive joint vetch resembles a yellow-and-red orchid atop a 6-foot stem. The plant is extremely rare, yet the largest population known in the world can be found along the Maurice River near Belleplain's western border. Barred owls maintain a stronghold in Belleplain, and bald eagles can often be seen at East Creek Pond. Rarer still are state endangered and threatened species such as the eastern tiger salamander, northern pine snake, and Pine Barrens tree frog. Deer, wild turkeys, beavers, muskrats, foxes, flying squirrels, and opossums inhabit the forest, and any visitor who pitches a tent in the spring will be serenaded by the nighttime calls of the whippoorwill.

Surrounding Points of Interest

Belleplain is within 20 miles of numerous saltwater fishing destinations, two of New Jersey's oldest lighthouses, and one of North America's most productive birding areas at Cape May. The fishing ranges from brackish inlets, bays, capes, and coves to deep-sea destinations well off the coast. Most birders are familiar with Cape May, where thousands of migrating birds stop to rest during their journey along the Atlantic Flyway. Some birders may not be aware of the 1 million birds that flood New Jersey's coast on a full moon in May, all in pursuit of the eggs of one marine animal—the horseshoe crab.

Nearby Boating and Fishing

Travel any direction but north from Belleplain, and you are bound to strike an area known for its saltwater fishing. New Jersey's inland waterway to the east extends from Cape May to Atlantic City and beyond. The saltwater fishing is unrivaled, and record catches of fluke, weakfish, striped bass, bluefish, and others are common. The Cape May area produces great sea bass fishing as well as offshore king mackerel, greater amberjack, and barracuda. The Delaware Bay, to the south, is heavily trafficked but produces massive fish, including black drum and striped bass. Head west, and you will hit the Maurice River Inlet, Fortescue State Marina, and Cohansey Cove, areas known for weakfish, flounder, and striped bass. The vast subject of saltwater and deep-sea fishing is not covered below in great depth, so check with local marinas for detailed information. Boat launches and marinas are prevalent all along the coast.

Tuckahoe Wildlife Management Area

This 14,710 acres of salt marsh, hardwood swamp, and pine-oak forest is a popular hunting destination, but it is also a prime birding spot for anyone seeking solitude. Three brackish-water impoundments attract waterfowl of all kinds. Rare birds seen here include rough-legged hawks, tundra swans, golden eagles, American white pelicans, and short-eared owls. About .2 mile inside the entrance, turn right and drive 1.3 miles to the impoundments on the right and left. The road along the impoundment to the right dead-ends after .3 mile, but the mudflats south of the road are good places to see sandpipers and plovers by the hundreds when the water level is low. The left impoundment holds deeper water, surrounded by a 1.6-mile access road that returns to the park's main dirt road. Take Route 550 east from Washington Avenue in Woodbine, drive 2.4 miles to Route 610 (Petersburg Road), and turn left. Proceed 4.4 miles to Route 631 (Tuckahoe Road) and turn left. Continue .8 mile to the Tuckahoe entrance on the right.

Corson's Inlet State Park

A stretch of pristine coastal dunes and a public beach are the highlights of Corson's Inlet State Park, an area known for guided beach walks and sunbathing. A concrete boat ramp caters to anglers, and gas-powered outboards are welcome. The saltwater fishing is good for bluefish, king mackerel, striped bass, and weakfish. Piping plovers, black skimmers, and least terns nest along the dunes in spring, and a variety of gulls, terns, and shorebirds can be seen throughout the year. Follow the directions for Tuckahoe Wildlife Management Area until you reach Route 631 (Tuckahoe Road). Turn right on Route 631, drive 3.9 miles, and turn right on Route 623 (Roosevelt Boulevard). Proceed 2.6 miles to Route 619 (Central Avenue) and turn right. Follow Route 619 for 3.2 miles to the park entrance on the left.

Cape May Point State Park

This 235-acre park lies on the southern tip of the Cape May Peninsula, home to the Cape May Lighthouse. About 4 miles of hiking trails stretch through a series of wetlands, coastal dunes, and ocean beach, where fishing is good for weakfish, bluefish, flounder, tautog, and striped bass. Climbing to the top of Cape May Lighthouse has been a ritual of visiting the southern tip of New Jersey since 1882, when the keeper began showing visitors the scene of Cape May Point from the top of the 157-foot tower. Built in 1859, the present lighthouse is still used by the Coast Guard as a beacon to passing ships. Picnic tables, restrooms, and a nature center surround the parking area. Drive about 20 miles south on the Garden State Parkway to the end, then cross over the Cape May Bridge onto Lafayette Street. Proceed 1.7 miles and bear right on Route 606. Continue 2.2 miles, turn left on Lighthouse Avenue, and drive .6 mile to the park entrance on the left.

Cape May Birding

Ask any birder about Cape May, and he or she will not tell you about its history, beaches, or restaurants. For birders, the annual migration tops all of the other combined attractions of Cape May. Dozens of world-class birding sites are scattered throughout the area. Cape May Bird Observatory, near the southern end of the peninsula, is the place to start for information. The bookstore, wall to wall with birding guides and maps of Cape May, is staffed with lifelong birders who are ready with advice.

Cape May Point State Park, at the tip of the peninsula, supports a bird blind and several observation towers that overlook a variety of ponds, marshes, dunes, and woodland. One of the largest raptor migrations in North America occurs each autumn, when birders from around the world arrive to view rare eagles, hawks, owls, vultures, and falcons. The Cape May Hawk Watch is held from an observation tower overlooking the Atlantic Ocean just south of the park office. Walk east along the beach from the hawk watch tower, and you can't go wrong for shorebird sites.

Cape May Migratory Bird Refuge, located south of Sunset Boulevard, is another highly praised birding area. Salt marshes and dunes are home to the endangered least tern and piping plover. A boardwalk and observation platform give access to almost a mile of shorefront, where gulls, terns, egrets, and herons stop to feed and rest during migration. Nesting shorebirds line the dunes in spring, when piping plovers and least terns arrive to dig depressions in the sand for their eggs. The behavior of nesting on beachfront property, and on open sand, has left these species especially vulnerable to coastal development and predation by domesticated animals.

A few additional areas gain attention from birders as well. Higbee Beach Wildlife Management Area, at the western shore of the peninsula, sees more than 1 million migratory birds every year and offers a wide variety of habitats: coastal dunes, meadows, farm fields, woodlands, hardwood swamps, and ponds. The eastern end of the wildlife management area is known locally as Hidden Valley (south of New England Road and west of Bayshore Road), a great place for migratory warblers, sparrows, and gnatcatchers. You can see shorebirds from your parked car at the end of Sunset Boulevard, where a World War I shipwreck sits offshore and plovers, sandpipers, and terns mingle with the surf.

Horseshoe Crab Spawning Areas

You don't have to be a birder to be awed by this spectacle, considered one of the natural wonders of New Jersey. During high tide in May, tens of thousands of horseshoe crabs crawl up on the beaches of Delaware Bay to breed. Surrounded by a group of males, the female digs a nest in the sand and lays thousands of eggs. This natural phenomenon attracts an estimated 500,000 to 1.5 million migratory birds to the southern shores of New Jersey every year. The peak spawning period is mid to late May, when a new or full moon creates higher tides.

Spawning occurs during high tide, and the best birding is at low tide, when the horseshoe crab eggs are exposed.

The spawning areas are all on the southwest coast, stretching from Norbury's Landing in the south to Fortescue Wildlife Management Area farther north. Fortescue's half-mile-long beach is one of the best areas to see a wide variety of shorebirds. Buff-breasted sandpipers, marbled godwits, ruddy turnstones, willets, semipalmated plovers, American oystercatchers, and many more flock here by the thousands during low tide. Take Fortescue Road to New Jersey Avenue and drive .5 mile south to the Raybins Beach area.

You can combine several points of interest by viewing the spectacle from Heislerville Wildlife Management Area, located south of Route 47 at the end of East Point Road and home to the East Point Lighthouse. The Maurice River flows through Heislerville's 7,166 acres of tidal marsh, coastal mudflats, and upland forest. On a single day one recent year in May, the naturalists at Heislerville counted 2,000 short-billed dowitchers and 2,000 dunlins on Thompson's Beach (east of the lighthouse), in addition to 300 black-bellied plovers, 50 least sandpipers, 10 greater yellowlegs, and 2 spotted sandpipers on the mudflats next to the Maurice River. East Point Lighthouse, New Jersey's second-oldest lighthouse, built in 1849, overlooks the scene.

Continue south along the coast, and you will come to Reeds Beach, then Norbury's Landing, about 15 miles south of Heislerville on Route 47. Both spots are usually staffed with naturalists during the spawning period and are good places to see red knots. Red knots are sort of the star of the show, migrating nonstop from the tip of South America to land and refuel on Delaware Bay crab eggs before continuing north to their breeding grounds in the Arctic. These birds must double their weight within days in order to continue their journey, a task that is completely dependent on the high energy provided by consuming horseshoe crab eggs.

Cape May National Wildlife Refuge

The Cape May National Wildlife Refuge was established to protect vital habitats for migrating and nesting birds and is made up of a dozen disconnected pieces of land totaling more than 11,000 acres. The largest section lies along the Delaware Bay, encompassing many of the horseshoe crab spawning areas between Reeds Beach and Norbury's Landing. Two short trails give access to the area, both beginning near the intersection of Routes 47 and 658. The .4-mile Songbird Trail leaves from the park headquarters on Kimbles Beach Road, and the 1-mile Woodcock Trail lies just to the south at the end of Woodcock Lane. The refuge will ultimately protect 21,200 acres of coastal habitat when the planning and land acquisitions are complete.

Other Wildlife Areas

A variety of lesser-known nature preserves and wildlife areas are worth a detour for those with selected interests. Eldora Nature Preserve, a natural area devoted to the conservation of rare moths, is a good destination for butterfly lovers. The preserve maintains a butterfly and hummingbird garden that attracts rarities such as marbled underwing and precious underwing moths and rare skipper butterflies. As you travel south on Route 47, the office is the first building you encounter on the left after you enter Cape May County. Egg Island Wildlife Management Area juts into the Delaware Bay near the Maurice River, where a series of trails gives access to salt marshes and tidal creeks. A pair of bald eagles has been nesting at Beaver Swamp Wildlife Management Area since 2004, and Dennis Creek Wildlife Management Area encompasses 6,146 acres of tidal flats, salt marshes, and drainage canals. Both areas lie about 10 miles south of Belleplain, near the town of Goshen.

Where to Buy Supplies

The tiny town of Woodbine is only 1.4 miles east of the park office on Route 550. Here you will find a pizza parlor, small deli, and outdoor hamburger stand. The nearest gas station is on the corner of Routes 611 and 47 in Dennisville, about 3 miles south of Woodbine. Anything more substantial requires a trip to Millville or Seaville. Millville is 16 miles north on Route 47 and offers almost anything a camper needs, including banks, pharmacies, car repair, grocery stores, sporting goods, fast food, hotels, restaurants, and delis. Seaville is 5.5 miles east of Woodbine on Route 550, then north on Route 628 (Corson's Tavern Road) for another 2 miles. The small city contains banks, fast food, and a few small grocery stores and restaurants. If you find yourself in Seaville and are not satisfied, the larger retail centers of Sea Isle City and Ocean City are only a few miles east of Seaville across the Sea Isle Boulevard bridge. Drive 2.7 miles south of Seaville on Route 9 and turn left on Sea Isle Boulevard. Proceed 2.8 miles to Sea Isle City.

Camping Regulations

The following regulations are paraphrased and subject to change. Individual parks may impose unique restrictions. Check with the New Jersey Department of Environmental Protection, Division of Parks and Forestry, for a complete list of regulations.

Minimum age: A campsite, lean-to, shelter, yurt, or cabin must be occupied by at least one person eighteen years of age or older. Group campsites and cabins require one supervisor, eighteen years of age or older, for every nine underage campers.

Limit of stay: Fourteen consecutive nights.

Check-out time: 12 noon at all campsites, and indicated on permits for lean-tos, shelters, and cabins.

Fires: Permitted in existing fire rings at campsites, and in fireplaces and woodburning stoves at shelters, lean-tos, and cabins.

Pets: Not permitted in camping facilities.

Vehicle limit: No more than two vehicles (including trailers) may be parked at a camping facility. More than two vehicles may be parked at group campsites and group cabins, subject to the approval of the superintendent.

Visitors: Allowed at camping facilities between 8 A.M. and 8 P.M.

Trailer hookups: Water, electric, and sewer hookups are not provided at New Jersey's public campsites.

Food storage: At parks where bears are present, all coolers must be stored in a vehicle and out of sight at all times.

Reservations: To reserve a campsite, lean-to, shelter, yurt, or cabin, contact the appropriate state park office.

Payment: Pay at the appropriate park office upon arrival or reserve by telephone. Reservations and cancellations may be subject to an additional fee.

Handicap Access: The disabled who require special considerations should contact the appropriate park, forest, or recreation area, whose staff will assist in making arrangements.

Bibliography

Becker, Donald William. *Indian Place Names in New Jersey.* Cedar Grove, NJ: Phillips-Campbell Publishing Company, 1964.

Boyle, William J., Jr. *A Guide to Bird Finding in New Jersey.* New Brunswick, NJ: Rutgers University Press, 1997.

Luftglass, Manny, and Ron Bern. *Gone Fishin': The 100 Best Spots in New Jersey.* New Brunswick, NJ: Rutgers University Press, 1998.

McPhee, John. *The Pine Barrens.* New York: Farrar, Straus, and Giroux, 1978.

New Jersey Department of Environmental Protection, Division of Fish and Wildlife. *Fish and Wildlife Digest.* Published annually by the New Jersey Department of Environmental Protection, Division of Fish and Wildlife, P.O. Box 402, Trenton, NJ 08625.

———. *Guide to Wildlife Management Areas.* Trenton: New Jersey Department of Environmental Protection, Division of Fish and Wildlife, 1985.

———. *New Jersey's Endangered and Threatened Wildlife.* Trenton: New Jersey Department of Environmental Protection, Division of Fish and Wildlife, 2004.

———. *Reptiles and Amphibians in New Jersey.* Trenton: New Jersey Department of Environmental Protection, Division of Fish and Wildlife, 2006.

Parnes, Robert. *Paddling the Jersey Pine Barrens.* Guilford, CT: Globe Pequot Press, 2002.

Perrone, Steve. *Discovering and Exploring New Jersey's Fishing Streams and the Delaware River.* Somerdale, NJ: New Jersey Sportsmen's Guides, 1994.

Peterson, Roger Tory. *Peterson Field Guides: Eastern Birds.* New York: Houghton Mifflin Company, 1980.

Walton, Richard K., and Robert W. Lawson. *Birding by Ear: Eastern and Central North America.* Audio CD. New York: Houghton Mifflin Company, 2002.

Useful Websites

Camping regulations, www.state.nj.us/dep/parksandforests/parks/camprules.html.

Delaware Water Gap National Recreation Area, www.nps.gov/dewa/index.htm.

Fish and Wildlife Digest, Freshwater Fishing Issue, New Jersey fishing regulations, www.state.nj.us/dep/fgw/digfsh.htm.

Fish and Wildlife Digest, Hunting Issue, New Jersey hunting regulations, www.state.nj.us/dep/fgw/dighnt.htm.

Hackettstown State Fish Hatchery, fish-stocked waters by lake and river, www.state.nj.us/dep/fgw/hacktown.htm#summaries.

New Jersey Division of Fish and Wildlife, www.state.nj.us/dep/fgw/index.htm.

New Jersey endangered and threatened species, www.nj.gov/dep/fgw/tandespp.htm.

New Jersey Pinelands Commission, information about the Pinelands National Reserve, www.state.nj.us/pinelands/.

New Jersey state parks index, www.state.nj.us/dep/parks/index.html.

NY-NJ-CT Botany Online, a list of plants found in New Jersey's wildlife areas, www.nynjctbotany.org.

State park fees, www.state.nj.us/dep/parksandforests/parks/feeschedule.htm.

Wildlife management area maps, www.state.nj.us/dep/fgw/wmaland.htm.

Index